THE ELDERLY
CAREGIVER

OTHER RECENT VOLUMES IN THE
SAGE FOCUS EDITIONS

THE ELDERLY CAREGIVER

Caring for Adults With
Developmental Disabilities

edited by
Karen A. Roberto

SAGE PUBLICATIONS
The International Educational and Professional Publisher
Newbury Park   London   New Delhi

For information address:

 SAGE Publications, Inc.
2455 Teller Road
Newbury Park, California 91320

SAGE Publications Ltd.
6 Bonhill Street
London EC2A 4PU
United Kingdom

SAGE Publications India Pvt. Ltd.
M-32 Market
Greater Kailash I
New Delhi 110 048 India

Printed in the United States of America

Library of Congress Cataloging-in-Publication Data

The elderly caregiver : caring for adults with developmental
    disabilities / edited by Karen A. Roberto.
        p. cm.—(Sage focus editions : 160)
    Includes bibliographical references and index.
    ISBN 0-8039-5029-9.—ISBN 0-8039-5021-7 (pbk.)
    1. Developmentally disabled—Care—United States.
    2. Developmentally disabled—Home care—United States.
    3. Caregivers—United States. 4. Aging—United States.
    I. Roberto, Karen A.
    HV1570.5.U65E43   1993
    362.1'968—dc20   93-25062

93 94 95 96 97 10 9 8 7 6 5 4 3 2 1

Sage Production Editor: Diane S. Foster

Contents

Foreword

The progressively increasing population of older Americans with developmental disabilities is mirrored by the aging of the overall U.S. population. Given that historically little attention has been given to the aging of persons with mental retardation and other developmental disabilities, this book, which addresses caregiver issues, should be a welcome addition to the literature and a ready handbook for workers in the fields of both gerontology and developmental disabilities.

Over the past 10 years there has been a significant shift from an emphasis on early childhood concerns for persons with developmental disabilities to one on life-span issues. Certainly the trends observed within the United States that show a marked movement from institutional to family and community living systems auger well for the lifestyle and quality of old age among persons with developmental disabilities. In many communities, service agencies have begun to look not only at housing supports but also at a range of supportive retirement environments and options and at accessible and affordable health-care services for older adults with developmental disabilities. Included among these are supports to caregivers in a variety of situations.

Paramount among caregiver concerns are issues related to the aging in place and provision of options for making the best use of one's day. Although the pathologies of old age take a disproportionate share of the attention of caregivers, the wellness and enlightenment of Third Age activities require substantial attention as well. Many caregivers are finding themselves in the situation of accompanying older persons to the very same retirement activities and health-care providers of which they themselves would take advantage. Many caregivers also are finding that the effects of aging can be mitigated by careful planning, foresight, and compensatory activities. The types of analyses presented in this text should enable the range of caregivers, providers, family members, and professionals involved with older adults with developmental disabilities to address current needs and to foresee and anticipate the changing needs of the senior generations to come.

This text addresses the gamut of concerns and challenges that are found in our field today. It provides an excellent synopsis of the current issues and trends and explores with depth the areas that are becoming the challenges of a new generation of older adults. Research has taught us that for the most part people age in general terms and that only in special situations does lifelong disability present a different course for the aging process. Certainly one of these differences, and one that is most noticeable, is the effect of the genetic structure of Down syndrome. Aptly, work in this text charts the nature of this condition and its interaction with the aging process. Unfortunately the effects of Down syndrome are such that many persons with Down syndrome not only experience premature aging but also may begin to show the signs of Alzheimer's disease. Thus the consideration of Down syndrome and the interaction with the aging process and its potential pathologies is a worthy aspect of this text.

As a text on this subject, *The Elderly Caregiver: Caring for Adults With Developmental Disabilities* not only will enlighten with its contemporary knowledge but also will serve as a milestone to the work already done and yet to be done in this unfolding field.

MATTHEW P. JANICKI, PH.D.
DIRECTOR FOR AGING SERVICES
NEW YORK STATE OFFICE OF MENTAL RETARDATION
AND DEVELOPMENTAL DISABILITIES
ALBANY, NEW YORK

Preface

The "aging" of the United States encompasses every segment of our population, including individuals with developmental disabilities. The number of persons with developmental disabilities living into their later years has shown a steady increase over the past several years. Their increase in life expectancy plus a strong support for community integration presents new challenges for older families providing in-home care for their relatives with disabilities.

For past generations, the caregiving situation tended to end by the time caregivers reached their middle years. Now, for many parents, providing in-home care for a son or daughter with a developmental disability is a lifelong task. As both parents and children pass through the life cycle, they must confront changes in their lives as a result of the aging process (e.g., health limitations, exiting the workforce, loss of a loved one). When parents, and particularly mothers, are not able or available to provide care, a sibling usually takes over the responsibility of providing day-to-day care. Entrance into this caregiving role often is assumed, and places sibling caregivers in conflict with their family and career responsibilities. Although providing care can be burdensome, caregivers are reluctant to turn to individuals outside the immediate family or the formal service system for assistance until a crisis occurs.

This book brings together the empirical work of researchers in the fields of both gerontology and developmental disabilities to provide insight into the physical, psychological, and social needs of this growing segment of our population. The book is divided into four sections. The first section provides a review of the caregiving literature as it pertains to this special population of caregivers. The intent of this chapter is to provide a basis from which to understand and further explore issues confronting caregivers of aging adults with developmental disabilities.

The second section is comprised of five chapters that focus on the issues and concerns facing elderly caregivers. Heller examines family perceptions of caregiver burden using both qualitative and quantitative data to describe the ways older family caregivers cope with their caregiving responsibilities and plan for their relative's future. Roberto describes changes in the type of caregiving activities provided by family members as both they and their care receivers have aged. Brubaker and Brubaker examine the financial, residential, social, and emotional concerns of elderly parents caring for adult children with mental retardation. The final two chapters in this section focus on caregivers of aging adults with Down syndrome. Hawkins, Eklund, and Martz identify age-related changes experienced by adults with Down syndrome that influence the need for care and provide an overview of assessment strategies that can be used by older caregivers to identify these changes. Noelker and Somple present a clinical view of elderly caregivers of aging adults with Down syndrome and Alzheimer's disease. Through the use of case studies, they describe the process for assessing Alzheimer's disease in adults with Down syndrome and the problems a dual diagnosis presents for aging family caregivers.

The third section of the book focuses on interactions between older caregivers and the service community. It consists of four chapters. Wood describes social and psychological issues facing older families as they plan for the transfer of care. She discusses the types of plans family caregivers have made and the preparation of aging individuals with developmental disabilities to deal with the death of their primary family caregivers. Lehmann and Roberto examine the current and future service needs of individuals with developmental disabilities living with elderly relatives. They discuss the need for a planning process and the design of mechanisms to facilitate the use of formal services. The last two chapters in this section focus on older families and formal case management. Rinck and Calkins describe a statewide survey of the older parents' perceptions of the case management system. Special attention is given to urban/rural differences in the case management process and the delivery of services. Smith and Tobin explore case managers' perceptions of practice with older parents of developmentally disabled adults. They discuss older parents' involvement in case-related activities and special services needed by older parents.

In the final section of the book, Ansello and Roberto summarize the practice concepts and directives for future research presented by the contributing authors. They conclude their chapter with a discussion of the research as a stepping stone for policy development.

Acknowledgments

The idea for this book emerged as a result of a meeting of the Aging and Developmental Disabilities Formal Interest Group of the Gerontological Society of America in 1989. During our session, individuals from the fields of both gerontology and developmental disabilities formally and informally shared reports of their current work. Afterward, I mentioned to a colleague that much of the work focusing on aging caregivers of adults with developmental disabilities was scattered across a variety of journals and various project reports and how it would be nice if all of this work were incorporated into one volume. She looked at me and said, "So do it!" With that, the challenges of developing a clear focus for the book, getting commitments from a variety of talented (and busy) researchers, and finding a publisher began.

Now that the book is complete, I would like to take this opportunity to thank the many individuals who directly and indirectly assisted in its development. First, I am extremely grateful to each of the contributing authors for their willingness to prepare and revise their chapters. I appreciate all the time and energy they committed to this project. Next, I am appreciative of the support I have received from Sage, and particularly from Christine Smedley. Her continual encouragement and enthusiasm helped keep some of the frustrations of editing a book in perspective. Third, I am grateful for the help of my graduate students, Mary Jesukiewicz, Candi Johnson, Rene Paukstis, and David Sheehan who meticulously completed tasks associated with proofreading and referencing. I also appreciate the help with the preliminary copyediting I received from Becky Edgerton. Finally, I want to express my sincere appreciation to my husband, Steven Sheetz, for his continual support and encouragement throughout this project and our life together.

PART I

Review of the Caregiving Literature

1

Family Caregivers of Aging Adults With Disabilities

A Review of the Caregiving Literature

KAREN A. ROBERTO

The "graying" of the U.S. population does not preclude persons with developmental disabilities. The number of persons with developmental disabilities living into their later years has shown a steady increase over the past 40 years (Waltz, Harper, & Wilson, 1986). Attempts to count the actual number of older persons with developmental disabilities residing in the United States produce population estimates ranging from 196,000 to 1,417,320 depending on the definition of "elderly" and the prevalence rate of mental retardation used in the calculations (Janicki, 1991; Seltzer, 1985; Seltzer & Krauss, 1987; Waltz et al., 1986).

As in the general population, the prevalence of chronic disorders of the cardiovascular, musculoskeletal, respiratory, and sensory systems increases as persons with developmental disabilities age (Anderson, 1989; Hogg, Moss, & Cooke, 1988; Janicki & Jacobson, 1986). The deterioration of the body's systems results in a decline in the functional abilities of the individual. Variables associated with the amount of functional decline reported include age, level of retardation, and type of disability. For example, a comparison of persons with developmental disabilities age 55-64 with those over the age of 65 found a 25% increase in hearing, visual, and mobility loss for the older group (Jacobson, Sutton, & Janicki, 1985). Adults with mild or moderate retardation begin to

3

show changes in gross motor abilities and independent living skills after age 50, whereas a decline in personal activities of daily living (e.g., toileting, dressing, grooming, and eating) and cognitive abilities (e.g., language, reading, writing, and quantitative skills) does not appear until after age 70 (Janicki & Jacobson, 1986). Individuals with Down syndrome exhibit a greater amount of loss in their abilities to perform activities of daily living and intellectual capabilities at an early age than individuals with other types of disabilities (Zigman, Seltzer, Adlin, & Silverman, 1991).

Increased longevity coupled with the prevalence of chronic health conditions in later life presents new challenges to family caregivers of persons with developmental disabilities. For past generations, the caregiving situation tended to end by the time caregivers reached their middle years (Gold, Dobrof, & Torian, 1987). Now these families face a situation where both the caregivers and the care receivers are growing older, with many caregivers being well into their later years. The needs and concerns of older adults providing in-home care for aging family members with developmental disabilities are only beginning to be addressed.

This chapter reviews the literature that focuses on family caregivers of aging adults with developmental disabilities. It begins with a brief review of the general status of informal caregivers of the frail elderly population and the consequences of caregiving. (See Barer & Johnson, 1990, and Horowitz, 1985, for a more comprehensive review and critique of the caregiving literature.) The intent of this section is to provide a basis from which to understand and further explore issues facing caregivers of aging adults with developmental disabilities. Next discussed in greater depth, is the literature specific to caregivers of older persons with developmental disabilities. In the final section, the similarities and differences between the two groups of caregivers are summarized and the issues unique to older caregivers of family members with developmental disabilities are highlighted.

Caregivers of Older Adults

Over 90% of older frail and disabled adults who live in the community rely, at least in part, on family and friends for assistance (Bouvier & De Vita, 1991). Initially family care involves emotional support and minimal instrumental help such as providing transportation, assisting with minor household chores, and running errands. As the older person requires greater assistance, family members provide more concrete daily services such as cooking, cleaning, bathing, dressing, and feeding.

Who Are the Caregivers?

The older caregiver tends to be a spouse, usually a wife, who assumed the role of caregiver because of the failing physical or mental health of his or her partner. The role of "spousal caregiver" is thrust upon older adults at a time in their lives when they may be experiencing health problems of their own or the reduction of functional capacities associated with aging (Cantor, 1983; Crossman, Landon, & Barry, 1981; Johnson, 1983). Despite the physical, emotional, and financial hardships they often endure, spousal caregivers usually provide the most comprehensive care for more impaired individuals and resist institutional placement for longer periods of time than do nonspouse caregivers (Cantor, 1983; Hess & Soldo, 1985; Johnson & Catalano, 1983).

When a spouse is not available or is unable to provide care, adult children assume the caregiving responsibilities for their aging parents. Children of elderly parents provide long-term care for almost one quarter of their fathers and more than one third of their mothers (Day, 1985). When an adult child takes on the role of primary caregiver for an aging parent, it is usually a daughter or daughter-in-law who assumes the major responsibility (Brody, 1985; Horowitz, 1985; Stone, Cafferate, & Sangl, 1987). These women often face the competing demands of caring for an aging parent, managing their household, and working outside the home (Bowers, 1987; Horowitz, 1985; Lang & Brody, 1983).

Although most older adults have at least one living sibling with whom they share an emotionally supportive relationship, only a small percentage depend on a sibling for frequent help (Cicirelli, 1985; Scott, 1990). Instrumental support is more common between unmarried siblings, those with fewer children, and siblings reporting frequent contact with one another (O'Bryant, 1988; Suggs, 1985).

Assistance to frail elders from informal caregivers outside the immediate family is rare. Friends and neighbors may provide crisis or short-term help, particularly when family members are not available to provide direct care, but their involvement typically does not extend to the day-to-day tasks of caregiving (Cantor, 1983; Litwak, 1985; Stoller, 1990).

Researchers consistently report the use of formal services by older adults and their caregivers as low (Coyne, Meade, Petrone, Meinert, &

Joslin, 1990; Krout, 1985). The primary reasons for the apparent under-utilization are lack of awareness of programs and the unavailability of services (Caserta, Lund, Wright, & Redburn, 1987; Wallace, 1990). Whereas from one half to two thirds of older adults have heard of services such as senior centers, congregate meal sites, and transportation programs, much lower rates of awareness are found for programs such as information and referral, respite, home health, and other in-home helping services (Krout, 1986). For the elderly and their caregivers who report knowing about services, variables such as marital status, income, education, gender, degree of illness, and living arrangement distinguish service users from nonusers.

The elderly and their families also may not use formal services due to their personal belief systems (Noelker & Bass, 1989). Caregivers often believe no one can care for their older family members as well as they can. They feel guilty about transferring their caregiving responsibilities to so-called strangers. In addition, taking advantage of community programs may be viewed as an admission of failure in their role as caregivers.

Consequences of Caregiving

The physical, psychological, and social liabilities associated with providing care for an older family member are well documented (Horowitz, 1985; Zarit, Orr, & Zarit, 1985). Several studies suggest that caregivers of frail elders suffer from poor overall health (Brody, 1985; Silliman & Sternberg, 1988). Researchers consistently report that caregivers of frail elders experience emotional distress including depression (Fitting, Rabins, Lucas, & Eastham, 1986; Gallagher, Wrabetz, Lovett, Maestro, & Rose, 1988), burden (Barusch & Spaid, 1989; Zarit, Reever, & Back-Peterson, 1980), and stress (George & Gwyther, 1986; Quayhagen & Quayhagen, 1988). Fulfilling the role of primary caregiver often restricts the person's use of personal time (Kleban, Brody, Shoonover, & Hoffman, 1989; Montgomery, Gonyea, & Hooyman, 1985), interferes with employment responsibilities and obligations (Stone et al., 1987; Young & Kahana, 1989), and strains family relationships (Brody, 1985; Scott, Roberto, Hutton, & Slack, 1985; Stephens, Kinney, & Ogrocki, 1991).

Whereas the negative aspects of caregiving predominate in the literature, some researchers suggest that family members also achieve positive outcomes from the caregiving situation. By redefining their relationship with the care receiver, caregivers are able to focus on the positive aspects of their relationship (Blieszner & Shifflett, 1990). If asked, caregivers often express a sense of pride (Motenko, 1988) and emotional gratification when successfully fulfilling their caregiving responsibilities (Kaye & Applegate, 1990; Motenko, 1989; Reece, Walz, & Hageboeck, 1983).

Caregivers of Adults With Developmental Disabilities

It is only since the mid-1980s that empirical research addressing the concerns of older caregivers of adults with developmental disabilities began to appear in the literature with some regularity. The primary focus of this research is parental care, the role of siblings, and the family's interactions with the formal service system. Table 1.1 provides a summary of the major empirical work published in this area from 1986 to early 1992.

Elderly Parents

For many parents, providing in-home care for a son or daughter with a developmental disability is a lifelong task. As both parents and children pass through the life cycle, all must confront changes in their lives as a result of the aging progress. Providing in-home care becomes more difficult for many older parents as they experience a decline in their health, strength, and patience (Gold et al., 1987).

A qualitative investigation of the role elderly parents play in supporting their children with developmental disabilities identified five major complexities and dilemmas (Grant, 1990). Caregivers often express *indecision and ambivalence* about the future care of the person with a developmental disability, particularly should their own death occur. The caregiving situation often promotes an *enforced interdependence* in which parents perceive their children as their confidant and companion, thereby promoting strong family bonds and few, if any, links to the larger community. For some families, the care of their disabled loved one is assumed to be provided within the family. Therefore, when the parents can no longer provide care, siblings take over the responsibility as part of *maintaining family tradition*. Other parents express *high expectations of the state* for the care of their children and in some cases themselves as well. Giving up the care of a son or daughter to a more formal service system, however, is difficult and parents often needed to

(text continued on page 12)

Table 1.1 Summary of Published Empirical Research (1986-1992)[a]

Study	Subject(s)	Purpose	Findings
Begun, 1989	Sisters, $N = 46$; Age (sister), $M = 30$; Age (sibling), $M = 27$	To develop a conceptualization of sibling relationships	Positive but nonintimate relationship between siblings
Caserta, Connelly, Lund, & Poulton, 1987	Mostly female, $N = 198$; Age (caregiver), $M = 64$; Age (relative), $M = 33$	To evaluate the need for formal support services among older caregivers with individuals in their home who have a developmental disability	Need for a number of key supportive services; Differences in need fulfillment found according to age of the caregiver
Engelhardt, Brubaker, & Lutzer, 1988	Mostly female, $N = 388$; Age, $M = 60$	To analyze service utilization and characteristics of older caregivers	Ability to provide care related to service use
Engelhardt, Lutzer, & Brubaker, 1987	Families, $N = 155$; Age ≥ 56	To determine reasons for parental caregivers' reluctance to use formal services for care of adult children with developmental disabilities	Elderly parents require assistance in planning

Study	Sample	Purpose	Findings
Grant, 1986	Mothers, N = 100; Age = 36-86	To examine the nature, scope, and functioning of the informal care system	Interdependencies between caregivers and care receivers; Fear for the future
Grant, 1990	Mostly female, N = 100 (baseline sample); Age = 40-80	To illustrate roles, interdependencies, and varied strategies for future care	Importance of social support, SES,[b] and age as influences on anticipation of future care of adult child
Heller & Factor, 1988a	Families; Mostly female, N = 100	To provide a comparison of older black and white families' future planning efforts	Black families less likely to have future placements because of economic and sociocultural factors
Heller & Factor, 1991	Mostly female, N = 100; Age (parent), M = 67; Age (child), M = 40	To provide descriptions of permanency planning for adult child by family caregiver	Little specific planning steps, particularly among black, young, lower SES families; Majority preferred use of female sibling as caregiver
Hoyert & Seltzer, 1992	Female; Group 1 = 5900, no caregiving; Group 2 = 358, parent care; Group 3 = 122, husband care; Group 4 = 125, child care	To examine heterogeneity of female family caregivers	More stress over time; Less self-satisfaction; Less marital satisfaction

Table 1.1 Continued

Study	Subject(s)	Purpose	Findings
Kaufman, Adams, & Campbell, 1991	Parent/child, N = 57; Age (parent), M = 62; Age (child), M = 34	To examine issues of permanency planning for adult children with developmental disabilities	More than 50% had not planned for future care of adult child; Planning related to education, SES, informal support
Seltzer, Begun, Seltzer, & Krauss, 1991	Families, N = 411; Age (mothers), M = 55; Age (child), M = 34	To identify the relationship between older mothers, adult children with developmental disabilities, and other siblings	Siblings provide more affective support than instrumental; Sibling involvement related to family dynamics and mother's well-being
Seltzer & Krauss, 1989	N = 203; Age (mothers), M = 66; Age (child), M = 35	To identify risk factors that affect the well-being of the mothers and the function of support	Mothers dependent on strong family support and parenting role

Sherman, 1988	Group 1 (out of home), $N = 154$; Group 2 (in home), $N = 377$; Age, $M = 46$	To describe circumstances that predict residential placement for adults with developmental disabilities	The more disabled, the greater the likelihood of placement; Larger families have higher placement; Behavior precipitates placement
Zeltin, 1986	Siblings: $N = 35$; Age, $M = 34$	To explore the relationships between adults with developmental disabilities and their siblings	Reciprocity important to the adults with developmental disabilities, their sisters, and primary caretakers; Various types of relationships exist

[a]Journal articles
[b]Socioeconomic status

find ways of *legitimating the need for support from the state* such as not wanting to place the burden of care on other family members.

The use of a "cost/benefit" analysis provides a framework for the examination of older parents' ability to maintain a supportive and involved role with their disabled children (Seltzer, Krauss, & Heller, 1991). Sources of stress, or "costs," for older parental caregivers include the recognition of their aging and anticipated deterioration, the continued dependency of their adult child, social isolation, lack of adequate services, and economic concerns (Hogg et al., 1988; Jennings, 1987). Continuous caregiving also can negatively impact the providers' perceptions of themselves and their relationships. For example, older mothers who provided care for their children for more than a year and those who reside with their adult children report more stress, less satisfaction with themselves, and less satisfaction with their marriage than mothers who provided care less than a year or who live apart from their children (Hoyert & Seltzer, 1992).

Researchers suggest, however, that the caregiving situation also provides benefits for elderly parents. For some mothers, the role of caregiver positively contributes to a sense of purpose in their later years, as they have the opportunity to continue in an active parenting role (Seltzer, 1991a). Despite the longevity of their roles, older mothers appear more resilient, more optimistic, and in better health than other caregivers of older adults (Seltzer & Krauss, 1989). These mothers appeared psychologically well adjusted and adaptive in their capacity as long-term family caregivers. An additional benefit for parental caregivers is the assistance they may receive from their developmentally disabled children with daily household chores, such as shopping, cleaning, and laundry, that can become difficult to manage in later life (Grant, 1986).

The Role of Siblings

Most studies of siblings of people with developmental disabilities focus on adjustment during childhood and adolescence. Results of these studies indicate that having a sibling with a developmental disability can have both positive and negative consequences. In some families, siblings may benefit from the increased opportunity to perform teaching, helping, and caregiving roles (Brody & Stoneman, 1986). For others, living with a sibling with mental retardation can be emotionally distressing. Researchers note that nonimpaired children often resent the amount of attention parents give their impaired siblings, express feelings of guilt about the etiology of their siblings' condition, and resent their own caregiving responsibilities (Lobato, 1983; McHale & Gamble, 1987; Simeonsson & Bailey, 1986).

These childhood experiences do appear to influence relationships between siblings in later life. For example, as children, females generally report a closer relationship with their impaired sibling and receive more "parental" responsibilities for these siblings than males (Cleveland & Miller, 1977). These close relationships continue in the later years and tend to influence the women's life commitments more so than those of their male counterparts.

In an examination of relationships between mildly retarded adults and their siblings, Zeltin (1986) identified five types of sibling relationships. In relationships characterized by *very warm feelings/frequent contact/extensive involvement,* many siblings assumed the role of surrogate parent or that of "best friend" to their brother or sister with a developmental disability. The second type of relationship, depicted as *warm feelings/regular contact/moderate involvement,* appeared somewhat less demanding than the first, although the nonimpaired sibling often fulfilled the role of provider and their parents expected that, upon the parents' death, the sibling would take on full responsibility as the primary caregiver. The most common sibling relationship was described by *warm feelings/minimal contact/minimal involvement.* These siblings served primarily as "fill-ins" when parents were not available, and the impaired siblings often felt that they did as much for their nonimpaired siblings as the siblings did for them. The fourth relationship depicted a situation where there were *resentful feelings/minimal contact/minimal involvement.* In most of these cases, the relationship between the impaired and nonimpaired siblings was viewed as strained throughout its history. *Hostile feelings/rare or no contact/no involvement* characterized the final and least common relationship. These relationships also appeared stressed from the time the siblings were young children. These siblings were never sought as resources and there was no expectation of their active involvement in the future.

Sisters of moderately to profoundly developmentally disabled siblings depicted their relationships as positive but nonintimate (Begun, 1989). Their perceptions of the impaired siblings' competencies appear to impact the quality of their relationships. Relationships with least dependent siblings most closely resemble the affection, interaction, and roles of normative sibling relationships. That is, they were warmer and closer, more conflicted, and more satisfying and important than those involving more dependent siblings.

As is true of sibling dyads in later life, emotional or affective support is much greater between impaired and nonimpaired siblings than instrumental assistance. Seltzer, Begun, Seltzer, and Krauss (1991) profiled the "most involved sibling" as typically older than the adult with retardation, living near the family, and having at least weekly contact with his or her impaired brother or sister. Families where there were high levels of sibling involvement were more expressive and cohesive, more oriented toward achievement and independence, and more likely to participate in active recreational activities than families with lower levels of sibling involvement.

Other Informal Care Providers

In a discussion of research on informal caregivers of adults with developmental disabilities, Hogg and his colleagues (1988) report that most older caregivers do not rely on friends and neighbors for assistance with their daily caregiving tasks. Although caregivers highly valued the help received from friends, they did not expect it. Family members appeared concerned about being indebted to friends and neighbors because they did not see themselves in a position to return the help that might be offered.

The Interface With Formal Services

Only a small proportion of older caregivers turn to formal service systems to help alleviate the stress of providing care for their family members with developmental disabilities. Caregivers appear to recognize the need for services as they are less able to provide care themselves. Yet, this change in status does not necessarily lead them to seek help from service agencies (Grant, 1990). Variables identified in the literature that influence caregivers' perceptions of their current and long-term care needs for their family members included the caregivers' age, personal capabilities, race, socioeconomic class, and interpersonal relationships.

An evaluation of the need for formal support services among older caregivers of individuals with developmental disabities living with them in their homes revealed the need for a number of key services to help alleviate the stress and strain of caregiving (Caserta, Connelly, Lund, & Poulton, 1987). The areas in which the caregivers reported the most need included housekeeping, home repairs, personal counseling, and legal advice. For caregivers over the age of 60, health status was the strongest predictor of service need fulfillment, whereas for those caregivers between the ages of 50 and 59, difficulty in locating services and perceived personal competence were predictive of need fulfillment.

In a county-wide survey of family members caring for mentally retarded adults, older parents reported greater reluctance than younger parents to rely on another person to provide respite care for their adult child (Engelhardt, Lutzer, & Brubaker, 1987). The most common reasons these parents cited for not using respite services were the unavailability of qualified personnel, the belief that their child had too many problems, and the cost of services. In a related study, the researchers reported a significant relationship between the use of formal service and the caregivers' current ability to provide care (Engelhardt, Brubaker, & Lutzer, 1988). Families used more services when they reported being less able to provide care for their aging members themselves.

Families of different racial and socioeconomic backgrounds also differ in their use of the formal service system. White parents and those of higher estimated incomes are more likely to plan for their children's future than black parents or those with lower incomes (Kaufman, Adams, & Campbell, 1991). Heller and Factor (1988a) report that black families are less likely to consider future residential placement outside the home and also are less likely to make financial arrangements for the future care of their loved one than white caregivers. Caregivers who are older, white, have less support from relatives, and report higher burden resulting from the caregiving situations are more likely to perceive out-of-home placement for their children as an option (Heller & Factor, 1991).

Families more likely to use residential placements are larger, headed by a single parent, suffer greater disruptions in family life, receive fewer directed client services, or have more impaired members with more severe behavioral problems than families who do not use residential placements (Sherman, 1988). Heller and Factor (1991) suggest that greater use of formal services throughout the life span of the family also may increase the likelihood that older caregivers will prefer a residential placement to in-home care for their children.

The relationship between the caregiver and the family member with a developmental disability may impede the planning process. In their review of the literature, Smith and Tobin (1989) identified several issues that may prevent caregivers from engaging in the planning process, including interdependent ties between parents and their dependent offspring, parental overprotectiveness, a sense of purpose derived from caregiving, companionship, supplementary income derived from public entitlement, and parental feelings of guilt and shame. Parents who do not plan for their child's future also reported greater contact with family and friends (Kaufman et al., 1991). The authors speculate that these parents may assume that someone among these individuals will take over the responsibility for their child when necessary, though there are no formal or informal agreements as such.

Summary and Conclusions

The literature reviewed in this chapter reveals several similarities between family caregivers of older adults and those of aging individuals with developmental disabilities. First, the structure of both caregiving networks appears hierarchical. One member of the immediate family assumes the role of primary care provider. When that person is not able or available to provide care, the next immediate family member takes on the responsibility. For families caring for the elderly, the spouse or adult child is the most frequent care provider. For aging persons with developmental disabilities, parents and then siblings take on the primary responsibility of providing care. In both situations, women (i.e., wives, mothers, or daughters) tend to be responsible for providing day-to-day care for the recipient.

With advancing age, there is likely to be a decline in the health and functional capabilities of both the caregiver and the care receiver. The physical, emotional, and social stress associated with intense caregiving accumulates over time (Hoyert & Seltzer, 1992) and often is overwhelming. These changes make spousal caregivers of aging adults and parental caregivers of adults with developmental disabilities especially vulnerable to the burdens of caregiving. Yet, both groups of caregivers are reluctant to turn to individuals outside the immediate family or to the formal service system for assistance.

Siblings providing care for a brother or sister with a developmental disability can be seen in roles parallel to those of adult children who provide care for their aging parents. For both groups of caregivers, women are the primary caretakers more often than men. When families consist of multiple children or siblings, one person usually assumes the primary responsibility of care while the others vary in their degree of involvement (Cicirelli, 1985; Zeltin, 1986). Entrance to the caregiving role frequently is assumed, and may place caregivers in conflict with their family and career responsibilities.

Differences between the two groups of caregivers also became apparent. First is the time of onset. The role of spousal caregiver occurs in later life, usually after several years of sharing healthy, independent lives. For parents providing care for their sons or daughters with developmental disabilities, their caregiving responsibilities begin at the birth of their child. These caregivers may have an advantage over late-life spousal caregivers, however, because they tend to acquire an understanding of their care receiver's capabilities early in life. Barring any major health problems, the care receiver's physical and mental abilities remain fairly stable throughout his or her adult life (Zigman et al., 1991).

Related to the time of onset is the number of years spent in the caregiving role. Caregivers of older adults spend a limited number of years fulfilling their caregiving responsibilities. For parents, and some siblings, of individuals with developmental disabilities, caregiving is a lifelong task. The relationship between situational longevity and caregivers' perceptions of burden and stress is not well understood. Researchers present two opposing hypotheses. At one end of the continuum is the "wear and tear" hypothesis that suggests prolonged exposure to the daily tasks of caregiving results in the depletion of physical and personal resources (Johnson & Catalano, 1983; Perlin, Lieberman, Menaghan, & Mullan, 1981). At the opposite end of the spectrum is the "adaptation model." According to this model, caregivers exhibit stability or improvement in their mental health over time (Townsend, Noelker, Deimling, & Bass, 1989). The literature reviewed in this chapter presents supportive evidence for both interpretations.

A third difference between caregivers of older adults and those of aging persons with developmental disabilities is their relationship with their care receiver. Caring for one's spouse or aging parent may present conflicting feelings of obligation and responsibilities depending on the caregiver's own life situation and prior relationship with the care receiver. It can be argued that these same variables influence the relationship between caregivers and persons with developmental disabilities. The parental caregiver, however, may present different issues, based upon personal feelings of obligation, guilt, or appreciation for the continuation of the parental role.

In conclusion, the general geriatric caregiving literature documents several issues also of concern for older families of aging adults with developmental disabilities. Whereas much of caregiving literature is descriptive in nature and has methodological drawbacks (see Barer & Johnson, 1990), it provides researchers and practitioners with the groundwork from which to build a better understanding of needs of older caregivers of aging relatives with developmental disabilities. Researchers also have begun to identify the distinct needs and concerns of this group of elderly caregivers that must be addressed in the development of appropriate intervention strategies. As the literature on this unique group of caregivers moves out of its infancy stage, researchers must strive to improve upon current content and methodological limitations (see Seltzer, Krauss, & Heller, 1991) in order to enhance our knowledge and ability to meet the needs of this small, but growing, group of elderly caregivers.

PART II

Issues and Concerns of Older Caregivers

2

Aging Caregivers of Persons With Developmental Disabilities

Changes in Burden and Placement Desire

TAMAR HELLER

"My son is the son I always asked the Lord for. I have never felt handicapped or held back from anything in caring and loving him. He is truly loved by all who know him."

"We have no problem or hardships with our son. He brings us a lot of joy and he's very helpful."

"The physical aspect of her care is more difficult for us as we get older; we need time to be alone."

"I feel resignation and constant concern. I don't know how to cope with his behavioral outbursts."

These words of older parents of persons with developmental disabilities living at home reflect the variability in their attitudes toward caregiving

---
This research was supported by grant number 2-5-37074 from the National Institute on Disability and Rehabilitation Research and Training Center Consortium on Aging and Developmental Disabilities and by grant number HD 2302201 from the National Institute of Child Health and Human Development.

and their ability to maintain their adult child in the home. This chapter brings a life-span perspective to understanding the predictors and changes in burden and placement desire experienced by families of adults with developmental disabilities. It draws upon data from two studies that focus on family adaptation to having a member with developmental disabilities. The first is a study of family caregivers of persons of all ages with moderate to profound mental retardation (Heller, Rowitz, & Farber, 1992). It examines life-course phase differences in stressors and in perceived caregiving burden. The second study is a 2.5-year longitudinal study of parent caregivers of adults with developmental disabilities age 30 and over living in the family home (Heller & Factor, in press). It examines the effects of child and family characteristics and support resources on caregiving burden and out-of-home placement desire over time.

This chapter first reviews research regarding life-span predictors and changes in family burden and out-of-home placement and then presents the results of the two new studies conducted by the author and her colleagues (Heller et al., 1992; Heller & Factor, in press).

Life-Span Differences in Burden and Placement

Burden Over the Life Span

Most families of persons with developmental disabilities provide lifelong family-based care for them. As parents age, out-of-home placement increases, although it is still not the primary residential arrangement, at least until the parents' death (Meyers, Borthwick, & Eyman, 1985). With the increased longevity both of the general population and of persons with developmental disabilities over the past 20 years the period of family responsibility is longer (Janicki & Wisniewski, 1985; Seltzer, Krauss, & Heller, 1991). Hence, family members are the most consistent source of social support for persons with developmental disabilities throughout their life span.

The life-span impact of caregiving for a person with developmental disabilities is not well understood. Most of the earlier research focused on the first decade of the child's life or on the last decade of the parent's life. Little research has compared families either cross-sectionally or longitudinally across various life stages. A life-span perspective assumes that the roles, functions, and stressors of caregiving change over the life span. Research on families without a member with disabilities has underscored the importance of considering family stages in understanding family stress. A common finding has been that for families without a child with disabilities their children's adolescence is the most stressful period in family life (McCubbin & Thompson, 1987; Olson & McCubbin, 1983).

The mental retardation, family development, and gerontological literatures provide us with theories for examining the long-term impact of caregiving for a family member with developmental disabilities. Birenbaum (1971) and Farber (1959) have hypothesized that as the child with developmental disabilities gets older, coping by family members becomes increasingly difficult. Although a shift of responsibility from parents to their offspring is normative, parents of persons with developmental disabilities most often continue caregiving over a longer time period. Farber (1959) refers to this phenomenon as "arrest" in the family life cycle. Hence, with age, family caregivers are more likely to play non-normative caregiving roles. Concurrently families face their own aging process, which can result in poorer health and loss of social supports. Several studies found that parents of older children with developmental disabilities were less supported and more stressed than parents of younger children (Bristol & Schopler, 1984; Holroyd, Brown, Wikler, & Simmons, 1975; Suelzle & Keenan, 1981). Wikler (1986) found that the transition periods, in which persons with developmental disabilities were entering adolescence or adulthood, presented the greatest stress to families.

On the other hand, researchers of caregiving among families of impaired elderly persons have proposed an adaptational model of long-term caregiving (Townsend et al., 1989), which hypothesizes that over time families better adjust to their caregiving role. They found that the psychological health of children caring for elderly parents improved over time. Seltzer and Krauss's (1989) study of 462 older mothers caring for an adult with mental retardation lends some support for the adaptational model of caregiving. They found that many of the mothers in their study were healthier, had better morale, and reported no more burden or stress than did mothers in studies of younger families of persons with mental retardation or of family caregivers of elderly persons.

Predictors of Burden

In addition to the life stage of the family, other major factors that have been shown to influence the degree of caregiving burden experienced by families have included characteristics of the family and of the persons with disabilities as well as the family's support resources. Among studies of children with developmental disabilities, the child characteristics that have been shown to be risk factors for burden have included having a child with more severe mental retardation, poorer health, and maladaptive behavior (Beckman, 1983; Crnic, Friedrich, & Greenberg, 1983; Seltzer & Krauss, 1984). The positive effects of informal and formal support resources on the well-being of family members of children with developmental disabilities have been well documented (e.g., Dunst, Trivette, & Cross, 1986; Friedrich, Cohen, & Wilturner, 1987; Orr, Cameron, & Day, 1991; Waisbren, 1980).

Few studies have been conducted on factors contributing to burden among families of adults with developmental disabilities. As in the studies of children, the key characteristics of the person with disabilities that are associated with family caregiving burden are poor physical health, high maladaptive behaviors, more severe mental retardation, and lower adaptive behavior (Black, Cohn, Smull, & Crites, 1985; Heller & Factor, 1988b; Seltzer & Krauss, 1989). The few studies that have examined the impact of support resources on the caregiving burden of families of adults with developmental disabilities have had mixed results. In Seltzer and Krauss's (1989) study of older mothers providing in-home care to adults with mental retardation, informal social support rather than formal service support was related to perceived caregiving burden. Roccoforte (1991), on the other hand, found that among families of adults with developmental disabilities both informal support and degree of unmet formal service needs were associated with family caregiving burden and stress.

Out-of-Home Placement Over the Life Span

Cole (1986) has proposed a theory for understanding the roles of family stressors and resources in influencing the decision to place a child with developmental disabilities out of the home. Stressors related to the child combine with other family stressors to produce a crisis. The family may cope by removing the stressors, including placing the child out of the home. Family resources and positive perceptions of the circumstances buffer the impact of these stressors, enabling the family to cope via accommodation and maintenance of the relative within the family home. As the age of the child with developmental disabilities increases, the likelihood of out-of-home placement also increases (Meyers et al., 1985; Suelzle & Keenan, 1981). Suelzle and Keenan (1981) found that among children the risk of out-of-home placement is highest when the child is between 6 and 12 years old and between 19 and 21 years old. With the increasing trend to maintain children within the family home, the residential system for persons with developmental disabilities has become primarily an adult system (Lakin, Hill, Chen, & Stephens, 1989). Key characteristics of the child, other than age, that have been associated with out-of-home placement have included maladaptive behavior problems (e.g., Blacher, Hanneman, & Rousey, 1992; Borthwick-Duffy, Eyman, & White, 1987; Sherman, 1988) and low IQ or more severe retardation (Blacher et al., 1992; Eyman & Call, 1977; Meyers et al., 1985).

As Cole's theory would indicate, several studies have found positive effects of informal and formal support resources on reducing out-of-home placements of children (German & Maisto, 1982; Sherman, 1988; Sherman & Cocozza, 1984). However, two recent studies have found formal support to be a nonsignificant (Cole & Meyer, 1989) or only moderate predictor (Bromley & Blacher, 1991) of parents' plans to seek placement in the future.

In the few studies that have been done on adults with disabilities, their maladaptive behavior has been a key characteristic associated with their family's desire for out-of-home placement (Black et al., 1985; Heller & Factor, 1991). The findings on the impact of support resources on placement decisions of families of adults with developmental disabilities are equivocal. Black et al. (1985) found that low service utilization was related to out-of-home placement requests. However, in Heller and Factor's (1991) study of families caring for a relative with developmental disabilities over age 30 formal service use had an opposite effect. Greater rather than less use of formal services was related to caregivers' preference for a residential program placement. Informal support was associated with preference for family care.

In the only study to compare determinants of out-of-home placements in families of adults versus families of children with developmental disabilities, Tausig (1985) reported that different factors influenced the decisions of the two groups. For children under age 21 years behavior problems primarily influenced placement decisions, whereas for individuals over 21 years stressors within the family were more important.

Descriptions of Study 1 and Study 2

The two studies reported in this chapter addressed family adaptation to having a member with developmental disabilities. Study 1 used a large cross-sectional design including all age phases (Heller et al., 1992), and Study 2 was done on a select sample of older families using a longitudinal design (Heller & Factor, in press).

Study 1: Life-Span Differences in Burden

Study 1 was part of a large-scale study of family adaptation to having a member with mental retardation conducted by me, Louis Rowitz, and Bernard Farber (Heller et al., 1992). Interviews and written surveys were conducted with 489 primary caregivers of persons with moderate to profound mental retardation living at home or in out-of-home placement and ranging in age from less than 1 year to 63 years.

The study assessed (a) characteristics of the family (socioeconomic status) and the person with mental retardation (age, level of mental retardation, problem behaviors, and residential placement status), (b) support resources (collateral family, lineal family, friends, professional, service problems), and (c) caregiving burden. Problem behaviors were measured by Inventory for Client and Agency Planning (Bruininks, Hill, Weatherman, & Woodcock, 1986). Residential status refers to whether the person with mental retardation lives out of the home or in the home. The support scales were derived from the network subscales of the Telleen Parenting Social Support Scales (Telleen, 1985). The support scales included (a) lineal support (from immediate family members, including parents and children of caregivers), (b) collateral family support (from siblings and other relatives), (c) friends' support, and (d) professional support. Perceived caregiving burden was a nine-item scale developed for this project that asked families the extent to which they agreed or disagreed with statements concerning the effect the person with mental retardation has on their lives. Families were grouped into five age phases based on the age of the person with mental retardation: (a) preschooler (0-5 years), (b) young child (6-12), (c) adolescent (13-20), (d) young adult (21-30), and (e) older adult (over 30).

Study 2: Changes in Caregiving Burden and Placement Desire

Study 2 addressed the following questions:

1. To what extent do child and family characteristics and support resources affect caregivers' perceived burden and their desire for out-of-home placement of their adult child with developmental disabilities over a 2.5-year period?
2. Do family support resources, caregiving burden, and out-of-home placement preference change as families age over a 2.5-year period?
3. To what extent do changes in support resources affect changes in burden and placement desire over a 2.5-year period?

This study was a 2.5-year follow-up of an earlier study of 100 family caregivers of persons with developmental disabilities age 30 and older living at home (Heller & Factor, 1991). The follow-up sample included 77 parent primary caregivers, of which 62 responded at Time 2. Interviews addressed functioning level of the person with disabilities, caregiver's characteristics, support resources, caregiving burden, and permanency plans.

The functional level of the adult child was assessed with the Inventory for Client and Agency Planning, which includes a measure of adaptive behavior and maladaptive behaviors. Family characteristics included primary caregiver's socioeconomic status, age, and health. Support resources included informal support (from the spouse, other relatives, and friends) and unmet formal service need. The informal support scale developed for this project assessed "the degree to which you could count on each of the three types of people to assist you in six areas pertaining to the care of your disabled relative" (providing emotional support, transportation, daily respite, extended respite for 1-2 weeks, information on formal services, and personal care). Unmet service need was measured by asking respondents whether they needed but were not receiving in the past year each of 17 listed services developed to assist families in caring for a relative with mental retardation.

Caregiving burden was defined as the degree of perceived strain experienced in caring for a relative with developmental disabilities. It reflected subjective rather than objective burden. It consisted of statements reflecting the physical, socio-emotional, financial, and time-demand strains of caregiving. The preference for out-of-home placement was measured by asking families what future living arrangement they expected for their relative when they could no longer care for him or her.

Findings From Study 1: Life-Span Perspective on Stressors and Burden

Life-Span Differences in Stressors

In the life-span study described here primary caregivers were asked to rate the degree to which they currently were experiencing stressors related to their relative with mental retardation. Table 2.1 depicts the differences in stressors experienced at different stages. Younger families were more likely to report problems related to obtaining information on their relative's development and to obtaining family support services than were older families, whereas older families were more likely to report stressors related to finding needed services for their relative than were younger families. Of all the age groups, the families of adolescents reported the greatest difficulties in finding appropriate services, in maintaining ongoing contact with staff, in finding information on their relative's development, and in participating in parent groups. The oldest families (primary caregivers of relatives with mental retardation over the age of 30 years) were most likely to feel stressed about future residential placement issues.

The following comments depict the anxiety older parents often face in regard to planning for their adult child's future living arrangements, particularly for the time when they can no longer provide the care:

> "They need more dedicated people to help care for these children. It does take a lot of you to raise a special child. I would rather we don't die before my son because I don't know who could care for him as well."

> "I worry about where he's going to live after I cannot take care of him."

> "I wonder if my daughter would be fair to him when she takes over his care. I will put a condition that my house can't be sold until my son dies, so he'll always have a place."

Table 2.1   Stressors at Different Age Phases (Mean Scores)

Stressors	Age Phases				
	0-5	6-12	13-20	21-30	31+
Finding information on development[a]	.70	.68	.62	.36	.41
Participating in parent groups[b]	.43	.35	.52	.33	.21
Finding services for family[a]	.68	.72	.74	.36	.33
Finding residential placement[c]	0	.26	.17	.46	.74
Finding service for child	.51	.87	.89	.65	.74
Ongoing contact with staff	.12	.11	.27	.22	.16
Planning for own death	1.06	1.07	1.03	.82	.79

[a]$p < .05$
[b]$p < .10$
[c]At home only

Life-Span Differences in Caregiving Burden

The life-span study examined differences in caregiving burden as perceived by the family caregivers across the age phases. A multivariate analysis of covariance (MANCOVA) in which residential status was covaried indicated that caregiving burden differed significantly between the age phases [$F(4,419)=6.28$, $p<.001$]. The means and standard deviations are indicated in Table 2.2.

As found in the research on families without members with mental retardation, adolescence was the most difficult period for families. Both the gerontological theory of family adaptation over the long term and the Farber theory of increasing difficulty over time for families were partially supported. Perceived caregiving burden was lowest for caregivers of the youngest (under 6 years old) and the oldest (age 30 and over) members with mental retardation. It seems that adaptation to having a relative with mental retardation is easiest when the child is young and becomes more difficult as the child becomes an adolescent. On the other hand, as the child becomes an adult and the parent ages, families experience less burden. Perhaps at this stage there is greater acceptance of the family member and greater reciprocity in caregiving as the child with mental retardation is often a strong support for the parent. In a study focusing on such

Table 2.2   Means of Burden Scores by Age Phase

Age Phase	Mean Burden Score	Standard Deviation	N	Percent at Home
Birth to 5	22.9	9.1	44	89
6 to 12 years	25.9	8.0	61	80
13 to 20 years	26.4	8.2	79	48
21 to 30 years	25.6	8.5	122	46
31 and over	21.6	7.8	119	50
Entire sample	24.4	8.5	425	57

caregiving reciprocity, Heller and Factor (in press) found that parents who received greater support from their offspring with developmental disabilities perceived less burden in caring for that offspring.

In the life-span study presented in this chapter, the qualitative data richly describe how family caregiving perceptions change over the life cycle. When older parents were asked how their feelings toward their child with disabilities changed over the years there were three strong themes. One was that over the years it became easier to adjust to the caregiving demands:

> "I'm so used to the routine. I'd be at a loss for something to do. It comes naturally."

A second theme was that over time they have understood their child better and have known how to better help him or her:

> "At first I was very upset. I didn't know how to go about helping him. There were not many schools available. I accepted it a long time ago."
> "Since maturing and living with him, we have gotten to be very close and understanding of him, even accepting."
> "We are very proud of him. As time goes on we are better able to help and understand him."

A third theme presented by the parents was that they have grown to love and appreciate their child more:

"I'd rather raise three children with Down syndrome than one normal one; they give you more love back."

"At first I thought why me? What did I do? Now he's a blessing. I enjoy him and his company. You get to accept things."

"At first it was terrible. I started to cry; I didn't believe it. Now I don't know what I'd do without her; she's my right arm."

"At first I was devastated. I thought it was totally unfair. Why did I have it? Why did others have normal children? I don't resent the fact that he's handicapped anymore. I suppose I know he has brought us great joy."

Life-Span Differences in Predictors of Burden

A series of regression analyses were done examining the effects of child characteristics (age, residential status, problem behaviors, and level of mental retardation) and support resources (collateral family, lineal family, friends, professional) on caregiving burden perceived by parents. Separate analyses were done for parents of children (under age 21) and for parents of adults with mental retardation (age 21 and over). As indicated in Table 2.3 the impact of child characteristics and support resources differed for families of children versus families of adults. For parents of children support resources were significantly associated with burden, whereas for parents of adults the characteristics of the adult child were a stronger influence. The major characteristics of the adult offspring associated with burden were problem behaviors, level of mental retardation, and residential status. The families who experienced greater burden were more likely to have an adult child with maladaptive behaviors and with more severe mental retardation. The adult child also was more likely to be living in their home.

This analysis points to the importance of examining family adaptation to a child with mental retardation through a life-span perspective. It appears that the amount of social support received has less impact on the older than the younger caregivers. One possible explanation is that many of the older families already had placed their relative out of the home and hence felt less of a need for support in caring for that person. In the following study reported here, which focused only on parents caring for an adult offspring in their home, social support played an important role in alleviating burden for older families.

Table 2.3   Regressions of Family Characteristics and Social Support on Burden, for Children and Adult Dependents

| | Children and Teens | | Adults | |
	Beta Coefficients	Standard Error	Beta Coefficients	Standard Error
Family/child attributes	$(r^2 = .06)^a$		$(r^2 = .150)^c$	
Level of retardation	−.013	.076	.220^c	.065
Living situation	.002	.076	.225^c	.066
SES	−.041	.074	.005	.060
Problem behaviors	.233^b	.073	.311^c	.061
Support system	$(r^2\text{change} = .08)^b$		$(r^2\text{change} = .01)$	
Lineal relative's support	−.240^b	.090	.025	.066
Collateral relative's support	−.047	.096	−.037	.065
Friend's support	.077	.082	.099	.064
Professional support	.259^b	.085	.031	.069
Total	$r^2 = .137^b$		$r^2 = .16^c$	
	$df = (8,176)$		$df = (8,236)$	

$^a p < .05$
$^b p < .01$
$^c p < .001$

Findings From Study 2: Changes in Burden and Placement Desire

Study 2 examined the role of adult child and family characteristics and of support resources on caregiving burden and placement urgency and on changes over 2.5 years in burden and placement desire. It also provided descriptive data on the burden families experience and the extent to which families desire placements.

Changes in Burden and Placement Desire Over Time

The degree of perceived caregiving burden did not change significantly over time. However, there were a considerable number of people whose burden decreased (44%) and a considerable number whose burden increased (36%). At both times the major difficulties families reported were concern about future caregiving (80% at Time 1 and 73% at Time 2) and reliance of their offspring solely on them for recreation and leisure activities (88% at Time 1 and 77% at Time 2). Families reported having done very little planning in regard to their offspring's future living arrangements for beyond their lifetime. About half of the families wanted a residential program placement eventually and 7 actually made a placement during the 2.5 years. Of the 29 families who still wanted a residential placement at Time 2 and had not made one, over 40% had not yet discussed the matter with anyone, 28% were in the discussion stage, 10% were looking into residential programs, and 21% had placed their child on a waiting list. When asked when they would like the change in living arrangements to occur, the majority of the caregivers (about two thirds both times) wanted it to occur after they died; about one third (both times) wanted it to occur within their lifetime; and only 3% in Time 1 and 7% in Time 2 wanted it to occur within the next year.

Among families who continued caring for their relative in their home at Time 2 there was a high correlation between initial and later desire for out-of-home placement ($r=.63$, $p<.01$). Blacher (1986) has conceptualized placement as a process rather than a single act. This process may begin with occasional thoughts followed by decision making, active searching, and actual placement. The findings from Study 2, though based on a small sample, support this concept. All but one of the families who placed their child had reported desiring out-of-home placements at Time 1. Also, three of the seven persons (43%) who moved into a residential program had been on a waiting list at Time 1. Only 11% of the families who did not make placement had been on a waiting list at Time 1.

Predictors of Burden and Placement Desire

Regressions predicting Time 2 caregiving burden and placement desire were conducted using Time 1 child and caregiver characteristics as the first block, Time 1 support resources as the second block, and Time 2 support resources as the third block. To control for Time 1 of the dependent variable the respective Time 1 dependent variable was entered with the first block. The results are indicated in Tables 2.4 and 2.5.

Table 2.4 Hierarchical Regression of Burden, Time 2

Variables	Change in R^2 for Block	Beta
Time 1 child/caregiver	.48[b]	
Child adaptive behavior		−.22
Child maladaptive behavior		−.42[b]
Caregiver SES		.08
Caregiver age		.07
Caregiver health		.08
Burden, Time 1		.34[a]
Time 1 support resources	.03	
Informal support		−.04
Unmet services		.18
Time 2 support resources	.15[b]	
Informal support		.04
Unmet services		.43[b]
Total	.65[b]	

[a] $p < .01$
[b] $p < .001$

Characteristics of the Adult Child

Initial maladaptive behavior of the adult with developmental disabilities was the only child or family characteristic related to increased caregiving burden over time. This finding has been generally supported in the literature on caregiving stress in families caring for persons with developmental disabilities. Unlike in Heller and Factor's (1991) study, which included parent and sibling caregivers, maladaptive behavior did not significantly influence future placement desire. One possibility is that maladaptive behaviors may play a larger role in actual placements versus in placement desire.

Table 2.5 Logistic Regression of Future Placement Preference, Time 2

Variables	df	Chi-Square	Beta
Intercept	1	1.02	10.16
Time 1 child/caregiver	6	27.60[c]	
Child adaptive behavior			.00
Child maladaptive behavior			.00
Caregiver SES			.02
Caregiver age			.07
Caregiver health			−.05
Placement preference			−1.66[c]
Time 1 support resources	2	10.38[b]	
Informal support			.06
Unmet services			−.58[a]
Time 2 support resources	2	3.47	
Informal support			−.15
Unmet services			−.23
Total	10	41.45[c]	

[a] $p < .05$
[b] $p < .01$
[c] $p < .001$

Role of Formal Support Resources

The number of perceived unmet formal service needs was a key variable influencing parental well-being and placement desire. A high number of initial unmet needs was related to greater out-of-home placement preference 2.5 years later. Also increases in unmet needs over time were associated with greater caregiving burden at Time 2. Most previous studies that had obtained equivocal results defined formal support resources as service use. However, these findings indicate that parents' perceptions that they are not getting needed services (rather than merely degree of service use) influence their ability and desire to maintain their relative in the family home.

These families used few formal services (average of 3.5 services). Yet they had a considerable number of unmet formal service needs (average of 4 services). The highest unmet need both times was for information on residential programs. Other high unmet service needs included out-of-home respite, social recreational services, in-home respite, case management, information on guardianship, information on financial planning, and family counseling.

Service use and unmet needs did not change significantly over time. Nor did older parents report using or needing more services than younger parents. Age may be related to greater need for some specific services and less need for other services. Lutzer and Brubaker (1988) found that older parent caregivers (over age 56) had greater needs for out-of-home respite care than did younger parents, but had fewer needs for a parent cooperative or for training.

Informal Support

In the present study informal support at either Time 1 or Time 2 did not significantly affect Time 2 caregiving burden or placement desire, although it was significantly negatively correlated with Time 2 caregiving burden. During the 2.5 years informal support was the only variable that decreased significantly over time due to decreases in support from the spouse and other relatives. With age the likelihood of widowhood increased. Five spouses died during the study period.

These findings suggest that as caregivers age, there is a greater need for support programs that bolster their informal support networks. In particular these programs need to address siblings who are likely to assume greater responsibility for their brother or sister with developmental disabilities over time (Heller & Factor, 1988b; Krauss, 1990; Seltzer, Begun, Magan, & Luchterhand, 1993). Furthermore there is evidence that the siblings' level of involvement with their relative with developmental disabilities is related to maternal well-being (Seltzer, Begun, et al., 1991).

Implications for Practice and Research

Practice Issues

The studies reported here highlight the importance of a life-span perspective in understanding family adaptation to a member with developmental disabilities. The fact that different stressors occur at different life phases suggests either that certain events occur more at different phases or that families perceive the events differently at different phases. For example, families may have more difficulty finding residential placements for children, yet seeking residential placement may be perceived as more stressful as the child ages and parents worry about their ability to continue caregiving. In addition to variable reactions to stressors, families vary in their degree of perceived caregiving burden at different age phases. The finding that families of the oldest age phase report the least burden suggests that elderly family members are more likely to benefit from caregiving for their relative with developmental disabilities than are younger family caregivers. A third life-span difference is that support resources appear to have a greater impact on burden in the earlier life phases. In the older age phases the characteristics of the person with developmental disabilities play a larger role, particularly degree of maladaptive behaviors and residential status. These findings underscore the need to understand family perspectives at different ages in developing policies, conducting training, and providing family counseling. Older parents are more likely than younger parents to need help in future planning, in obtaining residential placements, and in finding services.

One of the limitations of the cross-sectional study is that it cannot control for cohort differences. Hence one must keep in mind that the oldest families have had very different experiences with the service system from those of the younger families. Their family member with developmental disabilities is much less likely to have received special education services or the benefit of community-based residential placements. Many families report their negative experiences with schools and professionals in the earlier years. Also these families appear to have lower expectations from service agencies and are less attuned to advocating for their relative. An effective mode of communicating current service options with these families is to conduct group informational meetings in which other family caregivers share their personal experiences in obtaining services.

The longitudinal research reported in this chapter suggests the need for both family support programs serving families of adults with developmental disabilities living at home and the development of residential options for those needing residential placements when families can no longer provide care in the home. Funding for family support initiatives has grown over the past decade. A recent survey of family support programs nationwide indicated that as of fiscal year 1988, 42 states had discrete mental retardation/developmental disabilities (MR/DD) agency-based family support initiatives (either cash subsidy, respite, or other family support) (Fujiura, Garza, & Braddock, 1990). Many, however, limited the family support initiatives to families of children. Key family supports needed to maintain the adult with disabilities in the family home include information on residential, financial, and guardianship planning; respite care; and social-recreational programs.

For families requiring placements out of the family home, there are large gaps in the residential service system. Families face long waiting lists and few acceptable options. An Association for Retarded Citizens study in 45 states indicated that over 63,000 persons were on waiting lists for MR/DD residential services (Davis, 1987). Also the 135,000 residents of large MR/DD facilities and the 50,000 nursing home residents with developmental disabilities are more likely to receive priority in any new residential initiatives for adults (Fujiura et al., 1990). Hence planning for the future residential service needs of the older adult with developmental disabilities is essential.

Research Considerations

Further research on placement issues needs to longitudinally examine factors that predict both placement preferences and actual placements over a longer time span. The present research primarily focused on parents' desires for out-of-home placement over time rather than actual placements. There also is a need for larger and more diverse samples that include persons not currently identified by the service system. A larger sample would also enable further study of cross-cultural and regional differences in family attitudes toward caregiving and residential placement.

3

Older Caregivers of Family Members With Developmental Disabilities

Changes in Roles and Perceptions

KAREN A. ROBERTO

Historically, the number of persons with developmental disabilities cared for in the homes of family members declines with age. Based on a national sample of residential release patterns of public residential facilities, researchers found that 12% of persons with mental retardation, ages 40 to 63, lived with their families whereas no one beyond the age of 63 did (Best-Sigford, Bruininks, Lakin, Hill, & Heal, 1982). In a study of older adults with developmental disabilities in the state of New York, Janicki and MacEachron (1984) found the percentage of individuals residing with family members decreased from 7% of those aged 52 to 62 to 3% for those between the ages of 63 and 72 to 1% of those over the age of 73. A more recent study suggests that we may be beginning to see a shift in the living arrangements of this population. Seltzer and Krauss's (1987) national survey of programs serving elderly persons with mental retardation (55+) found that 12.5% of the elderly with developmental disabilities participating in community day programs (i.e., vocational day activity, day activity, supplemental retirement, leisure and outreach, and senior citizen centers) lived with a family member.

This study was funded by a grant from the Colorado Developmental Disabilities Planning Council, Denver, Colorado.

Two national trends contribute to the growing numbers of individuals remaining at home with their families. First, is the increase in life expectancy of individuals with lifelong disabilities. Until recently, few persons with disabilities survived to old age. Second, there is strong support for community integration of individuals with disabilities. The range of community resources now available for individuals with developmental disabilities provide them and their families greater residential, service, and work options than ever before.

These two developments present new challenges for current and future generations of families. Specifically, as the number of persons with developmental disabilities living into their middle and later years increases, parents are likely to spend more years sharing their homes with their children. Currently, limited information is available concerning the provision of long-term, in-home care for aging relatives with developmental disabilities (Roberto, this volume; Seltzer, Krauss, & Heller, 1991). We know that parents are the primary care providers. During their later years, these caregivers must learn to cope with and adapt to physical and psychosocial changes that may interfere with their ability to continue in their caregiving roles. When parents are no longer able to provide care, they most frequently turn to one of their other children to assume their caregiving responsibilities.

The identification of the structure of the family caregiving network provides a framework from which to explore the issues and concerns of these caregivers. A greater understanding of the changes that occur within the caregiving situation is necessary to meet the needs of this growing population of older caregivers. How well elderly caregivers cope with these changes depends on their cognitive appraisal of their families' situation (Lazarus & Folkman, 1984). That is, the caregivers' perceptions of the significance of the changes taking place within their family will minimize or magnify the stressfulness of the caregiver role in their later years.

The purpose of this study was to examine perceived changes in the caregiving role as both the caregiver and the family member with a developmental disability have grown older. The information collected specified situations where the older caregivers perceived the most change. The following questions guided the research:

1. What type of changes in the caregiving situation do caregivers perceive as they grow older?

2. Are background characteristics of the caregiver and care receiver predictive of overall stability or change in the caregiving situation?
3. Is change more likely to be perceived in certain situations based upon the personal and social characteristics of the caregiver or care receiver?

Method

Sample

The sample for this study consisted of 48 older adults providing care in their homes for aging family members with developmental disabilities. The caregivers ranged in age from 60 to 89 ($M = 72.2$). The vast majority of the 10 men and 38 women were parents (85%) and the other 15% were sisters of the person with developmental disabilities.

Procedure

The State of Colorado Division of Developmental Disabilities assisted with the identification of caregivers. A staff member from the division contacted the 16 community center boards in the state and requested mailing labels for all clients at least 40 years of age and living with their families. Fifteen boards cooperated in the study, identifying a potential sample of 148 families.

To protect the confidentiality of the participants, the Division sent a packet containing a letter from the Principal Investigator explaining the study and requesting the primary caregiver to complete the enclosed self-report questionnaire. Data collection took place during the spring of 1988. Three weeks after the initial mailing, division staff sent a second packet to all potential sample members. A total of 61 family caregivers returned the questionnaire for a response rate of 41%. Excluded from the analyses reported in this chapter were 8 caregivers who were younger than age 60 and 5 who did not report their age.

Measures

A self-report questionnaire was designed specifically for use in this study. The questions included in the survey came from a review of the geriatric caregiving literature; Gold, Dobrof, and Torian's (1987) study of family caregivers of adults with developmental disabilities; and input from community leaders serving families providing care for their relatives with developmental disabilities. Pilot testing of the questionnaire occurred with several parents providing in-home care for their adult children, and the results were incorporated into the final version of the questionnaire.

The first part of the questionnaire elicited *background information* about the caregivers and care receivers. These questions identified the sex, age, marital status, health status, and work status of the participants.

To assess the *functional ability* of the person with a developmental disability, a modified portion of the *Developmental Disabilities Profile* developed by the New York State Office of Mental Retardation and Developmental Disabilities (1987) was used. Respondents rated their relatives' ability to perform 21 tasks of daily living (e.g., toileting, bathing, dressing, preparing foods, maintaining safety, managing money). The response code for each task was needing (a) total support (person is completely dependent), (b) assistance (person requires lots of hands-on help), (c) supervision (person requires mainly verbal prompts), or (d) independent (starts and finishes without prompts or help). The items were summed for a total activities of daily living (ADL) score. The scale had an alpha coefficient of .95 when calculated with this sample of aging persons with developmental disabilities.

To assess the *socialization patterns* of the care receivers, caregivers indicated whether their family member participated in any type of structured program outside the home including day programs, shelter workshops, part-time employment, or full-time employment. Caregivers also indicated the type of social activities in which they themselves participated. Participation in each of 10 activities (e.g., organizational meetings, church, going out to dinner, visits with friends) was coded on two levels. The caregivers first indicated whether they participated in any of the social activities. If the caregivers reported that they did participate in a particular activity, they then indicated whether it was something they did with or without their care receiver.

To determine *changes in the caregiving situation*, caregivers responded to a series of 14 questions that required them to state whether they perceived an increase or a decrease in the situation or whether the situation had remained the same over the past 10 years. If a change had occurred, the respondents wrote a brief explanation of why they believed there was a change in their situation.

Results

Elderly Caregivers

The number of years the caregivers had provided care for their relatives with developmental disabilities in their home ranged from 2 to 59, for an average of 39.6 years. The caregiver's mean yearly income was between $10,000 and $14,999 and they reported an average of 11.2 years of formal education. When asked to rate their overall health at the present time, approximately 2% of the caregivers reported their health as excellent, 40% as good, 46% as fair, and 12% as poor. Besides being a caregiver for their child or sibling, 10% also were caring for a spouse who had become disabled and 6% were caring for another child with a developmental disability.

The caregivers were involved in an average of three ($SD = 2.6$) social activities (see Table 3.1). The most common activities were dining out (60%), weekly visits with family (46%) and friends (46%), and attending church (24%). All caregivers involved in social activities participated in at least one activity with their care receiver. Dining out (70%) and attending church (55%) were the two most common activities in which the caregiver included the care receiver.

Care Receivers

The 27 men and 21 women with developmental disabilities ranged in age from 41 to 70 ($M = 48.3$; $SD = 7.9$). The vast majority of care receivers were considered mentally retarded (83%). In addition 21% had cerebral palsy, 14% had epilepsy, 2% were autistic, and 8% had another type of neurological impairment. Fifteen percent of these individuals currently participated in day programs, 70% reported participating in shelter workshops, 10% worked part-time, and 8% reported full-time employment.

The caregivers reported that approximately 6% of the care receivers were in excellent health, 65% in good health, 23% in fair health, and 6% in poor health. Total ADL scores ranged from 26 to 77, with a mean of 58.5. Approximately one third of the individuals, however, needed at least hands-on assistance with the 21 activities of daily living. The activities in which the largest percentage of individuals required help were managing own money (87.1%), shopping for a simple meal (77.3%),

Table 3.1 Socialization Patterns of the Caregivers

| | Caregiver Participation | | With Whom | |
Activity	No	Yes	With Care Receiver	Without Care Receiver
Organizational meetings	32	16	1	15
Volunteer work	40	8	1	7
Walks	29	19	7	12
Church	28	20	11	9
Hobbies	33	15	1	14
Dining out	19	29	20	9
Senior center	39	9	1	8
Cultural events	39	9	2	7
Weekly visits with family	26	22	7	15
Weekly visits with friends	26	22	2	20

NOTE: $N = 48$.

doing laundry (65.9%), and using the stove or microwave (64.4%). The most frequent areas in which the care receivers needed personal assistance were brushing or combing hair (44.7%), selecting clothes (40.4%), and taking a bath or shower (38.3%).

Changes Perceived by the Caregivers

Respondents indicated whether changes occurred in particular aspects of their caregiving role over the past 10 years. A one-sample chi-square test indicated whether significant differences existed between the observed number of responses in each category and the expected frequencies. Significant differences were found for most items. Table 3.2 provides a summary of the caregivers' responses to each aspect of the caregiving situation.

An examination of the results reveals an overall pattern of stability in the caregiving situation. Areas in which the greatest changes did take place were physical burden (39.6% increase), the emotional burden (40.9% increase), the amount of time the caregiver spends involved in social activities (25.6% decrease), and the financial burden of providing care (20.8% increase). The most common reasons the caregivers gave for the perceived changes were (a) that the caregiver was getting older and (b) the

Table 3.2 Perceived Changes in the Caregiving Situation[a]

	Direction of Change			X^2
	Increase	Decrease	No Change	
Overall stress	41.7	0.0	58.3	.78
Financial burden	20.8	4.2	75.0	32.91[b]
Emotional burden	37.5	2.1	60.4	20.77[b]
Physical burden	39.6	0.0	60.4	.38
Time spent providing direct care	16.7	4.2	79.2	36.00[b]
Amount of help needed from others to provide care	14.6	2.1	83.3	38.77[b]
Amount of help from formal services for care receiver	18.8	8.3	72.9	19.00[b]
Amount of help from formal services for caregiver	4.2	8.3	87.5	38.80[b]
Amount of time care receiver spends with other family members	6.3	10.4	83.3	35.74[b]
Amount of time caregiver spends with other family members	6.3	8.3	85.4	39.84[b]
Amount of time care receiver spends with friends	4.2	12.5	83.3	43.43[b]
Amount of time caregiver spends with friends	2.1	12.5	85.4	48.14
Amount of time care receiver spends involved in social activies	7.6	10.3	82.1	41.69[b]
Amount of time caregiver spends involved in social activies	10.3	25.6	64.1	18.00[b]

[a]Numbers represent the percentage of caregivers in each group ($n = 48$).
[b]$p < .001$

decline in the caregiver's health. The majority of caregivers, however, reported no change in their roles.

An examination of the perceived changes in the caregiving situation according to the identity of the caregiver revealed, with few exceptions, a

Table 3.3 Comparison of Mothers', Fathers', and Siblings' Perceived Changes in Their Caregiving Situations

	Mothers (n = 32) I^a D^b S^c			Fathers (n = 9) I D S			Siblings (n = 7) I D S		
Overall stress	10	-	22	5	-	4	5	-	2
Financial burden	6	-	26	1	2	6	3	-	4
Emotional burden	10	1	21	4	-	5	4	-	3
Physical burden	11	-	21	4	-	5	4	-	3
Time spent providing direct care	3	1	28	1	1	7	4	-	3
Amount of help needed from others to provide care	4	-	28	2	1	6	1	-	6
Amount of help from formal services for care receiver	5	2	25	1	2	6	3	-	4
Amount of help from formal services for caregiver	1	3	28	-	1	8	1	-	6
Amount of time care receiver spends with other family members	1	5	26	1	-	7	-	-	7
Amount of time caregiver spends with other family members	1	3	28	2	-	7	-	1	6
Amount of time care receiver spends with friends	2	4	26	-	1	8	-	1	6
Amount of time caregiver spends with friends	1	3	28	-	1	8	-	2	5
Amount of time care receiver spends involved in social activies	2	3	27	-	1	7	-	-	7
Amount of time caregiver spends involved in social activies	3	6	23	1	2	6	-	2	5

[a]Increase
[b]Decrease
[c]Same

response pattern similar to that of the entire sample (Table 3.3). For example, a greater percentage of fathers (56%) and siblings (71%)

reported an increase in the overall stress of caregiving than mothers (31%). The percentage of siblings reporting an increase in the financial burdens of caregiver (57%) was much higher than that of either mothers (19%) or fathers (11%).

Predictors of Stability and Change

Multiple regression analysis was used to predict which caregivers were likely to perceive the most change in the caregiving situation. Three variables were entered into the equation: marital status of caregiver (married/not married), health of caregiver (excellent-good/fair-poor), and functional ability of the care receiver (continuous variable). Derived from the 14 situation items, the dependent variable was the amount of change in the overall caregiving situation. Each situation was coded as either (0) stable or (1) changing and summed for a total change score. A significant regression equation was found ($p < .001$), accounting for 57% of the variance. Caregivers who were not married and whose relative needed greater assistance with tasks of daily living were more likely to perceive change in the overall caregiving situation.

Stress and Burden

A series of chi-square analyses were conducted to determine differences among the proportion of respondents who reported changes in the perceived stress and burden of caregiving. Changes in stress and burden were analyzed according to the sex, marital status, and health of the caregiver and the health of the care receiver. In addition to overall stress, three specific areas of burden were examined: financial burden, emotional burden, and physical burden.

No significant differences according to the gender, marital status, or health of the caregiver occurred. The health of the care receiver, however, did influence the caregivers' perceptions of stress and physical burden. Specifically, a greater proportion of caregivers reported an increase in overall stress ($p < .05$) and the physical burden of providing care when they rated their care receivers' health as fair or poor ($p < .05$).

The socialization patterns of the respondents and care receivers with respect to perceived stress and burden also were examined. Caregivers who reported an increase in stress or burden did not differ significantly in the number of social activities in which they personally engaged. Caregivers reporting an increase in stress indicated that their care receivers participated in fewer activities outside the home than those who reported no change in the overall stress of providing care [$t(46) =$ $-2.59, p < .01$].

Discussion

The picture that emerged from this study of elderly caregivers of family members with developmental disabilities was one of stability in many facets of the caregiving situation. It seems that this group of caregivers have accepted their role and have learned to cope with the responsibilities placed upon them. As almost one half of the sample had been caring for their relative for 40 years or more, time in the role of caregiver may be a decisive factor. The elderly caregiver of a child with developmental disabilities is likely to assume the primary caregiver role right from the birth of the child. By the time the child reaches adulthood, the caregiver is well aware of the capabilities of the child and what he or she must provide. Changes in either the caregiver's or the care receiver's personal health or personal abilities, however, influence the caregiver's perception of the situation and her or his ability to cope (George & Gwyther, 1986; Suelzle & Keenan, 1981; Zarit, Todd, & Zarit, 1986).

The functional abilities of the person with developmental disabilities were the strongest predictor of perceived change in the caregiving situation. Yet according to the comments made by the caregivers, it was a decline in their own physical health that was making the difference. This finding is consistent with those of Gold and her colleagues (1987), who found that the adult child's level of impairment and parental health were strong factors contributing to perceptions of increasing difficulty in caregiving. The combination of a more dependent person and failing health of the caregiver can have major consequences on the caregiver's ability to provide continuous care.

The specific areas where the respondents were most likely to report change are common among all caregivers. Increased stress and emotional, physical, and financial burden may be signs that the caregiving situation is creating negative consequences for the caregiver (Horowitz, 1985). Intervention from formal and informal support systems can help to alleviate the stress and strain of the situation. Many caregivers, however, reported little or no involvement in social activities outside their homes. This type of situation may lead to feelings of confinement and isolation that could make caregiving even more stressful. Maintaining an active involvement with the community and their informal network can serve as a positive coping mechanism for caregivers as they learn to adapt to changes in their caregiving roles (Lazarus & Folkman, 1984; Springer & Brubaker, 1984).

The small volunteer sample and retrospective nature of some of the information obtained limits the generalizability of the findings. The results do, however, provide some beginning insight into the lives of elderly caregivers of adults with developmental disabilities. If community integration is the goal of human service providers working in the area of developmental disabilities, it appears that more people will be living at home. Therefore it is important to learn what specific needs must be met to help families maintain and enhance their caregiving situations.

Implications for Practice and Research

Practice Considerations

Practitioners working with elderly caregivers must play a proactive role in supporting these families. First, members of the formal service system must be knowledgeable in the field of aging and developmental disabilities. Being aware of and able to recognize changes in the physical and social conditions that make it difficult for or prevent older caregivers from fulfilling their caregiving duties will provide practitioners a basis from which to build effective interventions.

The burden of caregiving often intensifies over time, as the family caregiver's emotional, physical, and financial resources become depleted. To maintain an effective caregiving environment, many caregivers will require assistance from the formal service system. The findings of this study and others reported in this book suggest that marital status, income, degree of illness, and living arrangements distinguish between elderly caregivers who are service users and those who are nonusers. Whereas the use of formal services increased from 10 years ago for many of the sample participants, linkages between the family and service community need to be established or strengthened to better assist the older caregiver in meeting the demands of the caregiving situation.

Using community supports is often the most difficult step for a family caregiver to take. However, taking advantage of available services can result in positive outcomes for all family members involved. Formal services can provide older persons with the care they need while relieving some of the burden inherently placed upon older caregivers. Therefore it is important to match the needs of the caregiver and the care receiver with services provided by formal systems. In all instances, the object should be to maximize the independence of the aging person with a developmental disability and to minimize the stress on the primary caregiver (Springer & Brubaker, 1984).

Future Research

Future research must further document the caregiving situation of this special group of caregivers. The use of more powerful and precise methodologies will enhance our knowledge base in this important area of study.

First, future studies need to use larger, more representative samples of caregivers. The respondents in this study were a small group of caregivers with at least some contact with the service system. Due to the sampling procedure it was not possible to compare the caregiving situations of the study participants and the caregivers who chose not to respond to the questionnaire. In addition, no attempt was made to identify and include parental caregivers who have never accessed the service system. Future studies that address these issues will provide greater insight into the lives of these caregivers.

A second area that needs further examination is the issues and concerns of the different family members who serve as the primary caregivers for aging individuals with developmental disabilities. Whereas mothers constitute the majority of respondents in this study, a preliminary comparison of perceived changes in the caregiving situation for mothers, fathers, and siblings suggests that differences may exist in their perceptions of need.

Finally, researchers must be encouraged to pursue longitudinal studies of caregivers of aging persons with developmental disabilities. This type of study is necessary to advance our understanding of true changes in the caregiving situation as well as the tasks of caregiving as both the caregivers and care receivers grow older.

4

Caring for Adult Children With Mental Retardation

Concerns of Elderly Parents

ELLIE BRUBAKER
TIMOTHY H. BRUBAKER

There is a similarity in the needs of individuals providing care to family members. All caregivers must balance the caregiving recipient's needs with other responsibilities and their own needs. Most caregivers have given up either planned activities, lifestyle, career, or even all three. Each caregiver may experience moments of frustration, anger, or hopelessness. However, despite the similarities in all types of caregiving, elderly parents providing care to their adult children with mental retardation experience unique needs.

Much like a caregiving spouse, older parents providing care to their adult child with mental retardation must deal with their own aging and the limitations it places on caregiving (Brody, 1990; Lutzer & Brubaker, 1988; Roberto, this volume), as well as with the aging of the care recipient. Like that of the spouse providing care, the caregiver's social support system may be aging as well. Yet, unlike the recipient of spousal care, the adult child is likely not to be as frail as the caregiver. The elderly caregiver

Frequencies and percentages presented in this chapter were also presented in a project report: J. L. Engelhardt, E. Brubaker, V. D. Lutzer, and T. Brubaker, *A Manual for Caregivers of Adults With Mental Retardation.*

51

may be providing transportation, physical care, and parental authority, as well as meeting the social needs for an adult who has more energy and stamina than the caregiver. Unlike the spouse who provides care, the caregiving parent is likely to have carried out caregiving activities for the child's entire lifetime. Unlike the younger caregiver of the adult with mental retardation, elderly caregivers also must deal with factors associated with aging.

For most older individuals, chronological age is used as a guide to determine activities and responsibilities (Brubaker, 1990b). Usually aging means decreasing responsibilities in relation to children. However, for elderly caregivers of children with mental retardation, the experiences and expectations of others are not replicated. Responsibility to the adult child continues, and, in the case of an adult child with associated disabilities, responsibilities and needs may increase (Lutzer & Brubaker, 1988). The related needs of the care receiver likely will continue throughout the caregiver's lifetime. Generally the caregiving is expected to continue until the death of the caregiver, and it is the caregiver's task to plan for care following this eventuality.

These unique features of caring for an adult with mental retardation illustrate the special needs of older caregiving parents. As long as the caregiving parents are living and able to provide care, the caregiving will not be relieved. The needs of the adult child will continue and must be met. As Seltzer and Krauss (1989) note, "Caregiving for an aging son or daughter with retardation can span 5 or 6 decades" (p. 304).

The fact that caregivers experience stress (Brody, 1990) and that caregivers of children with mental retardation experience stress both have been established in the literature (Flynt & Wood, 1989). Are the stresses of older caregivers of adults with mental retardation exacerbated by the fact of their own aging? What factors contribute to stress associated with aging experienced by older caregivers of adult children?

Theoretical Framework

Examination of stress in older caregivers has been conceptualized with a contextual approach, using the ABCX model (Brubaker, 1990a; Brubaker & Brubaker, 1992). Examination of younger caregivers of children with mental retardation has applied the double ABCX model (Orr et al., 1991). Within this chapter, the ABCX model is applied to findings regarding older caregivers of adults with mental retardation.

The ABCX model was originated by Hill (1949, 1958) and further developed by Boss (1987) and Walker (1985). The ABCX model functions to describe the responses of families to a stressor that they experience. The model examines the input of a stressor, the family's reaction to the stressor, and the resulting situation. Use of the ABCX model provides information concerning the outcome of interaction among a stressful influence, the family's perceptions of that influence, and their reaction to it.

The stressor is symbolized by "A" within the ABCX model. In this case, the stressor is the *aging* of the individual providing primary care to an adult with mental retardation. The aging of an older individual becomes a stressor when that person recognizes aging as a barrier to continued care of his or her adult child with mental retardation.

"B" represents the response of the family to "A" through the use of available resources. The input of a stressor calls for some response on the part of family members. The potential responses may range from ignoring the stressor to making numerous plans for the future. Whatever the response to the stressor, the family changes its level of organization and becomes less organized as it adjusts to the new situation. If the response is to ignore the stressor, then the level of care may decline. If the family's response is to make new plans, an increased number of systems is likely to become involved in the situation. Whatever the response, some change in the family's functioning will occur. The family's adjustment to the stressor is likely an attempt to regain the previous level of functioning, where the care of the adult child is continued. Many caregiver needs are shared by other caregivers of adult children with mental retardation and can be viewed objectively. Other needs are more subjectively defined by individual caregivers and their families. The definition of a situation as a problem resulting in a need may be largely dependent upon the caregivers' and families' perceptions.

The manner in which the stressor is defined by the family is represented by "C." The definition of the stressor has an impact on the family's response to it. Each older family may view the stressor of age differently. For those with financial resources to buy care or a large support system and other family members who can provide continued care, the stressor of aging may be perceived as less of a threat. Those individuals with fewer financial resources or who are more isolated may see aging as an overwhelming problem. "X" represents the extent of crisis felt by the family as it adjusts and reorganizes in response to the stressor.

Research Questions

How does the stressor of aging influence older families providing care to their adult members with mental retardation? This study examined the financial, residential, social, and emotional concerns of older caregivers in relation to care of their adult family member as the caregivers aged. The study also questioned whether caregivers responded to aging by making increased plans for the future in the financial, residential, social, and emotional areas.

In an analysis of caregivers of adults with mental retardation who were 40 years of age or older, we examined the needs of elderly caregivers as related to caregiving. Research questions determined the caregivers' perceptions regarding their current and future concerns.

Many caregiver needs are shared by other caregivers of adult children with mental retardation and can be viewed objectively. Other needs are more subjectively defined by individual caregivers and their families. The definition of a situation as a problem resulting in a need may be largely dependent upon the caregivers' and families' perceptions.

Method

Sample

Respondents for the study were 388 caregivers of adults with mental retardation. Of the caregivers, 75% were mothers; 13% were siblings, aunts, uncles, foster parents, or other relatives; and 12% were fathers. Sixty-eight percent of the respondents were married. The respondents ranged from 40 to 87 years. The mean age was 59.6. Thirty-six percent of the sample were retired and 16% were unemployed. Thirty-four percent had completed high school and 22% had graduated from college. The caregivers' income ranged from less than $15,000 a year (28%) to greater than $55,000 a year (10%), with the largest group of caregivers in the $25,000 to $30,000 income range (30%).

Each respondent was a caregiver to a 40-year-old or older adult with mental retardation. Of the sample, 83% of the respondents provided care to an adult still living at home. Six percent of the adults for whom care was provided lived in a group home, another 6% lived in a developmental center, and 5% had other living arrangements.

Caregivers classified the level of mental retardation in their dependent adult. The levels ranged from profound mental retardation (5%) to mild (28%). Forty-eight percent of the caregivers classified the recipients of their care as having moderate retardation. Caregivers indicated that 58% of the recipients required some help with daily living skills and 23% required total care, whereas 20% did not require help with daily living skills.

Data Collection

Survey questionnaires were mailed to caregivers of adults with mental retardation in southwestern Ohio. The questionnaires were mailed by 10 mental retardation boards and 2 independent agencies to ensure anonymity of the caregivers. The questionnaire consisted of 86 items that questioned the specific needs of the respondents in regard to caregiving. The needs measured included present and future service, financial, residential, social, and emotional needs for the adult child as well as demographic information concerning the caregiver.

In addition 96 caregivers participated in in-depth interviews conducted over the telephone. The interviews were undertaken with the purpose of gaining more in-depth information from respondents than a questionnaire could provide. Respondents were questioned regarding a series of issues related to the questionnaire. The telephone interviews ranged from 20 to 40 minutes. The interview sample was selected to represent a range of ages, from 50 to 80 years and older.

Results

Respondents were asked about their concerns regarding current and future provision of care to their adult children. The research questions focused on three areas: financial, residential, and social and emotional arrangements.

Financial Needs

Respondents indicated that they view the financial costs of caring for an adult with mental retardation as a concern. Caregivers identified financial concerns in the areas of medical care, transportation, out-of-home respite care, in-home care, and equipment needs. The largest percentage (48%) of caregivers indicated medical costs as the greatest area of current financial concern. Caregivers also expressed concern about future financial costs. The greatest financial concerns expressed by respondents were concerns about their and their dependent's financial future. Fifty-six percent of the sample indicated that they worry about future medical expenses for the individual to whom they provide care.

Residential Concerns

As noted, the majority of caregivers (83%) had the care recipient living with them. Although caregivers reported that they were concerned about meeting future time demands (49% strongly agreed) and future physical demands (40% strongly agreed) of caregiving, 34% of the sample had made no residential plans for the future. Caregivers were asked whether care could be adequately provided for the adult with mental retardation outside of the home. Fifty percent of the respondents agreed that adequate care could not be provided outside of their home.

Social and Emotional Concerns

The area of greatest concern to the respondents was the social and emotional needs of the adult for whom they provided care. Respondents were asked what their greatest concern was as they grew older. Forty-three percent indicated that their concerns centered around their dependent's future social and emotional needs. This also was the area of least planning by caregivers. Although 80% of the sample had made future financial plans and 66% had made residential plans, only 63% of the sample had made plans for future companionship for their child.

Discussion

Results from the study indicate that for this sample, aging brings on concerns regarding future care for the adult to whom they provide care. Although financial and residential concerns about the future are important to caregivers, the greatest concern of this sample is related to the future social and emotional needs of the care recipient. Individuals who are currently and successfully providing care, and have done so in the past, experience a new stressor. Although these caregivers have been aging throughout the caregiving process, they recognize that they will not always be able to provide care to their dependents. Consequently, the fact of their own aging holds new meaning for them. Integration of the findings with the ABCX model reveals that for these respondents, aging may be viewed as a stressor.

In in-depth interviews, respondents indicated in numerous ways their concerns about future care for the current recipients of their care. As caregivers discussed this area of concern, many revealed the feeling that the future was beyond their control. This is particularly difficult for persons who have controlled the care of their child for the child's whole lifetime. Others stated that they had attempted to plan for the future in order to provide continuity of care for the adult with mental retardation. For those who feel hopeless and for those who take action, their perception of aging, as well as their response to it, will influence the level of crisis they will experience.

Those who had made plans for the future expressed concern about their adult child's future situation, particularly in the social and emotional area. The manner in which each caregiver deals with these concerns may be related to plans already made or not made, family and social support, the area on which caregiving has been primarily focused, the physical status of both caregiver and care recipient, and the perceptions of the caregiver.

Engelhardt, Brubaker, and Lutzer (1988) reported a significant relationship between utilization of service by older caregivers of adults with mental retardation and the caregivers' assessment of their ability to carry out the tasks of caregiving. In addition, as these caregivers "anticipated less ability to care for their dependent adult in the future, they reported more utilization of services" (Engelhardt, Brubaker, & Lutzer, 1988). Perception of and expectation concerning need ("C") appears to influence caregivers' utilization of service.

Perception of need may influence and be influenced by the gender of the caregiver. Interestingly, older fathers who provide care reported more concern about their ability to provide physical care for their dependent children in the future than did mothers (Brubaker, Engelhardt, Brubaker, & Lutzer, 1989). It may be that male caregivers are more focused on the instrumental needs of their dependents and perceive needs related to this area.

The perception caregivers have concerning their ability to provide care and the needs of care recipients may influence the level of crisis ("X") they experience as their age begins to limit their ability to care. Caregivers who respond to stress by seeking out services based on their perception of need may find those needs met and experience a lower level of crisis than those who perceive a need but do not plan for it.

The perception of the stressor ("C") may influence the making of future plans. In addition the existence of plans may lessen the caregiver's concerns about future care. In-depth interviews revealed that some individuals who had made financial plans spoke with more confidence about the financial future of the adult with mental retardation than did those who had not yet planned in this area. For these individuals the level of crisis experienced ("X") may be lessened.

The area in which it was most difficult to plan concretely for the future is the social and emotional area. Caregivers can teach their adult dependents friendship skills for the future, but they cannot ensure that these skills will be successful when employed in their absence. In-depth interviews revealed that caregivers' concerns about social and emotional issues centered on whether their dependent would have continuity of emotional and social support. One mother stated that no other person would ever love her adult child as she did. Other parents worried that their child would lack friends if they were not there to encourage and arrange social interaction.

These concerns may be realistic. Adults with developmental disabilities have been found to lack meaningful social relationships (Clegg & Standen, 1991). Anderson, Lakin, Hill, and Chen (1992) investigated the social patterns of older individuals with mental retardation who lived in residential facilities. They found that over half of the sample did not visit friends other than family or staff members. Some caregivers in our sample counted on family members to meet future social and emotional needs of the adult with mental retardation. Others planned creatively in this area. One mother stated that she had left an insurance policy to a friend in the hope that the friend would visit and show an interest in her child in future years. Regardless of plans, aging brought the caregivers serious concern about the social and emotional future of their dependent. This issue, perceived by caregivers as a serious problem, is likely to result in a higher level of crisis experienced.

As noted, caregivers with family support were better able to plan for future care. Support systems may result in other benefits as well. Flynt and Wood (1989) suggest that family and social resources "can offset the detrimental effects of a stressor on the family unit" (p. 281). Interviews with our sample indicated that when other family members were involved with the adult with mental retardation, the caregiver felt a sense of shared burden. In these situations, the response of other family members tempered the caregiver's definition of stress, and the level of crisis experienced by the caregiver was lowered.

Finally, although age brings on a new stressor for the caregiver, that of concern about the future, age also appears to have its advantages. Flynt and Wood (1989) found that of the mothers they interviewed, older mothers of children with mental retardation reported less family stress than younger mothers. When compared with other older caregivers, mothers of adults with mental retardation were found to be in better health and to have better morale. It may be that lifelong caregivers develop strengths and skills to deal with crises not yet developed by "new" caregivers. If this is the case, older caregivers who have successfully weathered previous crises may find that the stressor of age will not result in a higher crisis level.

Implications for Practice and Future Research

Practice Implications

Older individuals providing care to adults with mental retardation revealed needs centered around their concerns for the future. The concerns of this sample were the greatest in terms of future social and emotional support for the recipient of their care. Practitioners can support caregiving families as they struggle with these concerns. Professional involvement can include family life education, support groups for caregivers, and activity groups for adults with mental retardation. In addition practitioners can facilitate caregiver planning through assessment and case management.

Family life education to both caregivers and adults with mental retardation can provide information about how these adults can gain skills for developing friendships. Activity groups for adults with mental retardation have the potential to provide participants with the opportunity to practice friendship skills with one another in a supportive environment. Through this experience, skills can be attempted and refined. Support groups for caregivers dealing with concerns about the future can reduce the sense of isolation some caregivers may feel and allow caregivers to learn from each other.

Service providers can assist older caregivers through an awareness that caregivers may have concerns about the future. Assessment should include questioning about potential concerns. This will allow the appropriate targeting of services. Assessment also should focus on the care recipient's current friendships and ability to make friends.

Case management is another practitioner activity that can alleviate the concerns of caregivers. A major objective of case management is to increase continuity of care (Intagliata, 1992). For caregivers whose primary caregiving concern is continued social and emotional support of their child, case management has much to offer. Case managers also can function to ensure that current services are being coordinated to meet the needs of caregivers as they age.

Future Research

Future research is needed that focuses on older caregivers' *reactions* to the crisis that they may experience as a result of their perceptions and responses related to aging. In addition, research that investigates caregivers' perceptions and responses in relation to actual availability of resources would be useful. Caregivers may be aware of resources available to their adult child for current use but lack knowledge about resources that can aid them in planning for the future.

Service providers would benefit from information from researchers as to what services are needed for older caregivers as these caregivers deal with the aging process. Also, service providers and family life educators could better serve aging caregivers with knowledge about these caregivers' perceptions of available services.

5

Aging Adults With Down Syndrome

Biological and Psychosocial Considerations for Caregivers

BARBARA A. HAWKINS
SUSAN J. EKLUND
B. L. MARTZ

Research on persons with Down syndrome is largely focused on pathological, biochemical, and genetic studies with considerably less information available regarding other aspects of bio-psycho-social functioning in adults affected with this disability (cf. Dalton & Wisniewski, 1990; Janicki & Wisniewski, 1985; Lott, 1982; Lott & Lai, 1982). Within the past 30 to 40 years, significant changes in life expectancy as well as life conditions have greatly influenced this segment of the adult population with mental retardation (Eyman, Call, & White, 1991). The extent of this impact now includes many individuals with Down syndrome who are surviving well past midlife and into older adulthood.

The process of aging, however, brings a mixed outlook. For example, aging in people with Down syndrome who are past age 35 is associated with an increased risk for senile dementia of the Alzheimer's type

Material for this chapter is based on B. A. Hawkins, S. J. Eklund, and B. L. Martz. (1991). *Detection of decline in aging adults with developmental disabilities—Research report 1991.* Cincinnati, OH: Research and Training Center Consortium on Aging and Developmental Disabilities.

(SDAT) (Dalton & Wisniewski, 1990). The phenomenon of precocious aging or "accelerated neurological aging" is a notable phenomenon in this group (Eisner, 1983). Other areas of human functioning, however, have not been widely researched in relationship to growing older, with very little empirical evidence available regarding the physical, adaptive, mental, and social functioning of the aging adult with Down syndrome. The evaluation of these areas of functioning is the focus of our longitudinal research on aging-related change in adults with Down syndrome. One intent of our research is to provide individuals with Down syndrome and their caregivers with information that will assist them in understanding and adjusting to the aging process. It also is anticipated that the resulting information can be used in the development of more age-appropriate care plans for this population group.

Background

The application of a model for the study of aging processes in the population with mental retardation is not widely available in the research literature. The model that serves to guide our longitudinal study is presented in Figure 5.1. This model is adapted from the Baltimore studies of normal aging (Shock et al., 1984), where age changes are simultaneously investigated in a wide range of physical, cognitive, and social variables on the same subjects over time. Our research is a combination cross-sectional and longitudinal, descriptive study of persons with Down syndrome based on this model. The purpose is to explore the variables in the domains (physical, cognitive, social) for patterns of age-related change so that we may come to a better understanding of the effects of aging and its implications for program planning for adults with Down syndrome.

Physical Functioning

A number of physical performance variables are known to be correlated with age and are considered valid markers of biological aging in the general aging population (Borkan, 1980; Dean, 1988; Ludwig & Masoro, 1983; Mints, Dubina, Lysenyk, & Zhuk, 1984; Salthouse, 1982; Shock, 1981). The measures include height, weight, diastolic and systolic blood pressure, resting heart rate, hand-eye coordination, reaction time (simple and choice), vibratory threshold, far and near vision, trunk flexibility, and audiometric assessment.

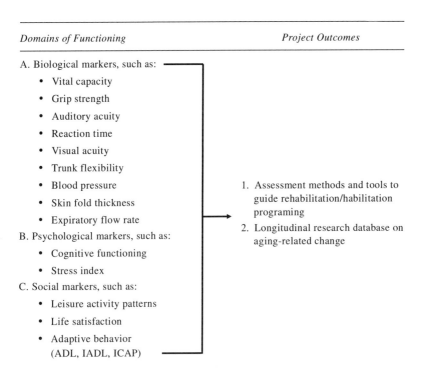

| *Domains of Functioning* | *Project Outcomes* |

A. Biological markers, such as:
  • Vital capacity
  • Grip strength
  • Auditory acuity
  • Reaction time
  • Visual acuity
  • Trunk flexibility
  • Blood pressure
  • Skin fold thickness
  • Expiratory flow rate
B. Psychological markers, such as:
  • Cognitive functioning
  • Stress index
C. Social markers, such as:
  • Leisure activity patterns
  • Life satisfaction
  • Adaptive behavior
    (ADL, IADL, ICAP)

1. Assessment methods and tools to guide rehabilitation/habilitation programing
2. Longitudinal research database on aging-related change

Figure 5.1. Conceptual Framework for the Study of Aging Processes in Aging/Aged Persons With Developmental Disabilities

Generally, height, weight, vital capacity, visual and auditory acuity, flexibility, vibratory threshold, grip strength, percent body fat, and coordination can be expected to decline with age. For example, Asmussen, Fruensgaard, and Norgaard (1975) found a decrease in heart rate for the nonretarded population. Systolic blood pressure has been shown to increase with age in the general population (Asmussen et al., 1975), but for people of comparable age with Down syndrome it has been shown to be lower (Hollingsworth, Hashizume, & Jablon, 1966). Reaction and choice reaction time also are expected to increase with age. These objective measures are preferred over self-report measures in instances where the individual is known to have impairment in cognition (Guralnik, Branch, Cummings, & Curb, 1989). Comparable research data is needed on the performance of adults with Down syndrome on these specific markers of aging-related change in physical functioning.

Cognitive Functioning

Age-related change in the cognitive domain is well documented for non-mentally-retarded adults (Arenberg & Robertson-Tchabo, 1977; Botwinick, 1977; Craik, 1977; Labouvie-Vief, 1985; Perlmutter, 1986, 1988). Longitudinal studies tend to show stability in overall IQ scores until the late 60s with a gradual decline thereafter. More detailed studies that investigated component cognitive abilities find earlier and more rapid decline in some abilities compared with others. The growth and decline of intelligence among individuals with mental retardation show that persons with higher mental functioning continue to grow in mental age for longer periods of their life, at least into their late 30s (Fisher & Zeaman, 1970). After age 60, mental ages for all levels of retardation show a tendency to decline, whereas between age 16 and 60 IQ is relatively stable.

Studies of the population with Down syndrome show a somewhat different pattern of cognitive aging. The loss of vocabulary, recent memory loss, impaired short-term visual retention, difficulty in object identification, and loss of interest in surroundings are exhibited in individuals with Down syndrome over the age of 35 (Wisniewski, Howe, Williams, & Wisniewski, 1978). In another study of persons with Down syndrome aged 19 to 49 years (Fenner, Hewitt, & Torpy, 1987), intellectual deterioration occurred in less than one third of the individuals over age 35. Increases in mental age were found for those in their 20s and 30s, followed by a decline with the 45- to 49-year-old cohort. These findings are consistent with other research that shows significant intellectual deterioration begins in the late 40s for persons with Down syndrome and that it occurs in less than 50% of these individuals (Dalton & Crapper, 1984; Hewitt & Jancar, 1986). Clear and consistent age-related deficits with a significant age by etiology interaction for persons with Down syndrome over age 50 can be expected (Zigman, Schupf, Lubin, & Silverman, 1987).

In the cases of specific cognitive abilities, evidence of memory loss in persons with Down syndrome age 44 to 58 years can be similar to that exhibited by nonretarded people with Alzheimer's disease (Dalton & Crapper, 1977; Dalton, Crapper, & Schlotterer, 1974). In addition Down syndrome individuals may exhibit increased deficits with age in auditory processing and auditory memory (McDade & Adler, 1980), visual memory (Eisner, 1983), and the ability to comprehend spoken language but not in verbal skills (Young & Kramer, 1991).

In the research there is great diversity of method, instrumentation, and analysis technique. Nevertheless a picture does emerge of differences between the population with Down syndrome and the mentally retarded population without Down syndrome. Among persons with Down syndrome, age-related cognitive decline appears to have onset in the 30s to 50s, whereas in mentally retarded groups without Down syndrome there appears to be little decline until the 60s.

Social Behavior

The relationship between life satisfaction and adjustment to changing social roles is well documented in the literature on aging and social function (Lawton, Moss, & Fulcomer, 1986-1987; McGuire, 1979, 1984; Riddick & Daniel, 1984; Tinsley, Teaff, Colbs, & Kaufman, 1985). From this perspective social behavior is defined as less dominated by work and increasingly circumscribed by leisure. The availability of discretionary time, the awareness of options of how to utilize this time, sufficient opportunities, and the availability of necessary resources influence social involvement. Each of these factors, along with individual need, interest, preference, and motivation, supports the attainment of fulfillment through leisure involvement in late life.

The occasion to indicate a preference and the freedom to make a choice are fundamental aspects of participation in leisure (Goodale, 1990; Iso-Ahola, 1980; Neulinger, 1974). However, opportunities for personal "choice making" are not a widespread attribute of programming for people with mental retardation (Houghton, Bronicki, & Guess, 1987; Shevin & Klein, 1984). The availability of autonomous behavior or choice making during leisure, therefore, is problematic, especially in older adulthood (Mahon & Bullock, 1992). Models are needed that (a) identify different strategies for assessing preferences, (b) enhance choice making, and (c) develop the skills needed to participate effectively in the decision-making process as adults with mental retardation move into and through retirement.

Research is needed that addresses the problems associated with assessing and understanding choice making during leisure by people with mental retardation (Dattilo & Schleien, 1991; Shevin & Klein, 1984). The study reported herein explores (a) strategies for assessing leisure participation, interests, preferences, and constraints; (b) the relationship of gender and age to the leisure behavior and interests of aging adults with Down syndrome; and (c) the relationship of leisure to perceptions of life satisfaction.

Research Question

Specific patterns of the different physical, cognitive, and social abilities that constitute overall functional status of aging adults with Down syndrome have not been systematically investigated in a prospective, longitudinal study. There is evidence from the gerontological literature on people without mental retardation that if declines in many areas of functioning can be reliably identified at an early stage, they can be modified or even reversed. Thus this study focuses on assessing and interpreting physical, cognitive, and social measures of human functioning in regard to the aging process in adults with Down syndrome, and on comparing the results with normal aging.

Methods

Study Participants

Subjects were 58 adults with Down syndrome ranging in age from 33 to 56 ($M = 43$) recruited through contacts with 31 local agencies in a midwestern state. All potential subjects were identified within these agencies who met the following criteria: (a) They were not residing in large, self-contained institutions for people with mental handicaps; (b) they were receiving services from the disabilities services system; (c) they were diagnosed as having mental retardation of Down syndrome etiology and were over the age of 30; and (d) they possessed the receptive and expressive communication skills necessary to understand simple directions and provide understandable responses to questions.

Twenty-seven females ranging in age from 33 to 56 years ($M = 44$) and 31 males ranging in age from 34 to 50 ($M = 42$) agreed to participate in the study. In all cases mental retardation was in the moderate to severe range. Twenty-two individuals resided in group homes, 35 persons lived with their parent(s) or a relative, and 1 person resided in a nursing facility but attended a community-based day program.

The study was cross-sectional based on age and gender, and longitudinal over three annual assessments. Data analyses from Year 2 and Year 3 are presented in this chapter. Year 1 data were treated as pilot data and were not included in the longitudinal comparisons.

Instrumentation

Physical Assessment Instruments

Table 5.1 presents a summary of the physical measures investigated in this study with assessment instruments. Each instrument provides an objective measure of the person's physical self and performance.

Cognitive Assessment Instruments

The battery chosen for assessing cognitive function was the Woodcock-Johnson Tests of Cognitive Ability—Revised (WJ-R) (Woodcock & Johnson, 1989) in addition to the Digit-Span and Digit Symbol subtests from the WAIS-R. The WJ-R was thought to be particularly appropriate for use in a longitudinal study because it provides "a record of individual growth across a wide time span" (Woodcock & Mather, 1989, p. 9). The primary reason for selection, however, was its theoretical base: "The WJ-R COG is in fact a model, i.e., an operational representation for a particular theory of intellectual processing—the Horn-Cattell Gf-Gc theory" (Woodcock & Mather, 1989, p. 13).

The Horn and Cattell (Cattell, 1963; Horn, 1972, 1976, 1985, 1986, 1988; Horn & Cattell, 1966) theory of intelligence distinguishes between crystallized and fluid abilities. Crystallized abilities represent a person's breadth and depth of accumulated knowledge about culture. Fluid abilities involve a broad ability to reason when faced with a new task that requires one to discover the essential relations of the task for the first time. When studies of intellectual performance and aging are divided into crystallized and fluid abilities, performance in fluid abilities is found to decline with age whereas crystallized abilities continue to show improvement until quite late in life (Horn, 1970). A large body of research involving aging in subjects who were not mentally retarded has focused on these and other age differences in adult cognitive functioning (cf. Arenberg & Robertson-Tchabo, 1977; Botwinick, 1977; Craik, 1977; Labouvie-Vief, 1985; Perlmutter, 1986, 1988).

Table 5.1 Physical Measures and Assessment Instruments

Variable	Instrument
Weight (lbs.)	Standard weight scale
Height (in.)	Standard height measure
Resting heart rate (BPH)	Standard resting pulse rate
Blood pressure (mmHg)	Standard blood pressure cuff
Anthropometric % body fat	Fat caliper
Grip strength (KG)	Hand grip dynamometer, Lafayette Model 78010
Vital capacity (L)	Pocket spirometer, P. K. Morgan Co.
Reaction time	Lafayette 63035 Visual Choice Reaction Time Apparatus
Choice response time	Lafayette 63035 Visual Choice Reaction Time Apparatus
Hand-eye coordination	Photoelectric Rotary Pursuit, Lafayette Model 30014, Digital stop clock; Lafayette Model 54030, Gralab Timer Model 51013
Hand-tapping	Lafayette Model 32012
Vibratory threshold	Bio-thesiometer, Model PVD, Biomedical Instrument Co.
Vision	Snellen Eye Chart, Tumbling E Chart
Audiometry	Beltone Audiometer
Flexibility	Box, Product of Health and Education Services

The WJ-R Cognitive Standard Battery consists of seven subtests, each representing an area of cognitive ability: Memory for Names (long-term retrieval), Memory for Sentences (short-term memory and attention), Visual Matching (processing speed), Incomplete Words (auditory processing), Visual Closure (visual processing), Picture Vocabulary (comprehension—knowledge or crystallized intelligence), and Analysis-Synthesis (reasoning or fluid intelligence). The Wechsler subscales of Digit-Span Forward and Backward and Digit Symbol also were used because they have been demonstrated to be sensitive to age-related decline in the generic aging population (Perlmutter & Nyquist, 1989).

Social Functioning Assessment Instruments

Standardized instruments to assess leisure participation, interests, and preferences, as well as constraints on leisure participation in adults with Down syndrome, are not available in the research literature (cf. Hawkins, 1988). Formal leisure assessments that do exist, such as the *Leisure Diagnostic Battery* (Witt & Ellis, 1987) or the *Leisure Activities Blank* (McKechnie, 1975), are not easily applied with individuals who have moderate or severe mental retardation (Bullock, Bedini, & Driscoll, 1991). Based on previous research on effective measurement approaches with subjects who have mental retardation (Sigelman et al., 1983; Sudman & Bradburn, 1974), a structured interview procedure using 50 picture-cued leisure activities was developed. The interview was attentive to specific task issues including (a) question wording (avoiding difficult or emotionally laden words), (b) difficulty of concepts, (c) length of questions, and (d) structure of questions (open- or close-ended questions). The *Leisure Assessment Inventory* evaluates (a) activity participation, (b) activity preference or those activities in which the subject desired to increase participation, (c) activity interest or those activities in which the subject would like to initiate participation, and (d) constraints on participation in leisure activity.

Life satisfaction was assessed using the *Life Satisfaction Scale for Aging Adults with Mental Retardation—Modified LSS (LSS-M)*. The *LSS-M* is a composite scale consisting of the *Lifestyle Satisfaction Scale* (Heal & Chadsey-Rusch, 1985) plus 46 additional items designed to tap areas that have been recognized as salient in measuring life satisfaction in older adults (cf. George & Bearon, 1980). The *Lifestyle Satisfaction Scale* contains subscales that assess (a) friends and free time, (b) services, (c) community, (d) job, and (e) general satisfaction. The additional 46 items that completed the *LSS-M* were selected from the work of Bradburn (1969); Lawton (1975); and Wood, Wylie, and Sheafer (1969). The items probed satisfaction in the following areas: (a) work or retirement, (b) happiness and worry (e.g., money, getting older, friends, death and dying), and (c) perceived health. A structured interview procedure was used wherein question wording was consistent with the previously described attributes (Sigelman et al., 1983; Sudman & Bradburn, 1974).

Results

Physical Functioning

Results from the analyses of data on physical functioning showed that vital lung capacity as measured by peak expiratory flow rate and grip strength were negatively related with age. Other significant age relationships included higher diastolic blood pressure, less trunk flexibility, poorer performance with two-point tapping and hand-eye coordination, and poorer auditory acuity at 6000 Hz, all with age. In general these findings would be consistent with the presence of mental retardation from other etiologies.

The data were analyzed separately for males and females because there were no males in the 50- to 59-year-old cohort. Two separate one-way repeated measures analyses of variance were carried out, one for males with two age levels for Year 2 and Year 3, and one for females with three age levels for Year 2 and Year 3. Age was a within-subjects effect and time of testing was a between-subjects effect.

For males the only significant main effect for age was on the two-point tapping test, where the younger group was better than the older group. There were time-of-testing effects for the following measures: diastolic blood pressure, which was higher in Year 3; vibratory threshold in the big toe, which was higher in Year 3; flexibility, which was poorer in Year 3; far vision, which was poorer in Year 3; reaction time, which was slower in Year 3; and auditory acuity at 6000 Hz, which was worse in Year 3. One item had significant time-of-testing and time-by-age effects. The peak expiratory flow measure of vital capacity showed higher capacity in Year 3 due primarily to the 30s age group, which showed marked improvement from Year 2 to Year 3.

For females the only significant main effect for age was for hand-eye coordination, where there also were effects for time-of-testing and age-by-time interaction. The younger groups performed better than the older. Performance was better in Year 3, and the best performance was for the females in their 40s in Year 3. A number of differences were found based on time-of-testing. Percentage of body fat declined significantly from Year 2 to Year 3. Vital lung capacity as measured by peak expiratory flow rate was better in Year 3. Flexibility was poorer in Year 3. Far vision was poorer in Year 3. Auditory acuity at 2000 Hz, 4000 Hz, and 6000 Hz was better in Year 3. Diastolic blood pressure increased from Year 2 to Year 3, but this change was statistically nonsignificant ($p < .05$). All of these changes are consistent with age-related decline except for the improved vital capacity and hearing indices.

Cognitive Functioning

Preliminary analysis showed that gender differences were present in Year 1 data. Consequently all further analyses were carried out comparing males and females. Results from the ANOVA showed no significant effects for age group (cohort) when comparing males and females in their 30s and 40s. There were, however, several gender and sex-by-age group effects. Memory for Names showed a significant effect for sex, with females scoring higher than males. The difference was primarily due to the higher scores of females in their 40s when compared to males in their 40s. For the Incomplete Words subtest there was also a significant sex-by-cohort interaction, with the difference primarily due to higher scores for females in the age 40 to 49 cohort when compared to males in the same age group. The same pattern was found for Picture Vocabulary, Analysis-Synthesis, and Broad Cognitive Total.

Significant sex and sex-by-age group interactions were then explored by graphing cohort gradients estimated separately for males and females for each of the cognitive abilities studied in each year. Patterns of gender differences were quite consistent in each of the three years of testing, with females having highest performance in the 40- to 49-year-old group or, in some cases, in the 50- to 59-year-old group (Picture Vocabulary, Visual Closure, in Years 2 & 3, for example). Males consistently showed peak performance in the 30- to 39-year-old group across all subtests of the Woodcock-Johnson. Although there are no 50- to 59-year-old males wth Down syndrome in this sample for comparison purposes, the crossover in age of peak performance for those in their 30s and 40s was clearly evident. Results indicated a mixed picture for females in their 50s (some subtests had lower scores for females with Down syndrome in their 50s, some were no different from those in their 40s, and some were higher).

Results for Digit-Span Forward showed a similar pattern, with peak performance for males with Down syndrome in the 30s and peak performance for females in the 40s. Digit-Span Backward was not productive in that all subjects performed so poorly that no meaningful patterns emerged. For Digit Symbol, females were highest in the 40s and males were highest in the 30s.

All of the findings discussed so far were based on cross-sectional analyses. For longitudinal comparisons, Year 2 and Year 3 were compared.

Results of the Year 2/Year 3 comparison using MANOVA with two age groups (30-39, 40-49) and two times-of-testing for male participants showed a significant effect for age group only for the Memory for Names subtest, wherein the highest performance was found in the younger group on this variable. A time-of-testing effect was found for Memory for Sentences and for Broad Cognitive Score. On Memory for Sentences improvement was shown for both age groups from Year 2 to Year 3. For the Broad Cognitive Score small but significant gains were found for both age groups. None of the age-by-time interactions were significant.

For females the MANOVA included three age groups (30-39, 40-49, 50-59) and two times-of-testing. For the females significant age differences were found for Memory for Names, Picture Vocabulary, and Analysis-Synthesis. Highest performance on Memory of Names was for the 40 to 49 cohort. On Picture Vocabulary there was a linear relationship with age wherein the highest performance averaged across both years appeared in the 50 to 59 age group.

For the Year 2/Year 3 comparison there was a significant difference on two tests for the female subjects, Incomplete Words and Digit-Span Forward. Incomplete Words increased for the 30 to 39 group and also for the 50 to 59 group. The Digit-Span Forward decreased from Year 2 to Year 3 for all three age groups. Age-by-time interactions also were significant for Incomplete Words and Analysis-Synthesis. On Incomplete Words peak performance appeared for the 50 to 59 age group in Year 3. For Analysis-Synthesis the same pattern was evident.

Social Behavior

Analyses of the structured interview data on leisure participation, interests, preferences, and constraints were directed toward determining whether any significant changes in leisure patterns occurred from Year 2 to Year 3 of the study. Leisure behavior measures consisted of (a) *leisure activity participation;* (b) *leisure preference,* which is the desire to increase activity participation; (c) *leisure interest,* which is the interest in initiating activity participation; and (d) *leisure constraint,* which is the level of internal and external constraints that impede activity participation. Each of the leisure behavior scores was entered into ANOVAs to explore for gender, age, and time-of-testing effects. Significant findings included (a) no significant gender differences, (b) no significant age-group or time-of-testing effects for male subjects, and (c) significant age effects for females with Down syndrome on the total number of activities participated in [$F(2,27) = 3.84$, $p = .034$]. Based on univariate follow-up tests, females with Down syndrome in their 30s had significantly higher total activity involvements compared with the females in their 50s at both testing times of the study.

A significant time-of-testing effect also was found among the females with Down syndrome for the number of activities in which subjects were not participating but indicated an interest in initiating [$F(1,27) = 7.06$, $p = .013$]. This difference can be characterized as a decline in the mean number of activities that subjects were interested in initiating from Year 2 to Year 3 of the study.

The number of constraints on leisure for Years 2 and 3 were analyzed in a one-way repeated measures ANOVA for age-group, gender, and time-of-testing effects. No significant effects were found for these variables.

Data from the *Life Satisfaction Scale for Aging Adults With Mental Retardation—Modified LSS (LSS-M)* were analyzed using the same framework for differences between Years 2 and 3 data only. There was a significant age-group effect on perceived satisfaction with life among males with Down syndrome [$F(1,29) = 4.24$, $p = .049$]. This difference can be characterized by higher life satisfaction, on average, among the males with Down syndrome who were in their 40s compared with males who were in their 30s. Follow-up univariate tests supported this finding for Year 3 only.

Additional analyses were conducted to explore the relationship of leisure activity to life satisfaction. No significant correlations between each leisure-behavior measure and life satisfaction were found for this sample of aging adults with Down syndrome.

Discussion

Physical Functioning

Blood pressure and resting heart rate were within normal limits; however, blood pressure readings were lower in this Down syndrome sample, especially in the females, compared with the general population at comparable ages (Hollingsworth et al., 1966). Systolic blood pressure increased with age, just as it does in the general aging population, but at earlier ages for individuals with Down syndrome (Asmussen et al., 1975). Resting heart rate showed no relationship to age in this sample.

Body fat percentages were higher for females than males, which is consistent with the general population findings for gender differences. Males with Down syndrome were in the above normal to very high fat range, and females with Down syndrome were at the high end of normal on gender-specific norms.

The measures of blood pressure, resting heart rate, weight, and percentage of body fat discussed so far are objective measures not related to degree of subject understanding, cooperation, and motivation. Measures of these variables appear to be reliable and accurate. All of the other measures of physical variables, however, are strongly influenced by subject cooperation. Subjects varied in their ability to understand directions and in their motivation to provide maximal performance. The vital capacity measures depended upon the subject's ability and willingness to blow into the spirometer as hard and fast as he or she could. The vibratory threshold tasks required that the subject respond the instant he or she perceived (felt) the vibratory stimulus in the thumb or big toe. Often, it was thought that subjects were waiting to be really sure that they felt it (a type of cautiousness in responding sometimes seen in the older population in general) before they would respond, thus providing higher threshold readings. Numerous problems were encountered with auditory assessments, again having to do with conveying the notion of responding as soon as they heard the tone. Large standard deviations were associated with all hearing assessments, such that caution should be used in their interpretation. Similar problems were encountered with some subjects on reaction time and choice reaction time tasks. Being sure that they were responding as quickly as they could, and that they understood that speed was important, was problematic. Great care was taken by the examiner to try to ensure communication. Given these caveats, the results were generally in line with expectations based on the literature on normal aging.

Grip strength values were in the low average range and better for males than females. The younger subjects (30s) had better grip strength than the older subjects. These findings are consistent with gender and age differences found by Hollingsworth et al. (1966). Vital capacity measures showed the usual gender difference, with males having higher capacity. There was a trend toward lower capacity for older subjects, thus reflecting a picture in accordance with age-related decline.

Reaction time and choice reaction time, which have been shown in studies of the general population to consistently increase with age, showed no age-related effects whatsoever in this population. All reaction time results were considerably slower than results on the general aging population at comparable ages, usually by a factor of two or three times. These results are in agreement with a large body of literature on reaction time deficits in people with mental retardation (Baumeister & Kellas, 1968).

On the tapping measures, the only significant finding for age was for the males with Down syndrome, where the younger males performed better. Hand-eye coordination scores were poor for all groups and showed no consistent relationship with age. The trunk flexibility measure showed consistent gender differences similar to those in the general population, with males less flexible than females. The subjects had greater flexibility than does the general population at comparable ages; however, both males and females with Down syndrome participants had declines in flexibility from Year 2 to Year 3.

In the vision and hearing assessments, near vision was not related to age. Far vision, though not showing main effects for age on any analysis, did correlate significantly with age. In addition significant declines in ability to see at a distance occurred from Year 2 to Year 3. This finding is in accord with findings on the aging population in general (Corso, 1971), but onset was earlier in persons with Down syndrome. Finally, the auditory assessments showed no consistent relationship to age. It is believed that these assessments were too unreliable to be valid. A consistent finding in the aging population at large is one of decreased sensitivity to high-pitched tones with age (Corso, 1971).

Cognitive Functioning

Cross-sectional findings support a picture of gender differences in patterns of cognitive functioning with age for subjects with Down syndrome. Clear age differences were found when comparing males and females in their 30s and 40s. Male performance appeared to peak in the 30s, whereas female performance was not seen to peak until the 40s (or in some cases the 50s). Such evidence of earlier decline in males, although decline is inferred here from cross-sectional evidence of age differences and not actual within-subject change over time, may be tentatively compared with quite recent findings of earlier brain deterioration in males than in females. A recent report in the *Proceedings of National Academy of Sciences* (Gur et al., 1991) stated that a study of males and females, aged 18 to 80, found that deterioration in the brain, especially the left side, which controls language and verbal abilities, is two to three times faster in men. The data (Gur et al., 1991) "suggest that women are less vulnerable to age-related changes in mental abilities, whereas men are particularly susceptible to aging effects on the left hemispheric functions" (p. 2845). These findings involved magnetic resonance imaging (MRI) research on only 34 men and 35 women and have yet to be replicated but might shed light on the present findings.

Comparing testing performance from Year 2 to Year 3, the overall picture was one of stability for this group of subjects who ranged in age from the 30s to the 50s. However, the Wechsler items for Digit-Span memory, although found useful in prior research with the general aging population, were not useful in the present study because scores were so universally low and show very little variability. Digit Symbol was highly correlated with Visual Memory from the WJ-R and did not seem to add anything of significance.

Social Behavior

The leisure behavior measures were useful in exploring general patterns or changes in patterns as a function of age, gender, or time of testing. The measures also can be used in exploring the relationship of leisure behavior to life satisfaction. Selected findings showed that younger female subjects with Down syndrome were significantly more involved in leisure activity than were older female subjects. However, the interest of females with Down syndrome in increasing leisure involvement decreased significantly from Year 2 to Year 3. No significant findings for changes in the leisure-behavior measures were found for the male subjects. Both males and females did not vary significantly from each other in their level of perceived constraints on leisure based on age group or on time of testing.

The measurement of life satisfaction provided mixed and interesting results. Older males were significantly higher than younger males in perceived life satisfaction. Also, life satisfaction was significantly higher in Year 3 compared with Year 2. No significant correlations were found between the leisure measures and perceived life satisfaction.

The findings from this study demonstrated that the older females were significantly less involved in leisure activity and that these individuals indicated a higher level of desire to increase involvement with a lower perception of life satisfaction. Other research has demonstrated support for this relationship in older, non-mentally-retarded adults (Backman & Mannell, 1986; O'Brien, 1981; Ray & Heppe, 1986;

Smith, Kielhofner, & Watts, 1986; Sneegas, 1986). The results of the present study suggest the need to further pursue inquiry on the relationship between leisure behavior and life satisfaction for people with Down syndrome, as no clear correlation between the measures used herein was found.

Implications for Practice and Research

Practitioners and Caregivers

Overall the results from this study support a picture of earlier onset of age-related changes in bio-psycho-social functioning for individuals with Down syndrome. Although onset appears to be earlier (40s for males, 50s for females) than in the general population, the pattern of change appears to be quite similar to the nondisabled aging population. Whereas other research has shown high incidence of Alzheimer-type changes in the brains of people with Down syndrome, actual behavior manifestations of senile dementia were not frequent in the present study. Much of what gerontologists have learned about enhancing or maintaining functions in later life should apply to individuals with Down syndrome as well, although caregivers do well to recognize the earlier age onset of aging-related change in this population. The general principle to be followed may be stated quite simply as, "Use it or lose it."

In the physical area moderate exercise is a necessity to maintain cardiovascular and muscular function. A minimum of three brisk 20- to 30-minute walks per week will help to maintain function. Diet is also important, especially for those males with Down syndrome who are found to be overweight. A low-fat diet combined with exercise would be a basic part of the regimen of all adults with Down syndrome. Modification of compulsive eating behavior may be a target area for intervention across all daily program and living environments.

In the cognitive area the same principle applies of using one's abilities in order to maintain them. Individuals will need to continue to practice their cognitive skills or they may expect to experience declines. Simple word games and memory exercises should be encouraged or built into daily routines. These activities need to be emphasized earlier for males with Down syndrome because they are showing declines in their 30s, whereas females appear to maintain function well into their 40s and 50s.

In addition to regular exercise (both mental and physical) and a low-fat diet, three other areas are important to successful aging: meaningful work, love and companionship, and social/leisure activity. The sense of satisfaction derived from work (not necessarily a job) in which an individual finds meaning is related to aging well in older adults in general and can be viewed as contributing to aging successfully for individuals with Down syndrome. Day activity in environments that satisfy the need for meaningful involvement should be maintained until the individual is no longer capable of carrying out the associated tasks due to marked intellectual or physical decline. It should be noted that the present study indicates that such declines may occur up to 10 years earlier for males than for females with Down syndrome. It also should be noted that in another part of the study not reported here, age-related decline was seen to have an onset of about 20 years earlier in the group with Down syndrome compared with persons with mental retardation not caused by Down syndrome (Hawkins, Eklund, & Martz, 1991). When a person with Down syndrome no longer is capable of work activity or indicates a strong desire not to continue in the workplace, retirement with a guided leisure activities program should be an option.

We all age better if we experience love and companionship in our lives. The opportunity to give and receive affection is as important to adults with Down syndrome as it is to any individual. The concern expressed by the study sample regarding the loss of roommates and house parents as well as family members reinforces the notion that interpersonal relationships have a great deal to do with how individuals cope with growing older. The opportunity to engage in social activities and social interaction, to experience the give and take of everyday exchanges with other people, also contributes to a sense of well-being in later life. Whether this type of interaction takes place in the workplace, in the home, or during leisure, it is important to maintain human contact. In summary, although aging appears to start earlier in persons with Down syndrome, it appears to follow much the same course as it does in the general population. Therefore the same kinds of interventions and coping strategies that have been found to be useful in the aging population at large (e.g., exercise, low-fat diet, meaningful activity, love and companionship, and leisure activities) should be employed by caregivers in meeting the daily-life needs of individuals with Down syndrome.

Future Research

The original purpose for using this battery of physical measures with these subjects was to find a way of assessing functional capacity and how it changes over time. Such a battery would be useful as a screening tool to assist in decision making about interventions needed when various physical capacities change; some can be remediated and some can be compensated for with assistive devices, such as glasses for presbyopia or hearing aids for presbycusis. Such a battery also could be useful in assessing the outcomes of interventions. Finally, we were interested in the establishment of a set of physical measures that could be used to gather descriptive information on the aging population with Down syndrome, information that could serve as a baseline for future longitudinal follow-ups as this population continues to age. Based on current findings the measures of weight, percentage of body fat, systolic and diastolic blood pressure, grip strength, vital capacity, vibratory threshold, far vision, and trunk flexibility seem to have the most promise for these purposes. Auditory acuity, an important age-related factor, should be assessed by an audiologist with special training in evaluating persons with mental retardation and under more ideal conditions than are generally available in field-testing sites. All of these recommended measures can be administered by a caregiver with brief training on these specific procedures.

The Woodcock-Johnson Revised appears to be an instrument that is useful for longitudinal study of cognitive functioning because of its wide age-range of standardization and its theoretical base. The original intention of analyzing changes in fluid versus crystallized abilities, however, did not prove viable for several reasons. First, the test developers warn against interpretation of any of the separate factors on the test on the basis of less than two subtests per factor, and we used only one. Second, the subtest that loads most strongly on fluid ability is Analysis-Synthesis. Although subjects' standard scores on Analysis-Synthesis appear to be relatively high compared to some of their other scores, it was possible for them to receive standard scores as high as 65 with raw scores of 0. Thus these scores are spuriously high and not useful for looking at change in fluid ability. In the future it is recommended that the Early Developmental Battery of the WJ-R, which drops Visual Matching and Analysis-Synthesis, be employed with this population. Further, if performance on specific factors is of interest, two measures of each of the five factors on the Early Developmental Battery should be utilized. If only the Broad Cognitive Score is of interest, the five-subtest Early Developmental Battery has been found to correlate .96 with the full Standard Battery in the adult age range (Woodcock & Mather, 1989).

The present study has established a base for the continued longitudinal follow-up of people with Down syndrome. Follow-up at intervals of 2 to 3 years would help in determining the actual patterns of change in functioning in this group. With an adequate time interval for conducting additional longitudinal research, the assessment protocols developed and applied in this study probably would provide far greater information about aging-related change in the population with Down syndrome. Two or three years of assessment does not represent a long enough interval to provide conclusive results regarding aging-related change. The model for the assessment of bio-psycho-social change that was applied in this study, however, was found to be useful for exploration of the aging process in this population.

6

Adults With Down Syndrome and Alzheimer's

Clinical Observations of Family Caregivers

ELIZABETH A. NOELKER
LAUREN C. SOMPLE

Approximately 4 million Americans suffer from Alzheimer's disease, including 10% of adults 65 years of age and older and 42% of individuals over the age of 85 (Alzheimer's Association, 1990). This progressive, irreversible, neurological condition impairs a person's cognitive abilities, behavior, and functional capabilities (Mace & Rabins, 1991; Price et al., 1982). Changes in the person's cognitive abilities include memory loss, inability to learn new information, a decline in judgment, language problems, and disorientation. Behavioral changes experienced by a person with Alzheimer's disease include agitation, irritability, anger, fearfulness, paranoia, suspiciousness, hallucinations, combativeness, and depression. The functional capabilities of persons with Alzheimer's disease also undergo changes. As the disease progresses, they are unable to perform activities of daily living such as personal care (e.g., bathing and dressing), housekeeping, cooking, handling finances, and driving.

Not all persons with Alzheimer's disease experience the same signs and symptoms of the illness, and the rate of progression varies for different individuals. Some individuals will demonstrate only a mild memory loss that is slowly progressive, whereas others will show a more rapid decline in cognitive abilities. The course of the illness averages about 8 years, but depending on the general health of the individual, a person may live for 20 or more years with Alzheimer's disease (Alzheimer's Association, 1990).

Currently there is not a specific diagnostic test for Alzheimer's disease. A definitive identification of Alzheimer's disease can be made only with a brain biopsy. A preliminary diagnosis is made by ruling out other forms of dementia and other conditions that mimic the signs and symptoms of Alzheimer's disease. For example, neurological disorders such as Parkinson's disease and Creutzfeldt-Jakob's disease must be ruled out. Other causes of dementia or conditions with dementia-like symptoms—including strokes and vascular disease, brain tumors, head injuries, central nervous system infections, thyroid disorders, vitamin deficiencies, nutritional disorders, alcoholism, anemia, metabolic disturbances, drug toxicities, heavy metal poisoning, and depression—also must be eliminated before making a probable diagnosis of Alzheimer's disease.

Alzheimer's Disease and Down Syndrome

Down syndrome appears in 1 per 1,000 live births (Mann, 1988). As recent as the 1930s, the average life expectancy of persons with Down syndrome did not extend beyond the early 20s. With advances in medical technological and personal care procedures, approximately 70% of persons with Down syndrome now live beyond their 50th birthday (Mann, 1988).

There is a significant incidence of Alzheimer's disease in persons with Down syndrome (Hurley & Sovner, 1986). By the time adults with Down syndrome reach age 40, they have neuropathological changes in the brain including senile plaques and neurofibrillary tangles that are similar to those found in the brains of persons with Alzheimer's disease (Epstein, 1983; Miniszek, 1983; Schweber, 1989; Wisniewski, Dalton, McLachlan, Wen, & Wisniewski, 1985). Clinical and behavioral manifestations of Alzheimer's disease appear in 40% of persons with Down syndrome by the time they are 60 years of age (Zigman et al., 1991).

Assessment and diagnosis of Alzheimer's disease in persons with Down syndrome require the same comprehensive medical and psychological screening used with older persons without Down syndrome. Caregivers, however, play a much more active and critical role. The person's primary caregiver provides a detailed history of changes in the person's cognitive, behavioral, and functional skills.

The pattern of cognitive and functional decline observed in persons with Down syndrome and Alzheimer's disease is similar to that seen in the general population of persons with Alzheimer's disease. The disease appears to progress more rapidly, however, in persons with Down syndrome (Evenhuis, 1990). According to Wisniewski and colleagues (1985), early signs of Alzheimer's disease in adults with Down syndrome include memory loss, behavioral changes, and visual-memory problems. Signs of progression to the middle stages of the disease include loss of social skills, an overall decline in function, and a loss of ability to care for personal needs. In the later stages of Alzheimer's disease, the person experiences mobility and gait problems, seizures, and incontinence. Caregivers of persons with Down syndrome and Alzheimer's disease often report the occurrence of behavioral problems earlier than specific cognitive changes (Evenhuis, 1990).

With the increasing life expectancy for persons with Down syndrome, the appearance of Alzheimer's disease in this population is rapidly becoming of interest to both the medical community and family caregivers. The dual diagnosis of Down syndrome and Alzheimer's disease is very complex and difficult to assess. This chapter describes the assessment process used by specialists at the University Foley ElderHealth Center of University Hospitals of Cleveland. Through the use of case studies, information is provided on the assessment methodology and examples of the issues facing caregivers of individuals with Down syndrome and Alzheimer's disease.

Clinical Assessment Procedures

At the Foley Elder Health Center, a team of neurologists, geriatricians, neuropsychologists, clinical nurse specialists, social workers, occupational and physical therapists, and geropsychiatrists provide comprehensive assessments for Alzheimer's disease and related dementias. Approximately 3,000 visits occur yearly by older adults and, in some instances, by younger individuals with unusual types of dementias. This figure includes new patients, follow-up visits, consults, and primary care patients. Almost 30% of these individuals are seen for dementia assessments by the Alzheimer's Center. Approximately 2% to 3% of the individuals assessed have Down syndrome.

The University Alzheimer's Center, a nationally recognized diagnosis and treatment center for Alzheimer's disease and related disorders, provides clinical and research participation options for patients and their caregivers. The University Foley ElderHealth Center, in collaboration with the Alzheimer's Center, conducts assessments for Alzheimer's disease with persons with Down syndrome. Following the assessment, a comprehensive plan of care is developed and the individual and family are provided with ongoing care and case management, as required, throughout the course of the disease. The assessment process used with persons with Down syndrome and suspected Alzheimer's disease includes an evaluation of their cognitive, behavioral, and functional abilities.

Cognitive Assessment

The cognitive assessment is performed by a neurologist and includes a comprehensive neurological exam, assessment of written and verbal skills, ability to follow commands and directions, identification of pictures and photographs, drawings, and a mental status exam. A detailed history of changes in memory (e.g., ability to think and reason, changes in judgment, a decline in visual memory, and a decline in word-finding abilities), as reported by the caregiver, provides important clues in the assessment of dementia in the person with Down syndrome. Tests typically utilized in the older adult population without Down syndrome, such as the Folstein Mini Mental State (Folstein, Folstein, & McHugh, 1975) or the Boston Naming Test (Kaplan, Goodglass, & Weintraub, 1983), are used on a limited basis due to the person's level of intellectual skills. The primary focus of the assessment is on changes in cognitive skills over a period of time as reported by the primary caregiver to the neurologist. The most frequent types of cognitive changes reported by caregivers are forgetfulness, confusion in making sense out of the environment, word-finding difficulty, and inability to understand directions that they once were able to follow. In addition, the neurologist may request blood work, a CAT scan, an EEG, a urine analysis, and neuropsychological tests to rule out any reversible forms of dementia.

Functional Assessment

The second phase of the assessment process, the functional assessment, is a significant part of the dementia work-up of the individual with Down syndrome. It identifies losses that often are difficult to document in the cognitive domain. The clinical nurse specialist or the social worker conducts the assessment. Information is obtained about the person's functional abilities using the Katz Activities of Daily Living

Scale (Katz, Ford, Moskowitz, Jackson, & Jaffe, 1963). This scale provides an assessment of the level of independence with which a person performs both *personal* (e.g., bathing, dressing, toileting, and feeding) and *instrumental* (e.g., use of telephone, food preparation, ability to perform housework/yardwork, and independence outside the home) activities of daily living. The caregiver provides information about (a) the person's level of functioning in each of these areas prior to when they began to notice any changes, (b) the period over which the changes occurred, and (c) the order in which the functions were lost. Other functional areas assessed include sleep patterns, mobility and falls, and weight gain/loss patterns.

This instrument provides assessment data that are very helpful in determining the current functional capabilities of the person with Down syndrome. Its success, however, in establishing the amount of *functional loss* depends on the person's intellectual level prior to any signs of Alzheimer's disease and the caregiver's ability to provide accurate information about recent changes in the person's performance.

Behavioral Assessment

The third component of the assessment process provides an evaluation of behavior and personality changes. The clinical nurse specialist or the social worker also conducts this portion of the assessment. The staff member obtains a detailed history of the past and current behavior of the person with Down syndrome through an explicit interview with the primary caregiver. Behaviors assessed in relationship to possible Alzheimer's disease include anxiety, fearfulness, agitation, irritability, verbal and physical aggression, inattentiveness, suspiciousness, paranoia, delusions, wandering, and preservation. The caregiver provides information about (a) the onset of any behavioral changes, (b) potential reasons for the changes, and (c) his or her major concerns regarding these behaviors. For example, a caregiver might report that the person with Down syndrome becomes more agitated and wanders as the evening sets in, becomes very fearful in strange environments, or hallucinates at night. Not all persons, however, experience major behavioral changes. Many individuals demonstrate only minimal behavior changes or problems typically associated with Alzheimer's disease.

Overall, the assessment of individuals with Down syndrome exhibiting signs of Alzheimer's disease is a complex process. Its success requires the involvement of both a skilled professional staff and the person's primary caregiver. The following case history illustrates our assessment process.

> Karen is a 42-year-old woman diagnosed with Down syndrome. Her sister initiated the assessment. Karen lives with her 75-year-old mother and participates in a sheltered workshop for adults. According to her family, she recently has shown some "mild" functional changes. Cognitive, behavioral, and functional histories, as described by the family and workshop staff, revealed progressive changes over time. For example, Karen became confused on the bus to the workshop. She showed a lack of initiation. The caregivers reported a decrease in her verbalization and a decline in her personal care habits. The assessment team followed Karen and her family for almost a year before making the diagnosis of probable Alzheimer's disease.

Psychosocial Assessment and Case Management

Once they reached the diagnosis of Alzheimer's disease, the team developed a comprehensive plan of care for Karen and her family. The behavioral changes exhibited by the person with Down syndrome and Alzheimer's disease are difficult for most caregivers to cope with and understand. As for many older caregivers, changes in the person's behavior often requires more attention than they can provide at this stage in their lives (Brubaker & Brubaker, this volume; Roberto, this volume). Therefore, in addition to the cognitive, behavioral, and functional assessment of the individual, the staff assesses the psychosocial needs of the individual and the family. Through the use of case management, the individual and the family are provided with information and support. Assistance is given in networking with community services that can help them with their caregiving responsibilities. As illustrated in Karen's case, accepting the diagnosis of Alzheimer's disease and making necessary changes in care arrangements often is a difficult process for families.

> At first, Karen's mother was reluctant to make any changes in the current system, claiming her health problems were minimal as were Karen's functional changes. Upon a follow-up visit, Karen's sister acknowledged the need for additional support due to her mother's declining health status and the described changes in Karen's abilities. Services were brought into the home to assist with the personal care needs of both Karen and her mother. The clinic staff continues to provide consultative services as to the family's current and future needs (e.g., living arrangements, financial support, and legal considerations).

Family Issues

The high and low emotional experiences described by families of individuals with Alzheimer's disease are well known and documented. Mace and Rabins (1991) describe the evolving anger, helplessness, guilt, grief, and depression that often grip the caregivers of persons with Alzheimer's disease. In *The Loss of Self,* Cohen and Eisdorfer (1986) note that caregivers often respond to the diagnosis of Alzheimer's disease with anger, frustration, guilt, and sadness.

For the family of an adult with Down syndrome, now diagnosed with Alzheimer's disease, the situation may appear as a déjà vu. Having already dealt with their feelings surrounding the birth and development of their child with Down syndrome, they now must revisit these emotions as their adult child approaches midlife. Parental caregivers often are not prepared to cope with the unexpected cognitive and behavioral declines inherent to Alzheimer's disease.

As Alzheimer's disease slowly impedes and impairs the level of functioning achieved by individuals with Down syndrome, family and professional caregivers report feelings of helplessness and frustration. For, as they have helped their impaired family member achieve a maximum level of functioning at home and in the community, the caregivers now can only stand by and watch as their loved one's cognitive and functional abilities decline. The caregivers often express feelings of guilt surrounding the diagnosis. Comments commonly heard from caregivers upon receiving the diagnosis include "I should have recognized this coming earlier" or "If only I would have helped him more." Guilt around the original diagnosis of Down syndrome also may reemerge. Caregivers frequently believe that if their sons or daughters did not have Down syndrome, Alzheimer's disease would not be occurring. Often their anguish surrounding the person's loss of functional ability is accompanied by anticipatory grieving (Rando, 1986). The family recognizes these losses as another indicator of the individual's limitations and ultimate mortality.

Caregivers experience isolation and feelings of depression, as the incidence and discussion of individuals with Alzheimer's disease and Down syndrome is a relatively new subject. These families often feel very alone in their search for services and report that very little of the educational literature about Alzheimer's disease addresses their needs. Anxiety accompanies the feelings of older parents as they must face not only the question of "Who will care for me as I age?" but also

"What will happen and who will care for my child if something happens to me?"

For aging parents of individuals with Down syndrome, the development of Alzheimer's disease presents several new issues. These caregivers are faced with uncertainty about their and their children's future. As one caregiver pondered her long-term care needs, she noted, "Perhaps we can get a room together in the nursing home . . . we've always been together." The need for daily care, not only for themselves but also for their children, is a primary concern of older caregivers. The following case illustrates the type of situation facing many parental caregivers.

> Sue is a 50-year-old single woman residing with her 70-year-old, widowed mother. Involved in a local workshop, Sue has begun to have difficulty with activities of daily living, including dressing, bathing, toileting, and personal care. Her mother acknowledges these changes in Sue and also voices her concern about her own health needs including a chronic heart condition and bouts of depression. She describes difficulty in assisting her daughter with personal care and her daughter's inability to help with household tasks. Due to cognitive declines, Sue is no longer able to vacuum the carpet or wash clothes. Sue's mother notes her frustration and sadness with her daughter's "slipping back." She is worried about Sue's future as well as her own. She asks about the long-term care options available for her daughter, acknowledging her fear of Sue's increasing need for assistance and her own need for care. She describes having suicidal/homicidal thoughts, and, on one occasion, driving her automobile off the road in an attempt to "solve" their care needs.

Aging in multigenerational households often presents new roles for the household members. One such role is the adult child becoming the caregiver for the aging parent. It is not uncommon to find adult children with Down syndrome assisting parents with activities of daily living. Alzheimer's disease, however, alters the child's abilities to perform household and other caregiving responsibilities. During the early stages of the disease process, family members report periods, or "windows," of wellness (i.e., a period of time when the affected person appears to have no additional cognitive impairments), almost as if the diagnosis of Alzheimer's disease was never made or was incorrect. Because behavioral changes may be minimal and their appearance inconsistent, families often view the person's actions as purposeful instead of a manifestation of the disease process. Parents often personalize their child's behavior as something they, the parents, have done to upset their child, rather than as a change within the child. At this stage, parents often deny or are reluctant to accept the diagnosis of Alzheimer's disease as an explanation for the changes in their child's behavior. This response is evident in the following case.

> The parents of a 35-year-old single woman brought her to the clinic because of changes in her behavior. She currently lives with her parents and attends an adult workshop during the day. Her parents describe her as lacking in initiative and becoming more isolated in the workshop setting. She had increasing difficulty with dressing, bathing, and performing her regular household tasks of making her bed and setting the dinner table. The family wanted to know whether these changes were "psychological." They reported that she no longer initiated conversation with them and that she "purposely" left clothing, workbooks, and papers in inappropriate places around the house. They felt she was "angry" with them for some reason and had tried, without success, to persuade her to discuss what is troubling her. Her parents acknowledge their concern with her decreased productivity in the workshop setting, but are reluctant to involve her in alternate activities such as adult day care, fearing she would not be able to rejoin the workshop at a later date because her job would be filled.

Professional Caregivers

The effect of this compounding illness on the professional "family" of caregivers should not go unnoticed. Caregivers of persons with Down syndrome and Alzheimer's disease residing in group homes experience many of the same emotions typical of families whose children live at home. Professional and lay staff also describe their frustration in observing declines from previously achieved levels of functioning. These caregivers, in the same manner as parental caregivers, often assume that a change in behavior is the resident's way of "acting out." For example, a worker discussing the disorientated behavior of one resident noted, "I just assumed her change in work habits was because we moved to a new building . . . that, perhaps, she was angry because of the move." Professional caregivers also experience feelings of guilt. They often believe the disease process could have been arrested if they would have recognized it earlier. Once staff members understand and recognize the symptoms of Alzheimer's disease, they are better able to accept the changes that occur with the residents. When they acknowledge the behavior as disease-related, it often is easier for the staff to change their routines and provide residents with the additional assistance they may now need. The following case illustrates this point.

Larry has been a resident of a group home for 5 years. Recently he began showing a decline in his ability to perform activities of daily living. The staff noted changes in his work abilities at the home and at the community workshop. He can no longer set the table or pack and assemble his own lunch to take to the workshop. The professional staff and family were very clear from the beginning of the assessment process that they wished to maintain Larry in this living arrangement. They made adjustments in the home's environment and in his work tasks to accommodate his progressive decline. For example, they broke down multiple-step tasks, such as setting the table, to one or two steps. This required much cuing and modeling on the part of the group home "family."

Implications for Practice and Research

Practice Initiatives

Education

For families and professional caregivers, the advent of the diagnosis of Alzheimer's disease for persons with Down syndrome presents many new issues and concerns. First and foremost, family caregivers require information regarding the diagnosis of Alzheimer's disease and the progressive nature of the disease. Health-care providers, social workers, and other practitioners need to help educate families about the type of functional and behavioral declines they can expect as their children advance through the stages of Alzheimer's disease.

Professionals, in both acute and long-term care settings, also need additional education and information to treat effectively individuals diagnosed with both Down syndrome and Alzheimer's disease. Acute care providers and their staff often lack the experience and exposure to patients with this dual diagnosis. For example, physician offices and clinics need to be sensitive to the timing of appointments for patients with Down syndrome and Alzheimer's disease. The person should not have an appointment scheduled when the office or clinic is crowded or at the end of day, when he or she may be overly tired. When in a new or strange environment, such as a clinic or hospital, persons with Down syndrome and Alzheimer's disease often become confused. They may be unable to express the pain, thirst, hunger, or fear they are experiencing. Physicians, nurses, and other staff members need to learn how best to communicate with these individuals to alleviate their fears and anxieties.

Both family and professional caregivers (e.g., group home staff, day-care providers, workshop leaders) need to understand that the gradual behavioral and functional changes exhibited by individuals with Down syndrome often represent a change in their cognitive abilities. The person is not being disruptive or noncompliant on purpose. With the onset of Alzheimer's disease, a once friendly individual may become withdrawn or easily agitated. Simple tasks the person once was able to accomplish now may require the assistance of other persons. Nurses, social workers, and other providers having experience with this population must share their knowledge and teach caregivers appropriate and effective techniques for communicating with these individuals and managing the changes they are experiencing.

Community Services

Providing additional support for middle-aged sons or daughters who can no longer care for themselves often is very stressful for parents who are simultaneously confronting their own aging. Practitioners need to be aware of the "tea kettle effect" among caregivers who have few outlets to "let off steam" or frustrations with their new roles. For these caregivers, the availability of community resources, such as support groups, respite programs, and adult day care, seems imperative to their ability to continue in their caregiving role. Unfortunately, community resources appropriate for individuals dually diagnosed with Down syndrome and Alzheimer's disease are lacking. Service providers must actively promote the development or expansion of services needed to assist these families in the provision of care. The launching of joint ventures among local chapters of the Alzheimer's Association, community center boards (CCBs), and the Association for Retarded Citizens (ARC) may be one way to address the needs of the individuals and their families.

Practitioners need to encourage families to serve as "pioneers" in the field, for they are the ones truly aware of the special needs of their sons and daughters. From the time of diagnosis, family caregivers should be involved in all care-plan conferences. They are most familiar with the history of the individual and can best describe changes in everyday behavior. They also need to be encouraged to join professionals in advocating for services that appropriately meet the needs of their sons and daughters and that help them manage their caregiving responsibilities.

Future Research

Adults with Down syndrome have a genetic predisposition to premature aging. Research on the aging of individuals with Down syndrome has confirmed that upon reaching their middle years, the majority of these individuals exhibit at least the neuropathological signs of Alzheimer's disease. As some scientists continue to pursue the biological and physiological relationship between Down syndrome and Alzheimer's disease, others must work toward finding solutions for the problems facing the current dual-diagnosed population and their caregivers. For example, we need more appropriate and accurate assessment instruments to evaluate the cognitive, behavioral, and functional abilities of persons with Down syndrome who are exhibiting signs of Alzheimer's disease.

Researchers must continue to focus on the issues and concerns of families caring for individuals with Down syndrome and Alzheimer's disease. Researchers need to address several questions:

1. Do mothers, fathers, and siblings differ in their roles, responsibilities, and abilities to provide care?

2. What types of services and assistance do persons with Down syndrome need as they progress through the stages of Alzheimer's disease?

3. What are the most effective strategies used by family and professional caregivers to cope with the behavioral and functional changes of persons with Down syndrome and Alzheimer's disease?

Answers to these questions are essential to our understanding of the disease process, the needs of the individuals, and the concerns of older caregivers.

PART III

Interactions Between Older Caregivers and the Service Community

7

Planning for the Transfer of Care

Social and Psychological Issues

JOAN B. WOOD

Family care is the primary residential support system for persons with developmental disabilities. Most live with their families throughout their entire lives. It is widely acknowledged that most persons among current cohorts of older adults with developmental disabilities are cared for in the home by family caregivers and that they are largely unknown to formal service providers. Thus most adults with developmental disabilities who are currently over the age of 40 are products of what is sometimes referred to as "postponed launching": They have not had the normative experience of departure from their family of origin. Instead they typically remain in the family home, being cared for by an aging female relative, usually the mother, until caregiver disability or death necessitates nonfamily placement. Often when families approach formal service systems for emergency residential placement under these circumstances, acceptable options are limited and the individual with a disability must experience the trauma of relocation without benefit of preparation for the transition (Janicki, Otis, Puccio, Rettig, & Jacobson, 1985).

Several studies document the failure of many families to make adequate plans for the long-term care of relatives with developmental disabilities beyond the lifetime of current caregivers. Goodman (1978), in one of the earliest studies in this area, reported that nearly two thirds of 23 caregivers surveyed indicated that they did not plan for their son's or daughter's future, tending instead to face each day as it comes. Lehmann and Roberto (this volume) found that less than 25% of the 61 caregivers in their study of family caregivers in Colorado had toured residential facilities, and only 43% had made future care arrangements with relatives. Heller and Factor (1991) found that only 27% of 100 caregivers interviewed in Illinois had made concrete plans, defined as making arrangements with another family member or arranging placement on a waiting list. In contrast, Gold et al. (1987) found, in a study of New York City caregivers, that two thirds of 42 caregivers had arranged placement in residential programs. Sixty percent wanted placement for their relative during their lifetime. Of these four studies, only Heller and Factor (1991) used random sampling techniques, and their sample was restricted to families identified by agencies serving individuals with developmental disabilities. However, all four studies clearly demonstrate that many families of older individuals with developmental disabilities have not made adequate preparation for the transition from parental care.

Few studies have investigated factors associated with planning. Heller and Factor (1991) found that age, race, and socioeconomic status of the family predicted permanency planning. Caregivers who were older, white, and of higher socioeconomic status were more likely to have made residential and/or financial plans.

A number of parent-child relationship factors are discussed in the literature, such as parental overprotectiveness, mutual dependencies between parent and adult offspring with disabilities, and parental feelings of guilt (Brunn, 1985; Carswell & Hartig, 1979; Dobrof, 1985; Gold et al., 1987; Seltzer & Seltzer, 1985). Smith and Tobin (1989) suggested that these factors may deter permanency planning. Grant (1986) noted that older parents who receive instrumental assistance or companionship from an adult son or daughter with a disability are more likely to postpone planning. Heller and Factor (1990) found that caregiving satisfaction and high morale among parents were related to deferred residential placement of their son or daughter with mental retardation.

Little is known empirically about the cumulative effects on aging parental caregivers of a lifetime of caregiving for a son or daughter with a disability. Seltzer and Krauss (1989) reported from a longitudinal study of 462 older mothers (mean age = 66 years) providing in-home care for an adult son or daughter with mental retardation that many of the women seemed to have adapted well to the caregiving role. Specifically these caregivers were healthier than noncaregiving women their age, had better morale than other caregivers of older persons, and reported no more burden or stress than either parents of young children with retardation or family caregivers to older adults. They viewed their experience in long-term family caregiving in largely positive terms.

These data support an adaptational model of long-term caregiving, proposed by Townsend et al. (1989). This model emphasizes stability or improvement in caregiver mental health over time, which may be predicted more accurately by caregivers' subjective appraisal of their circumstances than by the duration of caregiving. This would be consistent with the cognitive-phenomenological theory of stress and coping developed by Lazarus and his colleagues (Folkman, Lazarus, Pimley, & Novacek, 1987; Lazarus & Delongis, 1983; Lazarus & Folkman, 1984). Briefly, this theory suggests that stress is the result of a transaction (or interaction) between an individual and the environment that is perceived by the person as taxing or exceeding his or her resources. The meaning of the environmental transaction is determined by the individual in a primary cognitive appraisal. Through a secondary appraisal, the individual evaluates the adequacy of his or her coping resources and options. As applied to caregivers, potential stressors are "objective" phenomena in the caregiving situation, such as the degree of disability of the person being cared for (Cantor, 1983; Poulshock & Deimling, 1984). The caregiver appraises the environmental situation in terms of whether it is potentially threatening to her (primary appraisal). If the situation appears to hold potential harm, the caregiver evaluates, in a process of secondary appraisal, her resources for dealing with the potential stressor. Resources may include her own inner strengths (e.g., repertoire of coping strategies) and personal characteristics (e.g., physical health, income, education) and/or environmental factors, such as social support, that may be drawn upon in coping with stress (Lawton, Moss, Kleban, Glicksman, & Rovine, 1991). The subjective interpretation by the caregiver of the ongoing quality of the caregiving situation is thus the basis for the existence of caregiver stress. This evaluation is seen as a mediator between the objective characteristics of the caregiving situation and the outcome of psychological well-being or psychological distress (Poulshock & Deimling, 1984). The adaptational model of long-term caregiving suggests that caregivers have developed resources for coping and no longer appraise the caregiving situation as stressful.

Krauss (1990) and Heller and Factor (1991) report a very strong caregiver preference to continue in the caregiving role for as long as physically possible. This may reflect the functionality of the caregiving role for older women (Seltzer, Krauss, & Heller, 1991), meaning it may meet their need to feel needed and thus may promote caregiver mental health. Alternatively it may indicate the development of interdependencies between caregiver and care receiver. It also may signify parental concern about the lack of acceptable services and alternative arrangements (Heller & Factor, 1987; Seltzer, 1991b; Seltzer, Krauss, & Heller, 1991).

The preparation of adults with developmental disabilities for a change in caregivers or for the eventual loss of their family caregiver also has not been adequately investigated. Gold et al. (1987) and Smith and Tobin (1989) reported that very few parents had ever talked to their adult offspring about future changes in living arrangements. Indeed, Smith and Tobin (1989) found that some parents disregarded expressed preferences of the son or daughter with a disability if these preferences were incompatible with the parents' attitudes, fears, or anxieties.

The paucity of studies relating directly to caregiving for older adults with developmental disabilities and the many areas where findings are inconclusive suggested a need for further investigation. This study was conducted as a component of a larger study to determine the extent and characteristics of the population of aged and aging individuals with developmental disabilities in Virginia (Wood, 1991). Specific purposes of this study were (a) to investigate the extent to which families had made financial and/or residential plans for their older relatives with developmental disabilities in the event of illness or death of the family caregiver, (b) to examine experiences of aging individuals with developmental disabilities in dealing with death, and (c) to investigate psychological well-being and/or distress among family caregivers as indicated by levels of caregiver burden and/or depression.

Methodology

Personal interviews were conducted with 35 persons aged 40 or older who have developmental disabilities (i.e., consumers) and 44 family caregivers of persons with developmental disabilities. Family caregivers were self-identified as persons primarily responsible for the care of a relative with a developmental disability. Participants were referred to the study by service providers who were participating in the larger project, entitled The Aged and Aging Developmentally Disabled in Virginia (Wood, 1991). Individuals referred to project staff as potential partici-pants were initially contacted by the person making the referral to determine whether they were willing to be interviewed. Referrals were then contacted by project staff to schedule interviews at a mutually convenient time and place, often the participant's home. Consumers and caregivers were interviewed separately, although some represented caregiving dyads.

Information sought in the consumer interviews included demographic characteristics and information on lifestyle including informal support systems. Specific questions were asked about experiences related to the death of someone with whom the consumer had a close relationship. In addition to questions about demographics and lifestyle, family caregivers were asked about the steps they had taken to plan for the care of the family member with a developmental disability if and when they would no longer be able to provide care. Caregivers also were administered the Zarit Burden Interview (Zarit & Zarit, 1983) and the Center for Epidemiologic Studies Depression Scale (CES-D; Radliff, 1977). The Zarit Burden Scale is a 22-item self-report inventory that examines burden associated with providing care for an older relative. The CES-D is a 20-item self-report scale designed to assess depressive symptomatology in the general population. Scores may range from 0 to 60, with higher scores indicative of more depressive symptoms.

Results

Background Characteristics of Consumers

The age of the 35 consumer participants (i.e., individuals with developmental disabilities) ranged from 40 to 56 years (mean = 46). The sample was about equally divided between males (49%) and females (51%). Twenty-four percent were black, and 76% were white. Only 12% were married, and these were, without exception, individuals with physical disabilities. No persons with mental disabilities in our sample were married. Self-ratings of health ranged from excellent to poor, with the modal rating being good. The primary medical diagnosis for 79% of those interviewed was mental retardation. Other diagnoses were neurological impairment ($N = 2$), cerebral palsy ($N = 2$), and orthopedic impairment ($N = 3$). All consumer participants lived in the community with family or nonrelated persons. More than half (56%) were non-employed. Of those who were employed either full- or part-time, most (56%) worked in a sheltered workshop. Over half worked 31 to 40 hours per week, and 91% used a transportation service to and from work.

Lifestyle

Data on lifestyle of participants, though difficult to quantify, presented a profile of limited social activities. One person with an orthopedic impairment reported a wide variety of social activities (lunches with friends, volunteer work at a local hospital, leadership of a support group, participation in an advocacy group). With the exception of this individual, typical social activities included watching TV, going to the store with mother, helping with housework, and walking through the neighborhood to the fire station. A few reported enjoying helping to cut the grass. The social lives of those who attended a day program or a sheltered workshop were centered around these activities.

Support networks consisted almost entirely of family, professional service providers, and associates or supervisors at the sheltered workshops. Only a few named a best friend who did not fit into one of these categories. Forty-four percent indicated that they do "fun things" with relatives. Six persons (17%) responded that they do fun things with friends. Two thirds (67%) said that they like their daily social activities, although seven individuals responded that they would rather be doing something else. Eight individuals indicated that they would like to change their living arrangements, although they seemed not to have much awareness of where they might live. Many respondents also seemed not to have much awareness of social alternatives. Ten individuals (29% of those responding) said that they lacked transportation for social activities such as going to a restaurant or the movies. Eleven individuals (33% of those responding) said that they knew of no place to go to have fun. Only five persons said that they would like to be able to go out to have fun with others.

Experiences With Death

About one half (53%) of those interviewed had experienced a recent death of a person with whom they had a close relationship. These were usually family members, although in one instance the person who died was a friend at the workshop. The individual being interviewed had witnessed the death, as had other members of the work group. In another instance the respondent heard her father fall in the next room and found him dead on the floor. She believed he died from drinking too much "iced tea."

A quantitative analysis of the data from this section of the survey would have little meaning; however, the interviews yielded rich anecdotal information. Many of the participants seemed confused about the death experience and had difficulty describing their memories. Most (63%) had been excluded from the funeral and other activities surrounding the death. One individual told of family members returning from the hospital to talk about the death of a relative, while ignoring her presence in the same room. Although she learned of the death from their conversation, no one ever informed her directly of the death or spoke of it with her.

More than one half (53%) of the consumer participants reported that they had no one to talk to about their grief. A few indicated that they had been able to talk to their supervisors at the workshop. Many were unable to articulate feelings about the death or the person who had died. Some said they felt hurt, sad, or "funny."

Characteristics of Caregivers

Ages of the 44 family caregivers ranged from 44 to 88 (mean = 69.4). With the exception of one spouse caregiver who was 44 years old, all caregiver participants were 55 years of age or older. Nearly 90% were female, 78% were mothers, and more than 60% were single (widowed, divorced, separated, or never married). In a few instances this was the second or third family member to serve as caregiver for the older relative with a developmental disability. Nineteen percent were black and 81% were white. Educational level ranged from less than 8th grade to college graduate, with 51% having less than a high school education. Seventy-five percent had an estimated household income of less than $20,000 per year. Nearly 90% of caregivers were not employed. Most (56%) reported their health to be good or excellent, and 67% indicated that their health was about the same or better than it was 5 years ago. Conversely, 44% rated their health as fair or poor, and 33% said their health was worse than it was 5 years ago.

More than 83% had been providing care for the family member with a developmental disability for more than 25 years. More than half (52%) reported providing moderate levels of care (e.g., assistance with money management, reading, making appropriate choices). Nineteen percent provided assistance with personal care (e.g., eating, dressing, toileting), and 26% reported that the family member with a developmental disability was dependent on the caregiver for constant care.

Sixty-five percent reported that the aging family member with a developmental disability went out of the home for social or recreational activities no more than once per week. This included times when the caregiver also was present. Although transportation services were available for most of the individuals with developmental disabilities who work outside the home, 15% of the family caregivers reported that they provide transportation to and from work for the person for whom they provide care.

Most caregivers were not providing care for other disabled family members; however, three caregivers reported providing care for another son or daughter with a developmental disability. In one instance an aged mother was providing care for six adult children with developmental disabilities.

Planning for the Transfer of Care

Most caregivers reported that they had taken some steps to plan for long-term care of the dependent family member. Only five individuals (13%) said they had made no residential or financial plans. Nearly 65% had wills. Almost half (47%) had contacted a lawyer to discuss estate planning. Approximately 40% had investigated guardianship procedures, met with potential agency service providers, or toured residential facilities where the family member with a developmental disability might live. Sixty-two percent reported anticipating that another family member or close family friend would provide care when the current family caregiver is unable to continue providing care. Thirty-seven percent indicated that they did not know who would provide care when they were no longer able to do so.

Eighty-four percent of the caregivers indicated that they had made financial arrangements to provide for care of the relative with a developmental disability. These included savings accounts, trust funds, pension funds, life insurance benefits, and investments in real estate that the caregiver intended to be sold to acquire the funds needed to provide care. Sometimes these assets were willed to other family members who, it was hoped, would comply with the caregiver's wishes regarding their disposal. In several instances the financial "plans" of the caregiver consisted only of the hope that Social Security benefits would be adequate to secure care for the dependent family member. Seventy percent, or 30 of the 44 caregivers interviewed, said they had not discussed long-term care plans with their family member with a developmental disability.

Caregiver Distress

More than one half (56%) of the caregivers reported little or no caregiver burden as measured by the Zarit Burden Interview. However, 40%, or 17 caregivers, indicated burden in the mild to moderate range, and 2 caregivers reported moderate to severe burden.

Eighty-eight percent of the caregivers who participated in this study scored below 16 on the CES-D Scale, indicating low levels of depressive symptoms. Five caregivers (12%) reported significant symptoms of depression. Whether these symptoms are related to the caregiving situation is unclear.

Discussion

The data presented in this chapter are largely descriptive in nature, as this was an exploratory study undertaken for purposes of determining characteristics of the population in a given state, Virginia. Certain patterns may be observed, however, in family caregiving and in lifestyle of both caregiver and consumer that are consistent with findings from earlier research. Substantial numbers of older adults with developmental disabilities in this small sample are being cared for in the home by aged female relatives, often their mothers, with limited educational and financial resources. The aging individuals with developmental disabilities and, by inference, the family caregivers have a very restricted lifestyle, with limited social activities. Most reported that their social activities consisted of doing things in the home or neighborhood with families. Many of the consumers interviewed do not work for pay outside the home. Those who do report that their social lives revolve around the activities and personnel of the job site. Anecdotal evidence gathered by interviewers indicates that many of the adults with disabilities are infantilized by their caregivers. They often were referred to by "pet" names or in diminutive terms and spoken to in a patronizing tone.

Long-term planning for the transfer of care would include residential, legal, and financial arrangements that would be activated at some specified future time (Seltzer & Seltzer, 1985) and, presumably, also would include psychological preparation of both caregiver and care recipient for a time when the caregiver no longer may be able to provide care. This would be healthy for all parties concerned.

In this study the data indicate that substantial numbers of families have not made adequate plans for the transfer of care. Some family caregivers had made no plans other than to arrange with another family member to provide care. Sixty-one percent reported anticipating that another family member or close family friend would provide care when the current family caregiver no longer is able to do so. In many instances arrangements to accomplish the transfer had not been made and frequently had not even been discussed. Thirty-seven percent, or 16 of the 44 caregivers interviewed, indicated that they did not know who will provide care when they are unable to do so.

Most caregivers clearly did not expect to be survived by the person for whom they are providing care. They also seemed to have difficulty expressing their feelings regarding this issue. Some discussed examples of deteriorating health or the increase in chronic health problems in the family member with the developmental disability. They shared their concerns regarding the increase in visits to physicians for medical procedures or medication adjustments. Very few of the caregivers who indicated that another family member would take over caregiving responsibilitics had revised their wills to reflect the identification of the new caregiver or the financial adjustments that must be made to ensure the transfer of care. A few parents openly admitted that their choice would be for the person with the disability "to die the breath before I do," thereby relieving other family members of the responsibility of extended caregiving and also relieving the current caregiver of the need to make plans for the transfer of care.

Whatever the plans, 70% of the family caregivers had not discussed them with the family member for whom they were providing care. If financial and residential plans had not been discussed, it seems fair to assume that no emotional or psychological preparation has been made for the possibility of the caregiver's eventual death or potential inability to continue providing care. Other data showed that many of the care recipients did not attend funerals or participate in related activities when a family member died. This suggests difficulty in dealing with death or possible infantilization of the family member with the disability.

The findings of this study are consistent with those of Heller and Factor (1991) and Lehmann and Roberto (this volume), who also found that substantial numbers of families have not made adequate plans for transfer of care. A number of explanatory factors may be involved. First, as mentioned earlier, many family caregivers did not expect to be survived by the person for whom they were providing care. When currently aging or aged cohorts of persons with developmental disabilities were born and were growing up, this was a realistic expectation because most persons with developmental disabilities had a relatively short life span. Also, many spent much of their lives in public institutions. Consequently, planning for their care was not an issue of concern.

Second, many current older cohorts of individuals with lifelong disabilities experienced the stigma associated with being considered "handicapped" and had limited opportunities for participation in activities outside the realm of home and family. For this reason their caregivers may be overprotective and may experience a good deal of ambivalence about the prospect of transferring care.

Third, mutual dependencies between caregiver and care recipient may have developed. Continued involvement with the relative with a disability is a source of important emotional and psychological benefit (Seltzer, Krauss, & Heller, 1991), which the caregiver is reluctant to give up. The caregiving role may be a source of identity and ego satisfaction, especially for the female caregiver. Evidence also indicates that adults with disabilities provide assistance with household chores and serve as companions for caregivers, whose lifestyle often is constricted by their caregiving activities (Factor & Heller, 1992; Krauss, Seltzer, & Goodman, 1992). As caregiver and care recipient age together, a developmental factor may come into play. The stage of life of the son or daughter may relate to the parent's corresponding stage of life more closely than at any previous age. Thus resolution by family caregivers to continue providing care for as long as they live may meet mental health needs of aging caregivers.

A fourth factor in failure to plan for the transfer of care may be found in caregivers' appraisal of acceptable alternatives for providing care. Concerns may reflect limited awareness of the availability of services or actual gaps in available services, especially in the realm of housing alternatives.

In general, caregivers in this sample reported little psychological distress. These findings are consistent with results reported by Seltzer and Krauss (1989) and with the adaptational model of long-term caregiving. Caregivers interviewed in this study appeared not to appraise their situations as unusually stressful or, after many years of caregiving, believed that they had adequate resources for coping with the situation. It is important to note that two caregivers felt moderate to severe levels of burden and five caregivers reported high levels of depressive symptoms. Limitations in research design did not permit determination of causality in this study; however, it is possible that these individuals are experiencing changes in their own health or in the health of the relative for whom they are providing care that are perceived as taxing their resources for continuing to provide care.

Generalization of the findings from this study to a larger population must be restricted on two important accounts: the size and the nature of the sample. The 35 consumers and 44 caregivers who were interviewed in this study represent a sample of convenience; they were volunteers, all of whom were currently receiving some formal services. They were, therefore, known to the service delivery network and were, at least to some degree, familiar with the services that might be received. In this respect they perhaps were not typical of older adults with developmental disabilities and their families, the majority of whom may be unknown to formal service networks (Jacobson et al., 1985; Rose & Ansello, 1987; Smith & Tobin, 1989).

Implications for Practice and Future Research

Practice Considerations

Service delivery agencies increasingly report the "Friday afternoon phone call." In this scenario the formal service provider receives a frantic telephone call from a relative seeking emergency residential placement for an individual with one or more disabilities because the family caregiver has died or is seriously ill. The service provider is at a disadvantage in this kind of crisis atmosphere, and families may face few available options. Often the individual is given a temporary placement while suitable arrangements are explored. This may be traumatizing for the person with a lifelong disability who has received sheltered care from family members and who now has little opportunity to prepare for a transition.

This scenario points up several needs. Among these is the need for outreach activities to identify the "hidden" group of adults with developmental disabilities who reside in the community with their parents or other relatives and who are unknown to formal service networks (Jacobson et al., 1985). Demographic information developed from these activities would enable policy makers and planners to forecast population trends and predict future needs within this target group. Local service providers could monitor the needs of these families and assist them in proactive planning in order to avoid potential crises.

A second need is for the aging and disabilities service networks to be equipped to respond to the growing numbers of older adults with developmental disabilities and their families. In the past little reason has existed for the two systems to cooperate in the delivery of care because few clients with developmental disabilities survived to old age. Ansello (1992) has identified a number of practical barriers to inter-system cooperation, with the shortage of cross-trained personnel ranked as the most critical need. To facilitate effective collaboration, key staff need training not only in disabilities and in aging but also in the background and operations of both systems.

Heller and Factor (1991) found that information about use of formal services (e.g., respite, care management) increased the probability that caregivers would prefer a residential program placement. One can conclude from this finding that familiarity with support services for family caregivers may serve to decrease apprehension about formal services and, thus, may facilitate planning for the transfer of care. It clearly points up a need to develop programs for informing families about the availability of services.

Future Research

Research on older adults with developmental disabilities and their families currently is very limited. Much of the available information was generated from descriptive studies, using small samples of convenience. Theory-driven, longitudinal studies using large-scale probability samples are needed. Research is needed to examine the effectiveness of various interventions (e.g., support groups, counseling, information about services) in facilitating adequate planning for the transfer of care (Seltzer, Krauss, & Heller, 1991; Smith & Tobin, 1989). Studies also are needed to investigate both the short-term and the long-term impacts of planning on the well-being of older individuals with developmental disabilities and their family caregivers. It is especially important to assess the effect of care planning on the mental health of caregivers because it is believed that such planning can result in significant short-term stress (Seltzer, Krauss, & Heller, 1991). Developing strategies for intervention that include considerations for support and sensitivity to the psychosocial needs of older individuals with lifelong disabilities and their family caregivers is an important area of program development.

8

Current and Future Service Needs of Aging Individuals With Developmental Disabilities Living With Relatives

JEAN P. LEHMANN
KAREN A. ROBERTO

The successful transition of special-needs youth from school to work is a major goal for educational and human services agencies. The term *transition* presently is characterized by a model that predicts greater employment opportunities for persons with disabilities who receive adequate support and preparation (Will, 1984). Three factors critical to this model are the implementation of an individualized planning process (Albright & Cobb, 1988; Wehman, Kregel, & Barcus, 1985; Wehman, Moon, Everson, Wood, & Barcus, 1988); the provision of specific outcome-oriented training (Brolin, 1982; Falvey, 1989; Wehman et al., 1988); and collaboration among service delivery systems (Johnson, Bruininks, & Thurlow, 1987). Current service goals that enable individuals with developmental disabilities to experience normal lives highlight the need to look at another transition, that of losing a primary caregiver. Although this transition is difficult for most persons, it probably is more traumatic for the aging person with developmental

This study was funded by a grant from the Colorado Developmental Disabilities Planning Council, Denver, Colorado, awarded to the second author.

disabilities who has depended upon a single set of family caregivers throughout life. This transition also demands cooperative advance planning and assistance. Therefore, the purpose of this chapter is to explore the current service use and transition needs of families with aging members with developmental disabilities.

Community Service Utilization

Most persons with disabilities need support to live successfully in the community (Agosta, 1989). Community services to families of children with developmental disabilities have changed dramatically in the past 20 years. Families once told to institutionalize their children now are expected to raise them at home with the assistance of community-based services (Warren & Warren, 1989). Currently, however, no unified approach or even philosophy exists for supporting families who have chosen to be the primary caregivers for their sons or daughters (Singer & Irvin, 1989). More alarming are reports that the waiting lists for community-based services are burgeoning (Davis, 1987). Families desiring to keep their children at home or expecting their children to live in independent or semi-independent living situations will find a dearth in service availability.

The focus of research in this area is the efficacy of services whose overriding purpose is to prevent institutionalization. For example, Agosta, Bass, and Spence (1986) surveyed parents about the types of services they needed to maintain their children with disabilities at home. Overall, findings showed a widespread use of community support services. A sizable proportion of the respondents reported they received financial assistance from government agencies, including Social Security and food stamps. Families with older children were most concerned about where their children were going to live in the future. There is also some evidence that parents' expectations for their children's future use of community-based employability and residential services may reflect their understanding and the accessibility of services. For instance, Cox and Wilson (1985) found that the availability of housing was a factor in the decisions surrounding the adolescent's move away from home. Current limitations in the adult service systems are the reason parents of children with disabilities were not interested in having their children work in nonsheltered environments (Hill, Seyfarth, Banks, Wehman, & Orelove, 1987; Seyfarth, Hill, Orelove, McMillan, & Wehman, 1985).

According to Sowers (1989), professionals influence parents' expectations regarding service needs by suggesting children with disabilities
cannot work. Hence these parents have fewer expectations about future
opportunities for their children.

Issues for Persons Caring
for Aging Adults With Disabilities

Investigations into the family caregiving situation with aging adults
with developmental disabilities have examined caregiver characteristics, specific service needs, and service utilization patterns. Results
show that older parents often report a lack of qualified providers and
consider the cost of the service to be prohibitive (Engelhardt, Brubaker,
& Lutzer, 1987) and that there is no relationship between (a) caregiver
characteristics (e.g., age, income, health) and characteristics of the
dependents with developmental disabilities (e.g., behavior, level of
mental retardation) and (b) service utilization. The caregiver's assessment of his or her current ability to provide care is significant. Family
members used more services when they perceived themselves being less
able to provide care and when they anticipated being less able in the
future. Moreover, there is a relationship between perceived caregiver
ability and caregiver's perception of his or her health and level of depen-
dence of the child with developmental disabilities. Similarly, Roberto (this
volume) found that elderly caregivers reported an overall increase in their
stress levels and a need for formal services when there was a perceived
decrease in the functional abilities of the aging person with developmental
disabilities and an increase in the health problems of the caregiver.

A study by Gold and her colleagues (1987) examined several factors,
including the extent to which generic agencies for the aged served aging
families of persons with disabilities. Their findings suggest that the
caregivers had few, if any, contacts with the aging agencies. The
investigators concluded that this lack of service utilization could be due
to the families' more active involvement with services for individuals
with developmental disabilities. The majority of these families had
applied for residential placements for their children but expressed
confusion regarding the workings of this system. The parents also
expressed concern over the uncertainty of their son's or daughter's
future but did not seem able to prepare for this inevitable transition.

Gold and her colleagues also found that poor parental health also contributed to the caregivers' perceptions that their situations were bleak.

In summary, it appears that recent literature focused on the transition of individuals with developmental disabilities from school to work but largely ignored the difficult transition that occurs when a primary caregiver can no longer fulfill this role. Studies regarding families of children with disabilities indicated a need for community services to maintain their children at home and a concern about future residential opportunities. There are inconsistencies throughout the literature about determining which families are most likely to use services at the present time and in the future, due, perhaps, to differences in sample selection and data-gathering methods. However, the caregiver's perceived health is one variable that does appear to influence service needs. Current studies show that elderly caregivers underutilize both the services for the aging and the services for persons with developmental disabilities. These are services that might provide support when a change in primary caregivers occurs. Relatives also voiced fears about future care needs but indicated confusion regarding potential service use.

Research Questions

This study explores the current services in which aging persons with developmental disabilities living at home with their elderly relatives participate and the types of services perceived as being needed in the future. The questions asked were:

1. What services do families with aging children with developmental disabilities currently use and why do they not access other services?
2. Is there a relationship between persons with developmental disabilties persons' performance of activities of daily living skills and their current use of services or the perceived need for future services?
3. What alternatives for the future care of their son, daughter, or sibling with developmental disabilities are most acceptable to elderly caregivers?
4. What plans for the future of their relative have caregivers begun to implement?
5. What information would caregivers like that might assist them in planning for the future transition of their child or sibling with developmental disabilities?

Answers to these questions will provide us with a better understanding of the planning and training considerations necessary in facilitating a smooth transition from the family living situation to a community living situation.

Method

Sample

The State of Colorado Division of Developmental Disabilities identified the sample of relatives caring for aging persons with developmental disabilities. A staff member from the division contacted the 22 Community Center Boards in the state and requested mailing labels for all service recipients who were at least 40 years of age and living with their relatives. Twenty-one boards cooperated in this study, identifying a potential sample of 148 families. To protect the confidentiality of the sample, a letter explaining the study and requesting the primary caregiver to complete the enclosed self-report questionnaire was sent by the division during the spring of 1988. Three weeks after the initial mailing, potential sample members received a second survey packet. A total of 61 family caregivers returned the questionnaire for a response rate of 41%. Specific follow-up of nonrespondents was not possible due to the need for protection of subjects' anonymity by the Colorado Division of Developmental Disabilities.

The respondents ranged in age from 38 to 89 ($M = 68.8$). Most of the 13 men and 48 women were parents (79.0%) and the majority of the remainder were sisters (18.0%). The caregivers had a median income of between $10,000 and $14,999 and a mean educational level of 11.3 years. More than one half of the respondents rated their present health status as fair to poor whereas the remaining 40% reported their health to be excellent or good. The average number of years the person with developmental disabilities lived at home was 36, and ranged from 2 to 59 years. In addition to being a caregiver for their child or sibling, 8.2% also cared for a disabled spouse and 6.6% cared for another child with a disability.

The 36 men and 24 women with developmental disabilities ranged in age from 40 to 79 ($M = 48.3$ years). One person's gender was not reported. The majority were labeled mentally retarded (83.6%). Other or additional impairments reported were cerebral palsy (19.7%), epilepsy (13.1%), autism (3.3%), or some other type of neurological impairment (8.2%). Approximately 68.9% of these individuals were in good health and 31.1% were in fair to poor health. Eighty percent worked in sheltered workshops, 13.1% participated in day programs, and 23% had either full-time or part-time employment. Only 2 respondents indicated that the person with developmental disabilities was not working.

Generalizability of this survey is limited by the small, nonrandom sample upon which it is based. However, characteristics of both respondents and their family members with developmental disabilities compare favorably with populations described in other studies (see Caserta et al., 1987; Engelhardt et al., 1987; Gold et al., 1987) and were similar.

Survey Instrument

A self-report questionnaire consisting primarily of forced-choice questions was designed specifically for this study. A series of demographic questions elicited background information about the caregivers and their family members with developmental disabilities. A modified portion of the Developmental Disabilities Profile created by the New York State Office of Mental Retardation and Developmental Disabilities (1987) assessed the functional ability of the person with a developmental disability. Caregivers rated how independently their child or sibling could perform 21 tasks of daily living. Rankings on each task indicated the disabled person's need for (a) total support, (b) assistance, or (c) supervision or (d) being independent on each task. To better understand the relationship between care receivers' level of functioning and their current or future service needs, the activities of daily living were divided into two categories, personal and instrumental. Personal skills were those needed in caring for oneself such as toileting, bathing, and brushing teeth. The reliability coefficient for this scale was .97. Instrumental skills were those needed to function independently. They included cleaning, cooking, money management, caring for simple health needs and the ability to communicate needs, and doing laundry. The reliability coefficient for the instrumental scale was .93. The items from each category were added to make a total personal and a total instrumental score. Personal skills scores ranged from values of 7 to 28 with a mean score of 21.2 and instrumental skill scores ranged from 14 to 50 ($M = 34.2$).

Respondents identified all services being used by their child or sibling and selected services they anticipated needing in the future in order to determine current service utilization and future service needs.

They chose from the 16 services representing generic services typically available for older adults. Respondents selected one of five reasons for not utilizing services: (a) unnecessary, (b) unknown, (c) unavailable, (d) dissatisfactory, or (e) expensive.

A series of questions asking the caregiver to rate alternatives for the future of his or her child or sibling as acceptable or not acceptable explored future care issues. Caregivers also indicated the steps taken to plan for the future (e.g., contacting a lawyer or making arrangements with another family member to provide care). In addition, caregivers noted the type of information they wanted to obtain before designing or implementing future plans.

Results

Services

Respondents indicated all of the services the person for whom they were caring currently used (Table 8.1). An average of two services were used. The most frequently utilized services included Supplemental Security Income (SSI) (46%), medical care (30%), transportation (26%), and case management (26%). Companionship (2%) was the least used service. The majority of the respondents reported not using the services because they did not need them. Closer examination showed that 27% were not using advocacy services because they did not know about them and 21% were not familiar with companionship services. Multiple regression analyses examined the relationship among background variables of caregivers and their child or sibling with developmental disabilities and service use. The four variables entered into each equation—(a) caregiver's relationship to the person with a developmental disability (parent vs. sibling), (b) caregiver's marital status, (c) caregiver's annual income, and (d) the child or sibling's health rating—failed to produce significant regression equations for either current or future service use ($p > .05$).

Respondents indicated major future service needs to be housing alternatives (43%) and medical care (40%). Meals on Wheels was the service least needed in the future (11%). The mean number of services reported as being needed in the future was 3.6. This was a significant increase over the amount of current service use [$t(55) = 2.46, p < .05$].

Table 8.1 Percentages of Current Service Use Versus Anticipated Need

Services	Current Use	Future Need
Housing alternative	10.5	42.9
Medical care	29.8	40.4
Transportation	26.3	32.1
Housekeeping	7.0	25.0
Case manager	26.3	24.6
Home health care	8.8	24.6
Adult day care (seniors)	10.5	21.4
Legal assistance	8.8	21.1
SSI	45.6	19.6
Respite services	7.0	17.5
Counseling	7.0	17.5
Companionship	1.8	16.1
Advocacy	3.5	14.3
Congregate or group meals	3.5	14.3
Household repairs	3.5	14.3
Meals on Wheels	5.3	10.7

NOTE: $n = 57$

Care Receivers With Developmental Disabilities

The percentage tabulations of individuals needing assistance with personal and instrumental activities of daily living are shown in Table 8.2. Approximately one third (30%) of the caregivers indicated that their child or sibling with developmental disabilities needed total support when taking a shower or bath, brushing his or her teeth, or brushing and combing his or her hair. Most children with disabilities (64%) were completely independent in the area of toileting, and 71% fed themselves without any assistance. In terms of instrumental skills, 40% communicated their needs and 36% cared for simple health needs. The largest percent of individuals required total support or assistance managing their money (88%), shopping for a simple meal (80%), washing laundry (67%), cooking with the stove or microwave (66%), and using public transportation (60%).

Table 8.2 Caregivers' Perceptions of Their Relative's Ability to Perform Activities of Daily Living

Level of Functioning	1	2	3	4
Personal Skills				
Toileting	23.0	9.8	3.3	63.9
(bowels)	(14)	(6)	(2)	(39)
Toileting	21.7	8.3	1.7	68.3
(bladder)	(13)	(5)	(1)	(41)
Showering	30.0	10.0	10.0	50.0
	(18)	(6)	(6)	(30)
Teeth care	30.5	8.5	11.9	49.2
	(18)	(5)	(7)	(29)
Hair care	30.0	15.0	15.0	40.0
	(18)	(9)	(9)	(24)
Dressing	28.3	8.3	6.7	56.7
	(17)	(5)	(4)	(34)
Feeding	25.9	1.7	1.7	70.7
	(15)	(1)	(1)	(41)
Instrumental Skills				
Selecting	21.7	18.3	21.7	38.3
clothes	(13)	(11)	(13)	(23)
Doing laundry	50.0	17.2	15.5	17.2
	(29)	(10)	(9)	(10)
Communicating	22.4	19.0	19.0	39.9
needs	(13)	(11)	(11)	(23)
Using telephone	35.2	24.1	14.8	25.9
	(19)	(13)	(8)	(14)
Shopping	55.6	24.1	16.7	3.7
(simple meal)	(30)	(13)	(9)	(2)
Preparing food	40.4	14.0	15.8	29.8
(simple)	(23)	(8)	(9)	(17)
Using stove	41.1	25.0	16.1	17.9
	(23)	(14)	(9)	(10)
Caring for	33.9	15.3	15.3	35.6
health (simple)	(20)	(9)	(9)	(21)
Maintaining	26.3	15.8	24.6	33.3
safety (home)	(15)	(9)	(14)	(19)

Table 8.2 Continued

Level of Functioning	1	2	3	4
Maintaining	33.3	16.7	16.7	33.3
safety (community)	(18)	(9)	(9)	(18)
Crossing street	36.2	12.1	17.2	34.5
	(21)	(7)	(10)	(20)
Using public	45.5	14.5	12.7	27.3
transportation	(25)	(8)	(7)	(15)
Managing	58.6	29.3	6.9	5.2
money	(34)	(17)	(4)	(3)
Cleaning room	26.7	16.7	20.0	36.7
	(16)	(10)	(12)	(22)

NOTE: Numbers in parentheses are the actual numbers of cases used to calculate the percentage of responses.
1 = total support, 2 = assistance, 3 = supervision, 4 = independent

No significant relationship was found between ability to perform personal activities of daily living and the number of services that the individual currently used ($p > .05$) or anticipated needing in the future ($p > .05$). As expected, persons considered able to perform many of the instrumental skills participated in fewer services ($r -.26$, $p < .05$). No relationship, however, was found between the performance of instrumental skills and expected need for future services ($p > .05$).

Future Care Issues

Caregivers rated the acceptability of various living arrangements for their children or siblings (Table 8.3). Placement of their offspring/siblings into a group home was the most acceptable and asking a friend to live with their offspring/siblings was the least acceptable. The types of steps taken by caregivers to plan for the future also were explored. Findings showed that 43% of the sample had begun to make arrangements with another family member to provide care for the individual with developmental disabilities in the future. Thirty-six percent had met with potential agency service providers such as social workers or case

Table 8.3 Acceptability of Future Care Alternatives

Alternative	Percentages
1. Group home	77.1 (48)
2. Immediate family member	70.8 (48)
3. Semi-independent living situation	61.4 (44)
4. Nursing home for persons labeled developmentally disabled	50.0 (44)
5. Nursing home (seniors)	40.5 (42)
6. Foster home	31.0 (42)
7. Distant relative	25.0 (40)
8. Regional center	24.4 (41)
9. Friend	14.6 (41)

NOTE: Numbers in parentheses are the actual numbers of cases used to calculate the percentages of responses.

managers, but only 23% actually had toured facilities where their relative might live. A few caregivers (19%) had contacted lawyers regarding estate planning.

A series of chi-squares was made to determine whether there were differences in the steps taken for future planning and the caregivers' perceived level of health. Of the caregivers who reported poor health, fewer than expected had made legal arrangements ($X^2 = 5.94$, $p < .01$). There was no other significant difference between the health of the care-giver and the arrangements being made for the future care of the person with developmental disabilities.

Caregivers indicated the type of service (e.g., housing alternatives and community services for either aging or developmentally disabled) about which they desired information. Most caregivers reported that they did not want more information about services for the aging, but 46% wanted to know more about housing alternatives for persons with developmental disabilities and 39% were interested in community services for persons with developmental disabilities.

Discussion

The results of this study suggest that families of persons with devel-opmental disabilities face several dilemmas in planning for the future of their son, daughter, or sibling. For example, there appears to be some confusion regarding available services. Many caregivers indicated that they were not using specific services. Case management was being used by only 26% of the sample population. Although most respondents (82%) were not using this service because they did not think they needed it, 12% did not know what the service was. This is unusual because all of the study subjects have case managers. Further, the stated lack of need for services seems to contradict the fact that many of the persons with developmental disabilities needed much assistance with personal and instrumental skills. The findings suggest caregivers equated the term *need* with *crisis* and, therefore, did not utilize resources until all other avenues had been exhausted. Another explanation for the study's findings is that the current service offerings are not applicable or adequate to meet the needs of older individuals with developmental disabilities. Indeed, several studies report that families of young adults with developmental disabilities perceive a need for more or expanded services (Berger & Foster, 1976; Suelzle & Keenan, 1981).

It is evident from the data that aging persons with developmental disabilities who are living at home with parents or other family members depend on these caregivers for ensuring that many of their personal activities or daily living skills are performed properly. These results support those from a study conducted by Hirst (1985). Hirst found that young adults with disabilities relied on their families for assistance with many activities of daily living, including bathing and washing hair. It is surprising, then, that no significant relationship was found between the level of personal skill performance and the number of services used. These are skills that often determine the type of living situation for which a person with developmental disabilities is most suited. It appears that relatives need assistance preparing persons with developmental disabilities to become more independent.

Similar to the study conducted by Agosta and his colleagues (1986), caregivers expressed greatest interest in the area of residential placement. They wanted more information about potential residential opportunities, and they thought this would be the primary service their child or sibling would eventually need. Yet they seemed more willing to make arrangements with another family member for the future than to visit residential options. Transportation also remains an issue. Many of the respondents indicated they needed transportation now and anticipated needing it in the future. Clearly, adequate, affordable transportation is necessary for older persons with or without developmental disabilities to participate in services. This is an area in which both groups (i.e., community aging services and services for persons with developmental disabilities) might collaborate in advocacy efforts. It is hoped that the Americans with Disabilities Act (Public Law 101-336) will remedy many of the concerns in this area because public transportation will be more accessible.

Several questions remain at the finish of this study. For example, were relatives' responses to questions about future service needs influenced by their lack of information about opportunities, similar to the families interviewed by Hill and colleagues (1987)? Further, how might service providers facilitate a smooth transition for aging adults with developmental disabilities away from their immediate relatives? Some suggestions are offered in the next section.

Implications for Practice and Research

The role of parents with children with severe mental retardation has evolved over the past 20 years from that of minimal contributors in child rearing to primary caregivers (Farber, 1986). Historically, persons with mental retardation were removed from their families and bound over to state institutions for care (Kaufman & Payne, 1975). In response to growing concerns about discriminatory practices with persons with disabilities, an executive committee appointed by President John F. Kennedy decried institutionalization and recommended that services for persons with mental retardation be based in the community (President's Panel on Mental Retardation, 1962). Since the issuance of the panel's recommendation, the care and treatment of persons with mental retardation have undergone major changes. The push for deinstitutionalization created a system of community residential services such as group homes and foster homes for persons with developmental disabilities (Taylor, 1987). Moreover, formal recognition of the family's residence as a viable living alternative may have furthered parents' resolve to keep their children at home (Willer & Intagliata, 1984). Both the guiding policies and current efforts are based upon the premise that a comprehensive array of community-based alternatives exists. Unfortunately, the amount of persons requiring formal supports far outstrips available resources (Davis, 1987). Suggestions for improving the systems that provide assistance to aging persons and individuals with developmental disabilities are offered in this section.

Practitioners/Caregivers

The fields of early childhood education and special education offer several models for supporting families raising and living with individuals with disabilities. Summers, Behr, and Turnbull (1989) describe the major task of service providers to work with the entire family by identifying positive strategies for meeting each individual family member's needs. Suggestions for support include involving families in self-help groups that place them in contact with families experiencing similar decisions, developing educational programs that address critical issues (Summers et al., 1989), empowering families by informing them regarding available services, and allowing families to purchase the services they feel would be most beneficial through government-subsidized voucher systems (Agosta, 1989; Taylor, Knoll, Lehr, & Walker, 1989). The voucher system would enable families to select the formal services that best serve their particular needs. Thus they would be able to—in the words of Warren and Warren (1989)—"create order out of chaos" (p. 66). The ability to select and schedule assistance perceived as necessary for dealing with issues associated with aging would give families choices.

One caveat to this proposal is that there are not many available resources (Davis, 1987). Services for the aging population, as well as those for persons with developmental disabilities, are limited. Therefore, it behooves professionals to conduct a community assessment to identify all services designed for elderly citizens as well as those for persons with developmental disabilities, in addition to those generic services available to all community members that offer financial support, education, social and recreational opportunities, and medical intervention. The survey provides information about voids in the array of available service options.

The current philosophy in special education, inclusion, has implications for community service utilization and development. Inclusion efforts in the schools has meant students are integrated socially into regular classes and asked to participate even if only partially (Falvey, 1989). Persons with disabilities and their families therefore should be able to access a full range of supports from churches, social services, and other organizations in which nondisabled persons interact.

The development and provision of support services for families and their children with disabilities depend upon their specific needs. Caregivers in this study reported that their children were unable to perform many personal hygiene tasks such as brushing their teeth. It would be easy to design or even locate existing services that teach activities of daily living. However, parents' perceptions may reflect the focus of many professionals on the limitations of persons with disabilities (Falvey, 1989). The assessment of persons with disabilities must be refocused from being deficit driven to accentuating strengths. Families are not attuned to their children's strengths. An existing tool that allows families and service providers to consider persons with disabilities in light of their skills is the Magill Action Planning System (MAPS). Stainback and Stainback (1990) describe the MAPS process as a series of questions posed to families, children with disabilities, and all other persons intricately involved in the family situation. The group brought together for assessment is asked to describe the strengths of the person with the disability, her or his history, dreams for her or his future, nightmares about the future, and potential resources and barriers. This process may help families and service providers to become more aware of the skills and positive attributes of the person with disabilities, thereby capitalizing on skills versus becoming mired in doubt about deficits. This assessment also leads to the development of a transitional plan.

As the waiting lists for community services grow, it becomes more critical that families of individuals with developmental disabilities begin to prepare for the inevitable future transition they face in the caregiving situation. Perhaps implementing a planning process for aging individuals with developmental disabilities living with their relatives similar to that which is already occurring for students leaving high school is required. Formal planning may offer solutions to some of the barriers to future planning found in this study. For example, the plan should list training needs, agency involvement, and the steps required to facilitate a successful transition. According to Seltzer and Seltzer (1985), such a plan is viable and should include information on the desired residential, financial, and protective service outcomes. More specifically, Sample, Spencer, and Bean (1990) recommend the following areas be addressed in a transitional plan: (a) living arrangement; (b) work, education, or retirement options; (c) transportation needs; (d) social and recreational needs; (e) health and medical needs; (f) self-care issues; and (g) supports necessary for negotiating a successful transition. The information obtained from the MAPS process is useful for developing long-range outcomes and short-term goals for the transitional plan.

Clearly, planning efforts must address the needs of the entire family and not just the needs of the member with disabilities. The Individualized Family Services Plan (IFSP) mandated by the Reauthorization of the Education for All Handicapped Children Act (Public Law 99-457) is one existing mechanism that recognizes the importance of the family systems approach to service planning (Dunst, Trivette, & Deal, 1988). Although the IFSP is implemented for families of infants and toddlers with disabilities, its approach seems equally appropriate for elderly families of adult children with developmental disabilities. According to Dunst and colleagues (1988), the family services plan should contain (a) the name of a case coordinator who will function to empower families with the knowledge and skills to mobilize resources, (b) a statement of the families' strengths, (c) a prioritized list of family needs, (d) a statement regarding sources of support and resources, (e) a statement of actions that will be taken by all significant parties including the family, and (f) procedures for evaluating the success of the plan (pp. 132-133). This type of plan can be developed in conjunction with the transition plan.

A larger issue is involving families in the service systems. Possible solutions to this problem include requiring case managers to contact families regularly for an update and to discuss options if they do not already do so. Generic services for the aging also should be made aware of the needs of these potential service recipients. Relatives and siblings need to be assisted to take a more active role in planning for the future. Their dependent with developmental disabilities is at risk of being placed into large facilities where he or she does not perform many activities of daily living skills. One possible avenue for helping families and relatives understand the importance of future planning may be through physicians. Medical services were noted in this study to be a regularly used service. Medical practitioners such as physicians should be encouraged to refer their patients to the appropriate service agency when they detect a need for future planning. Because many physicians may not be aware of available services for families, this involves designing educational literature or programs for physicians.

Figure 8.1 summarizes the services the developmental disabilities system and agencies for aging persons could bring to families. Clearly, the use of a proactive assessment such as MAPS to identify strengths, the development of a transitional plan outlining future goals, and consideration of the entire family system expands the roles of service providers. Agencies serving the aging may have to collaborate with those who provide services

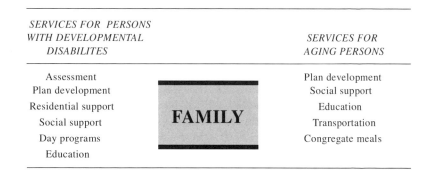

Figure 8.1. Service Provision to Support Elderly Families

to persons with developmental disabilities. Training across disciplines may need to occur so the two systems understand each other.

Researchers

The findings from this study shed some light on the lives of persons with developmental disabilities living at home with their elderly caregivers and the factors that have influenced the current and perceived need for future services. Few services are used that will enable individuals with developmental disabilities to leave their relatives and lead successful lives in other settings. It is apparent that their families require a proactive systematic process to engage them in the planning process for the future of their child or sibling. Future research must identify those factors that predict an orderly and smooth transition for aging persons with developmental disabilities away from their families and into diverse residential arrangements.

Multivariate designs, examining the influence of more than one variable, are called for so that the attributes of caregivers, care receivers, and service outcomes are compared. Qualitative methodologies could be employed to better understand families' perspectives regarding their children's futures, service desirability, and the types of assistance they would like to have available. In the tradition of Edgerton and his colleagues (Edgerton, 1967; Edgerton & Gaston, 1991), aging persons with developmental disabilities could be studied or interviewed about their preferences for their future. The qualitative information would enable relevant service systems to implement supportive strategies to meet the individual needs of families and consumers.

9

Family Satisfaction With Case Management and Service Provision

Rural and Urban Perspectives for Older Families of Persons With Developmental Disabilities

CHRISTINE RINCK
CARL CALKINS

For many decades the needs of persons with developmental disabilities were met in one of two ways. Families often kept their family members at home, receiving limited services from the state. Even educational opportunities often were denied. The other alternative was to place their family member in an institutional setting where many services were provided at the site. In the 1950s, services for persons who were mentally retarded were virtually nonexistent in a community setting (General Accounting Office, 1977). The purpose of this article is to outline the family's perspective of the case management system comparing both the age of the parents and their residential setting (urban/rural).

The authors express their thanks to the Missouri Planning Council for Developmental Disabilities for funding the research described herein and to the Missouri Department of Mental Health, Division of Mental Retardation/Developmental Disabilities, for their assistance in the project. Special thanks is given to Ms. Melinda Elmore, the division's coordinator, who provided valuable input to the development and implementation of the project and to the analysis of the results.

125

Service Provision

With the advent of deinstitutionalization, the need for services within a community context became paramount. Many individuals who had resided in an institutional setting for most of their lives were now placed in a community setting. Their need for speech therapy, vocational activities, and recreational services was no less in the community than in the institutional setting. Thus a service delivery system had to be established within the context of the community. The "delivery system," as it might be termed, developed in a haphazard fashion, with both duplication of some services and gaps in others (Weil, 1985a). A lack of coordination among service agencies is evident, particularly in a rural area (Willer & Intagliata, 1984).

Few individuals in rural areas receive comprehensive habilitation services. Medical services in the rural area also are limited. Family practitioners may be present, but the family must make a trip to an urban area for a specialist's visit. Other professionals (e.g., speech therapists, occupational therapists) rarely practice in rural settings. This was verified in a Missouri survey of case managers who assist infants and their families under a statewide pilot program of Part H of Public Law (P.L.) 99-457 (Rinck, Eddy, Lund, & Griggs, 1990) and in the independent assessment of the Medicaid Waiver for persons with a developmental disability in Missouri (Rinck, Eddy, & Torner, 1991). Single case studies typically document the effect of this shortage of rural professionals. Families have described long trips to visit therapists on a regular basis (Rinck, Eddy, et al., 1990) or even the lack of therapies due to the family's inability to find a therapist (Rinck et al., 1991). The published references reflecting the perceptions of older caregivers who reside in rural areas of services received have been sparse.

In recent years the provision of services has changed—from delivery in a segregated model to an integrated one. Full inclusion in the community is the goal for persons with a disability. This concept covers the life span from receiving preschool in generic day-care facilities to leisure services in Area Agencies on Aging programs (LePore & Janicki, 1990; Taylor, Racino, Knoll, & Lutfiyya, 1987).

Case Management

To best "tie together" the loose fabric of the service delivery system, a case management system evolved. Case management has been conceived of as a process or approach to care that ensures that "consumers are provided with whatever services they need in a coordinated, effective, and efficient manner" (Intagliata, 1981). This system is most valuable for individuals with multiple, often undefined needs, where diverse services must be provided. Some of the activities subsumed under this process include identification of needs and resources, coordination of services monitoring and follow-up on the services delivered, and evaluation of the effectiveness of the services and resources. Three key components of the case management system proposed by Caragonne (1984) are accountability, accessibility, and coordination.

Case management can be conceptualized as having a dual dimension: (a) cross-sectional, requiring comprehensive, coordinated services at any point in time, and (b) longitudinal assistance, providing long-term care for ever changing needs (Test, 1979). The case manager assumes a diversity of roles, all highly complex. These include advocate, broker, diagnostician, planner, community organizer, evaluator, consultant, and therapist (Weil, 1985b). Both formal and informal systems must be known to the case manager (Bertsche & Horejsi, 1980).

Evaluation of the effectiveness of case management systems, however, has not followed proliferation of these models. Positive benefits have been noted by case managers' facilitation of service provision (Maverick Corporation, 1976), linkages between program and consumers (Rosenberg & Brody, 1974), enhanced delivery of a complex sequence of services (Brody, 1974), and better documented service gaps and duplication (Perlman, 1975). In a previous AoA/ADD demonstration project, it was found that case manager services provided for individuals with disabilities through an age-segregated case management system were more successful in attending to the needs of this older population (Kultgen, Rinck, Calkins, & Intagliata, 1986). Where caseloads consisted of both children and elderly, more attention was focused on the younger age group. In the age-segregated model, the Individual Habilitation Plans reflected significantly more attention to functional skills, socialization, and health-care issues than in an age-integrated model. There have been no specific comparisons of rural and urban perceptions of the case management process or of older and younger caregiver perceptions.

The pattern of case management has undergone changes over the past several decades. Initially, emphasis was placed on the "needs" of the consumer with the professional "dictating" which services were needed. Recently, the family's role in determining the course of program planning has been emphasized through federal legislation (P.L. 99-457) and trends in the field (Turnbull, Turnbull, Bronicki, Summers, & Roeder-Gordon, 1989). The theoretical framework for this planning has shifted to a more ecological, holistic one (Singer & Irvin, 1991), where programs are tailored for the environment in which the person with a developmental disability lives or the environment itself is changed.

Research Questions

Based on the previous discussion and concerns, a research project was designed by the University of Missouri-Kansas City University Affiliated Program to track these outcomes for the Missouri Department of Mental Health (Rinck, 1989; Rinck, Tintinger, & Denman, 1990). Several research questions emerge from the preceding discussion.

1. What services do older families currently utilize for themselves or their family member with a disability?
2. How satisfied are older rural families with the services they receive?
3. What gaps in services are reported by families and how do these compare to those reported by younger and older urban caregivers?
4. How is case management viewed by older rural families and how does this compare to the viewpoint of urban and younger caregivers?

Method: Mail Survey

Subjects

Potential subjects included 5,456 families of individuals served by the division of mental retardation/developmental disabilities (MR/DD) from urban regional centers as well as 3,670 families from rural regional centers. The division of families was made into four groups: young families from urban centers, older families from urban centers, young families from rural center areas, and older families from rural center areas.

Procedures

Surveys were sent to all families whose members were served by the Missouri Division of MR/DD. The survey instrument addressed both case management and service provision issues. These components are defined as:

1. Case management: The survey items assessed the various components of case management: (a) intake and initial assessment; (b) Individual Habilitation Program planning; and (c) service coordination and monitoring.
2. Service provision: There are many services that a person with a disability can receive. Some of these are provided for and/or paid by the state. Others are provided by other agencies (e.g., county boards). Table 9.1 defines the services that could be provided that were included in the survey form.

Results

Mail Survey Demographics

A total of 1,438 surveys were returned, 795 from urban areas and 643 from rural areas. This represented a 14.6% return rate for urban areas and a 17.5% return rate for rural areas.

Demographic information about the parents showed that the majority of the parents were married (76.4%). Approximately 15% of the parents were either divorced or widowed. Eight percent of this group were single, never married. The majority of family members or wards were reported to be male (54.8%). The predominant ethnic background was white (92.4%). Approximately 7% were black and less than 1% represented other groups. The average age of fathers was reported as 48.7 years, with a range of 20 years to 92 years. One third of this sample was over 56 years of age. The average age of mothers was 47 years, with a range from 20 to 86 years. One third of this sample was over 55 years of age.

Families were divided into four groups. Some caregiver respondents did not list their ages. There were 371 young urban family respondents (under 50 years), 241 older urban family respondents (over 50 years), 421 young rural family respondents, and 118 older rural family respondents.

More than 90% of the sample was reported as mentally retarded. Other frequently cited disabilities included learning disabilities (28.3%), epilepsy (16.6%), cerebral palsy (19.6%), and slow learner/developmental delay (19.7%). There was a broad distribution of responses in regard to functional level. The most frequently chosen levels were moderate mental retardation (28.1%) and severe mental retardation (31.3%).

Table 9.1 Definitions of Services

Service	Definition
Information about disability	Information defining the disability and what to expect. This is especially needed in low-incidence disabilities (e.g., cri du chat).
Referred to needed services	Knowledge of the myriad of available services is essential for families.
Day programming/pre-vocational	Day activities for those not able to work competitively or in sheltered workshops.
Sheltered workshop	Employment setting for individuals with disabilities. Usually consists of piecemeal work.
Supported employment	Employment setting in community with supports (e.g., McDonald's).
Respite care	Provision of relief service for families by persons trained to care for persons with disabilities.
Individual/family counseling	Counseling provided by licensed specialist.
Family support groups	Peer groups that foster support to members and sometimes advocacy activities.
Specialized therapies	These include speech therapy, physical therapy, and occupational therapy.
Advocacy/legal services	Advocating through an educational or vocational system and providing legal advice (e.g., trusts and guardianship).
Transportation	Transportation is usually provided to day activities.
Recreational services	Previously, many recreational services (e.g., Special Olympics, bowling) were developed in segregated settings. The trend is for more integrated recreation.
Adaptive equipment	Assistive devices range from simple lever devices to wheelchairs to communication boards.

Case Management

The mail survey addressed perceptions of the case management system. A listing of different aspects of the case management system

Table 9.2 Parameters of Case Management

| | Urban | | Rural | |
	Young (under 50)	Older (50 and over)	Young (under 50)	Older (50 and over)
Percent who knows name of case manager	80.0	81.0	81.0	76.0
	(432)	(309)	(499)	(116)
Number of case manager changes	2.75	2.68	3.17	3.45[a,b]
	(355)	(277)	(381)	(86)
Effect of case manager changes[c]	1.72	1.57	1.48	1.48
	(321)	(255)	(416)	(89)
Percent transportation has affected attendance at IHP	39.0	38.0	44.0	47.0
	(243)	(157)	(446)	(96)
Percent who have attended last meeting	57.0	54.0	73.0	76.0[a,b]
	(243)	(173)	(464)	(100)
Percent who knew annual goals	65.0	61.0	89.0	88.0[a,b]
	(269)	(195)	(460)	(98)
Percent who know appeal process member during the IHP meeting	59.0	57.0	71.0	69.0[a,b]
	(200)	(134)	(387)	(85)

NOTE: Numbers of subjects for each item are in parentheses.
Significant differences: [a]urban/rural; [b] < .001
[c]Scale: 1 = not at all, 2 = somewhat, 3 = to a great extent, 4 = very much

was developed. Families rated these aspects. Tables 9.2 and 9.3 present the results of these family ratings.

A significantly higher percent of rural caregivers had attended the Individual Habilitation Plan meeting $[F(1,976) = 28.87, p < .001]$. These caregivers also were more cognizant about the goals and objectives developed for the year $[F(1,1018) p = 87.27, p < .001]$. There was a higher number of personnel changes in case managers $[F(1,1095) = 20.45, p < .001]$. These changes, however, had less of an impact than urban changes $[F(1,1077) = 13.55, p < .001]$.

Table 9.3 Family Perceptions of Case Management

How satisfied were you with:	Urban		Rural	
	Young (under 50)	Older (50 and over)	Young (under 50)	Older (50 and over)
Intake and Assessment				
The ease of completing the intake application process?	3.44^g $(413)^h$	3.63 (251)	3.16 (513)	3.95^a (119)
The willingness of the Regional Center staff to take the time to answer your questions about services?	3.70 (415)	3.84 (257)	3.62 (515)	3.44 (119)
How well the financial aspects of the process were explained (e.g., eligibility criteria, sliding scale)?	3.10 (413)	3.26 (514)	3.17 (254)	2.93 (119)
The initial assessment of your family member's or ward's needs?	3.21 (408)	3.40 (249)	3.22 (514)	$2.98^{a,f}$ (119)
How the results of assessment were explained?	3.45 (355)	3.68 (205)	3.88 (418)	$3.96^{a,f}$ $(92)^{b,d}$
Individual Habilitation Planning (IHP)				
Being able to discuss your concerns and suggestions during the reassessment and IHP process?	3.84 (222)	4.10 (143)	4.17 (430)	$4.18^{a,f}$ (91)
The goals and objectives decided upon for your family member during the IHP meeting?	3.78 (219)	4.05 (137)	$4.06^{a,e}$ (431)	$3.98^{c,d}$ (91)
The productivity of this meeting?	3.68	3.92	3.92^d	3.87^d

	(219)	(136)	(429)	(92)
Coordination and Monitoring of Services				
How the case manager arranged for and coordinated services needed by your family member or ward?	3.79 (275)	4.03 (201)	3.94 (456)	3.98[b,d] (90)
The match between the services your family member or ward needs and the services provided by the Regional Center?	3.64 (272)	3.80 (200)	3.86 (453)	3.83[a,d] (89)
Communication from the Regional Center about the progress of your family member or ward on a regular basis?	3.38 (266)	3.55 (183)	3.73 (439)	3.88[a,f] (88)
Overall				
How adequately case manager answers questions?	3.77	4.24	4.26	4.30[c]
How helpful case manager is?	3.67	4.14	4.23	4.20[c]
The support provided to you by the case manager (or other team members) in helping you and/or your family member or ward with any ongoing concerns, problems, or crises that may have occurred?	3.61 (227)	3.82 (191)	3.84 (456)	3.93[a,e] (91)
How would you rate the helpfulness of the information and referrals you received from the Regional Center in making decisions about your child?	3.07 (392)	3.32 (241)	3.63 (475)	3.50[a,f] (105)[c,d]

Significant differences: [a] urban/rural; [b] old/young; [c] interaction of age and geographic location.
[d] = < .05
[e] = < .01
[f] = < .001
[g] Scale: 1 = very dissatisfied . . . 5 = very satisfied.
[h] Numbers of subjects for each item are in parentheses.

Intake and Assessment

The intake process was viewed more favorably by urban families (see Table 9.3). Ease of completing the process $[F(1,1292) = 17.30, p < .001]$; the initial assessment of the family member $[F(1,1281) = 5.30, p = .02]$; and how the results were explained $[F(1,1066) = 30.96, p < .01]$ were significant.

Individual Habilitation Planning

Young urban parents noted the least satisfaction with the individual habilitation planning process. The ability to discuss concerns and satisfaction $[F(1,882) = 14.91, p < .001]$ and satisfaction with the goals and objectives decided upon for the family $[F(1,874) = 666, p < .001]$ were significantly lower for young urban families. On the latter item, there was a significant interaction between setting and age $[F(1,874) = 4.89, p = .03]$.

Coordination and Monitoring of Services

Differences in the perceptions of this case management function were between rural and urban families, with the former group more satisfied. The arrangement and coordination of services was rated significantly higher by older families $[F(1,1018) = 3.80, p = .05]$ as was the match between needs and services $[F(1,1010) = 5.08, p = .02]$. The communication from the regional center about the family member's needs also found a high rural satisfaction $[F(1,874) = .666, p = .01]$.

Overall

The young urban parents were the least satisfied with the support the case manager provided with ongoing concerns $[F(1,1011) = 6.75, p = .01]$ and with the helpfulness of the information and referrals $[F(1,1209) = 4.87, p = .03]$.

Service Provision

There were several questions about each potential service: (a) Had the family member utilized the service? (b) If yes, what was the family's level of satisfaction with the service (1 = very dissatisfied, 5 = very satisfied)? and (c) If they did not currently utilize the service, would

Table 9.4 Percent Currently Receiving Service

| Types of Services | Urban | | Rural | |
	Young (under 50) (N=371)	Older (over 50) (N=241)	Young (under 50) (N=421)	Older (over 50) (N=118)
Information about disability	23	16	35	21[a-f,b-f]
Referral to needed services	33	23	38	29[a-d,b-f]
Day programming/ prevocational	18	20	28	31[a-f,b-d]
Sheltered workshop	43	43	43	33[a-e,b-f,c-f]
Supported employment	4	8	10	1[c-e]
Respite care	21	23	13	25[a-d,b-d]
Individual/family counseling	14	10	13	13
Family support groups	8	2	10	10[a-d,b-d]
Residential placement	20	5	61	12[a-f,b-f,c-f]
Specialized therapies (O.T., P.T., R.T.)	16	7	26	13[a-f,b-f]
Advocacy/legal services	5	2	10	8[a-f]
Transportation	25	51	33	38[b-f,c-f]
Recreational services	21	21	31	25[a-f]
Adaptive equipment	2	8	14	6[a-f,b-f]

NOTES: Significant differences: [a]urban/rural; [b]old/young; [c]interaction of age and geographic location.
[d] = < .05
[e] = < .01
[f] = < .001

they like to? This section will describe the results for each category. Tables 9.4, 9.5, and 9.6 describe the results of these inquiries.

Information About the Disability

Younger families reported receiving more information about the disability $[F(1,1434) = 15.39, p < .001]$. Families in urban areas reported receiving less information than those in rural areas $[F(1,1432) = 12.04, p < .001]$. There were no significant differences in the satisfaction with the information received. Young families requested more information than older ones $[F(1,1434) = 19.37, p < .001]$.

Table 9.5   Satisfaction With Services

Types of Services	Overall Mean	Urban		Rural	
		Young (under 50)	Older (over 50)	Young (under 50)	Older (over 50)
Information about disability	3.99[g]	3.85	4.01	4.23	3.96
		(94)[h]	(172)	(43)	(24)
Referral to needed services	3.98	3.78	4.03	4.13	4.13[b,e]
		(133)	(192)	(67)	(32)
Day programming/ prevocational	4.10	3.79	4.37	4.02	4.42[b,f]
		(48)	(49)	(111)	(36)
Sheltered workshop	4.19	4.18	4.44	4.02	4.06[a,d]
		(61)	(107)	(131)	(33)
Supported employment	3.93	3.92	3.89	3.93	5.00
		(12)	(18)	(30)	(1)
Respite care	3.80	3.79	4.02	3.54	3.90[b,d]
		(89)	(63)	(59)	(29)
Individual/family counseling	3.90	3.81	4.39	3.72	4.00[b]
		(52)	(31)	(65)	(11)
Family support groups	3.54	3.61	4.00	3.45	3.50
		(33)	(6)	(49)	(12)
Residential placement	4.24	4.35	362	4.29	3.50
		(51)	(13)	(160)	(6)
Specialized therapies (O.T., P.T., R.T.)	4.06	4.10	4.26	4.11	3.25[c,f]
		(67)	(19)	(124)	(16)
Advocacy/legal services	3.51	3.60	3.45	4.10	3.00
		(25)	(49)	(10)	(10)
Transportation	4.16	4.10	4.35	4.09	3.95[c,d]
		(100)	(141)	(170)	(42)
Recreational services	3.97	3.90	4.00	4.05	3.66[c,e]
		(82)	(57)	(157)	(29)
Adaptive equipment	3.85	3.58	4.57	3.91	3.75[b]
		(33)	(7)	(70)	(8)

NOTES: Significant differences: [a]urban/rural; [b]old/young; [c]interaction of age and geographic location
[d] = < .05
[e] = < .01
[f] = < .001
[g]Ratings based on scale: 1 = very dissatisfied . . . 5 = very satisfied.
[h]Numbers in parentheses refer to number of families responding to the question.

Table 9.6 Percent Requesting Services

| | Urban | | Rural | |
	Young (under 50) (N=472)	Older (over 50) (N=326)	Young (under 50) (N=520)	Older (over 50) (N=120)
Types of Services				
Information about disability	14	4	11	8[a-f,b-f]
Referral to needed services	17	10	9	8[a-f,b-e]
Day programming/ prevocational	4	2	3	2
Sheltered workshop	4	6	4	4
Supported employment	10	8	7	7
Respite care	12	8	11	8[b-d]
Individual/family counseling	15	11	6	10[a-f,c-d]
Family support groups	16	14	6	8[a-f]
Residential placement	13	4	24	16[a-f,b-f]
Specialized therapies (O.T., P.T., R.T.)	16	12	7	8[a-f]
Advocacy/legal services	16	12	10	10[a-d]
Transportation	18	8	11	13[b-f,c-e]
Recreational services	21	11	14	14[b-f,c-d]
Adaptive equipment	12	9	4	5[a-f]

NOTES: Significant differences: [a]urban/rural; [b]old/young; [c]interaction of age and geographic location.
[d] = < .05
[e] = < .01
[f] = < .001

Referral to Needed Services

Rural families currently reported using more referral than urban ones [$F(1,1434) = 4.79, p = .03$], as did younger families [$F(1,1434) = 12.80$, $p < .001$]. Older families reported more satisfaction with this referral [$F(1,421) = 7.05, p < .01$]. Younger families [$F(1,1434) = 13.67, p < .001$] and urban families [$F(1,1434) = 7.86, p = .005$] requested more referral services.

Day Programming Prevocational

Rural families [$F(1,434) = 31.09, p < .001$] reported their members participating in this form of day activity significantly more often than urban families. There also was a significant difference between younger and older caregivers [$F(1,1434) = 11.05, p < .001$]. Older families were more satisfied with these programs [$F(1,242) = 11.05, p < .001$].

Sheltered Workshops

There was an equal distribution of urban and rural families who reported their family member participating in a sheltered workshop. Approximately 40% of individuals with disabilities over 21 years of age were employed in a sheltered workshop setting. Urban families reported more satisfaction with the sheltered workshop setting [$F(1,1434) = 3.91, p = .05$]. Few families requested a sheltered workshop setting.

Supported Employment

Few families reported their family member engaging in supported employment. Older urban and young rural families reported the highest usage (8% and 10%, respectively). The satisfaction ratings were similar across all settings, except in the rural older families, where only one person rated the item. Although similar requests for supported employment were present in all settings, these requests were higher than those for sheltered workshop placements.

Respite Care

Both older families [$F(1,1434) = 6.17, p = .014$] and urban families [$F(1,1434) = 4.54, p = .033$] reported higher use of respite care. Older families were significantly more satisfied with the service received [$F(1,238) = 4.45, p < .05$]. More younger families requested respite care [$F(1,1434) = 5.6, p = .018$].

Individual/Family Counseling

There were no significant differences in the percent using individual/family counseling. Nor were there differences in the satisfaction ratings of families for this item. Urban families requested this service significantly more often [$F(1,1434) = 12.88, p < .001$]. The interaction between rural/urban setting and young/old caregivers also was significant [$F(1,1434) = 5.41, p = .02$].

Family Support Groups

Rural families reported higher participation in family support groups [$F(1,1434) = 5.46, p = .02$]. The groups often were more attended also by younger families [$F(1,1434) = 4.57, p = .033$]. The satisfaction rating for family support groups was one of the lowest ratings. There were, however, no differences between the different age and setting groups. Urban families requested significantly more respite care than rural families [$F(1,1434) = 21.28, p < .001$].

Residential Placement

The highest rate of residential placements was reported by rural young families [$F(1,1434) = 208.3, p < .001$]. Residential placement received the highest overall satisfaction rating (mean of 4.24) with young families significantly more satisfied than older ones [$F(1,1434) = 8.64, p = .004$]. Out-of-home placement was requested more by rural families [$F(1,1434) = 23.79, p < .001$] and younger families [$F(1,1434) = 38.41, p < .001$].

Specialized Therapies

Rural families [$F(1,1434) = 16.49, p < .001$] and younger families [$F(1,1434) = 22.52, p < .001$] reported that their family member used some specialized therapy. Urban families noted more satisfaction with these services [$F(1,224) = 10.50, p < .001$]. Urban families requested this service significantly more frequently [$F(1,1434) = 15.37, p < .001$].

Advocacy/Legal Services

Rural families noted a higher use of advocacy/legal services [$F(1,1434) = 13.64, p < .001$]. This service received the lowest satisfaction rating of all services. Advocacy/legal services were requested by significantly more urban families [$F(1,1434) = 5.27, p = .002$].

Transportation

One of the highest utilized services was transportation. More older families reported utilization of this service than younger families [$F(1,1434) = 43.67, p < .001$]. There was a significant interaction, with older urban families reporting the highest use (51%) [$F(1,1434) = 13.55, p < .001$]. Older families provided the highest satisfaction rating (rural families—3.95) [$F(1,1434) = 4.13, p = .014$]. Younger urban families (8%) and older rural parents (13%) requested significantly more transportation than other groups [$F(1,1434) = 8.45, p = .004$].

Recreation Services

Rural families reported the highest utilization of recreation services [$F(1,1434) = 12.33$, $p < .001$]. Younger rural families reported the highest satisfaction rating with recreation services (mean of 4.05), and older rural families reported the lowest ratings (mean of 3.66) [$F(1,353) = 6.67$, $p = .01$]. Younger urban families noted the highest request for this service and older urban families the lowest request [$F(1,1434) = 5.55$, $p = .019$].

Adaptive Equipment

Rural families reported receiving adaptive equipment more often [$F(1,1434) = 10.86$, $p < .001$]. Older families rated their satisfaction as higher [$F(1,116) = 4.29$, $p = .04$]. Urban families requested more adaptive equipment [$F(1,1434) = 16.41$, $p < .001$].

Predictors of Satisfaction With Regional Center Services

An attempt was made to predict what variables were predictive of satisfaction with the quality of the regional center by older rural caregivers through a stepwise multiple regression. Demographic variables, the current services received, and the number of case management changes were entered into the equation (see Table 9.7). The major predictor of satisfaction with case management services from the regional center was the number of case manager changes within a 5-year period. The more changes, the lower the satisfaction rating. The second predictor was the age of the family member, with the families with older members reporting higher satisfaction. Families whose family members resided at home were less satisfied than those whose members lived in community placement. The final predictor showed that older fathers were more satisfied with regional center services.

Implications for Practice and Research

Practice Considerations

Older rural families reported utilization of many services for their family member to enhance the quality of both their lives and that of their adult family member. For the most part these families were quite satisfied with the services they were receiving. There were, however,

Table 9.7 Predictions of Satisfaction With Regional Center Services

	Correlation	R^2 Change	Total R^2	F Change	p	Beta in Regression
No. of case mgnt. changes	−.1983	.039	.038	32.60	<.001	−.1983
Referral to needed services	.186	.036	.073	30.79	<.001	.1893
Live in natural home	−.151	.012	.084	10.54	<.001	−.114
Father's age	.176	.008	.096	7.32	.007	.113

some services where at least 10% of the respondents noted a need that was not currently being fulfilled.

The highest request for service was in the area of residential housing. Approximately 16% of the rural caregivers cited the need for community placement of their family member. These families have learned, over the years, how best to cope with the problems and concerns as they arise. They often have traversed many service delivery systems; secured the optimal vocational situation, even if it is working on the farm; and lived full and rich lives. As parents age, however, they often are faced with the reality that more permanent arrangements should be made for their family member.

Traditionally, individuals with disabilities were placed in congregate settings. In recent years an alternative to congregate living has evolved. This alternative, termed "supportive living," is designed to fit the program to meet the individualized needs of the individual, rather than fitting the individual to meet the existing programs. Under this model the individual with the disability is provided with a home (be it a house, apartment, or trailer). The supports that are needed to maintain the person in this setting are provided. These supports can range from minor assistance with budgeting and shopping to round-the-clock full-time support. This model does not preclude individuals deciding to live together, if *they* so choose.

Implementation of this model has been conducted in Missouri in rural areas. Benefits of this alternative include less restrictiveness, the independence it provides to residents, and the lack of "bureaucracy" individuals feel when they live in more congregate settings. The success of this type of living arrangement can be seen in the quality of life reported by those who live in these settings (Taylor et al., 1987). More research could explore how these alternative residential settings affect the quality of life for both caregivers and consumers.

Similarly, in the employment domain the emphasis has been toward a more community-integrated work experience than toward the sheltered workshops. Survey respondents noted a higher request rate for supported employment than they did for sheltered workshop settings. Newer vocational models have been emphasized in the literature (Nisbet & Callahan, 1987). In supported employment, the individual works, with *supports,* in a *community* setting *for pay.*

From a previous survey that was conducted with consumers in two urban areas and one rural part of the state, it was found that rural consumers more often had worked in competitive employment, even if the work was only part-time (Rinck, Tintinger, & Denman, 1990). Many of these "jobs" involved waiting tables, cleaning dishes, cleaning warehouses, cutting grass, and housekeeping. There are many natural integrated settings for employment within the rural community. Oftentimes these rural businesses are less computerized and hire a smaller cadre of employees. There are several examples of successful supported employment programs in rural Missouri areas. In Ironton, Missouri, a day program that employed only in the segregate sheltered setting 5 years ago is now training and providing supported employment to persons with disabilities in such diverse locations as hospitals (clerk assistant), street maintenance, fast food restaurants, and maid service. Obtaining the cooperation of the town, funding through diverse mechanisms, and the appropriate staff are key ingredients in a successful integrated employment program.

Recreation services were a high request for older rural caregivers (14%). Limited recreational services are available for persons without disabilities in many rural areas. Few formal services such as YMCAs/YWCAs, bowling alleys, or hobby clubs exist. One problem that has been noted in previous studies is that older caregivers who have maintained their family member at home sometimes are reluctant to allow their family member to participate in community activities (Rinck, 1990). This may be due to the fact that the person with the disability now may be assuming the caregiver role. The parent(s) may be frail and infirm, sometimes with cognitive problems. In other cases, the "protection" the family has always provided to the person with the disability continues even until old age (Rinck, 1989). Case managers in the Smith and Tobin study (this volume) also noted parental emotions and feelings were barriers to permanency planning. Community activities are viewed as "too risky" for the person with a disability to engage in.

Several practices could be implemented in rural areas to enhance recreational activities. Needs assessments of leisure activities could allow for individualized programming (Carter & Foret, 1991). Integration into generic aging recreational services can be enhanced through the use of peer companions (Kultgen et al., 1986; Stroud & Sutton, 1988). Informal leisure activities (e.g., eating in restaurants, frequenting malls) also can provide positive experiences.

Families often have questions that require a lawyer or financial planner (Turnbull et al., 1989). This need becomes more crucial for older caregivers, who may not be aware of the full implications of estate monies that their family member could inherit. Even relatively small amounts of personal monies could mean interruption of residential services provided by the state because the person's monies could exceed the limit for eligibility. In addition, caregivers may wish to ensure that their family member is well taken care of and the monies are not frivolously spent. In many cases a guardian or conservator is appointed, the former to assist in decision making and the latter to help with money matters. The difficulty with these legal appointments is that the restrictions often imposed limit the autonomy of the person with a disability. Some states have protective services (through state social service or aging departments) that could assist in decision making. There are alternatives to these services that could be explored.

The legal services the rural families had received were the lowest rated service. This also was one of the services that was requested by 10% of the respondents. Creative delivery of legal and financial advice could be addressed in a family-oriented case management system, where individualized planning would meet each family's needs.

It is interesting to note that in Smith and Tobin's study (this volume), case managers reported a different set of needs for older parents. Respite care was the most frequent response. This study found respite as a lower priority. This could be explained by the fact that in this state a large number of older families noted the current use of this service. The high rate of requests for residential placement also should be noted.

Most components of case management were rated satisfactorily. The most prominent exception was intake and initial assessment. The reasons for the lowered rating were unclear. Practitioners should examine some of these intake and assessment items more closely. Some subjective responses indicated areas where future studies could probe. First was the comment that the eligibility process was too lengthy, often requiring several trips. Many of these rural families live long distances from the developmental disabilities center, thus making application a more arduous process. Second, the assessment of special populations (e.g., sensory impaired, autistic) drew criticism from several rural caregivers. These evaluations were seen as "incomplete" or not using specialized instruments for more specialized groups. Finally, the explanation of the disability was requested to be "in layman's terms" without more information being made available about the disability. In addition, the more case manager changes there were (a problem in rural areas), the more dissatisfaction was shown by families with the services received. Innovative strategies should be developed to address these components of case management.

Every case manager cannot be an expert in all disabilities, especially low-incidence disabilities. There are several potential approaches. The proliferation of national support groups and their dissemination of information specific to these low-incidence disabilities could be most helpful in rural areas. These support groups often have valuable information about the disability and about adaptations to enhance the life of persons with the disability.[1]

Many of the concerns reported by the older rural respondents could be addressed through family-oriented planning. The Individual Family Service Plan represents a process through which this can be accomplished.

Family-oriented case management has been mandated for early intervention services under Part H of P.L. 99-457 (Hanson & Lynch, 1989; Tingey, 1989). This same family orientation would be beneficial throughout the life span of the person with a disability. Family-oriented case management is particularly valid for older persons who continue to reside in their natural home. One innovative family-oriented planning tool is called "futures planning." In this model comprehensive planning is conducted in the presence of the individual's family, service providers, and social support system. Planning for the future should be in the context of those whom the person with a disability regards as important in her or his environment.

Research Implications

Research into older families who have members with disabilities has been sparse. There are several areas based on this study where further research should be conducted. These endeavors should explore not only needs of older families but also implications of case management decisions on long-term family interactions.

Case management studies on families should include an ecological perspective. Variables in the individual environment of the family may affect case management needs. Living in a large, close, extended family could require different case management solutions than residing in an isolated single-family setting. The fit between the needs of older families and their environmental context should be examined.

The perceptions of both the individual with a disability and the case manager should be solicited, in addition to those of the family. The perceptions of the first two may be divergent from those of the family, especially on issues related to independence. The perceptions of the case manager also could add to the research base of a needs assessment.

The effect of differing models of case management also should be studied. New paradigms that allow the individual and their family to determine what services are needed and place emphasis on full inclusion may alter the satisfaction with these services.

The challenge for both families and service providers in all areas, rural or urban, young or old, is to enhance the quality of life of persons with developmental disabilities. The mere provision of services will not ensure this. Full inclusion in residential settings, vocational placements, and other aspects of life, to the extent possible, will assist in reaching this goal.

Note

1. A national resource for this information can be obtained from the National Organization of Rare Diseases (NORD), P.O. Box 8923, New Fairfield, CT 06812. The UMKC-UAP also has published a national directory of family support groups that includes more than 180 different national organizations. This may be obtained from UMKC-UAP, 2220 Holmes, Kansas City, MO 64108.

10

Case Managers' Perceptions of Practice With Older Parents of Adults With Developmental Disabilities

GREGORY C. SMITH
SHELDON S. TOBIN

An expanding population of aging families with adult offspring with developmental disabilities is being served by a cohort of clinicians who have no established guidelines and minimal practice wisdom regarding issues relevant to later stages in the life cycle. In turn, despite increasing recognition of the prolonged longevity of persons with mental retardation and other developmental disabilities (Janicki & Seltzer, 1991; Janicki & Wisniewski, 1985), limited attention has been devoted to the needs of older parents who continue to care for their offspring with developmental disabilities at home (Sison & Cotton, 1989).

The sparse literature on these parents has focused primarily on their use of formal and informal social supports to continue in the caregiving role as long as possible, and less regard has been given to their concerns for the future well-being of their disabled offspring after they are no longer able to provide care (Roberto, this volume; Smith & Tobin, 1989). In turn, investigators (Carswell & Hartig, 1979; Gold et al., 1987; Goodman, 1978; Grant, 1986; Heller & Factor, 1987, 1988a, 1991; Kaufman et al., 1991; Krauss, 1990; Roberto, this volume; Seltzer, Begun, et al., 1991) who have studied these topics have done so from the

Supported in part by NIA Grant No. R01 AG09198.

perspective of older parents themselves, rarely considering the views of practitioners from the mental retardation and developmental disabilities (MR/DD) network.

The situation is similar within the clinical literature, with virtually no attention having been accorded to case management with older parents of adults with developmental disabilities to date. An exception is the recent paper by Kaufman, DeWeaver, and Glicken (1989), in which a case management practice model relevant to the aged with mental retardation living is presented. More recently, Sutton, Sterns, Schwartz, and Roberts (1992) described the components of the role of specialist in developmental disabilities and in aging, and Seltzer (1992) described techniques for training family members to serve as case managers for elderly individuals with developmental disabilities. Although Kaufman and colleagues (1989) delineated six distinct practice roles appropriate for this target population, as shown in Table 10.1, their work, as well as that of Sutton and colleagues (1992) and Seltzer (1992), was not based on input from case managers themselves.

There are several reasons why knowledge of how service providers perceive their work with aging families of adults with developmental disabilities is important. As noted by Seltzer, Krauss, and Heller (1991), "Family care is and always has been the dominant residential arrangement for persons with mental retardation" (p. 3). Yet, although the number of persons with developmental disabilities who are living long enough to have elderly parents remain as their primary caregivers is rising (Janicki & Seltzer, 1991; Rose & Janicki, 1986), extant family support services are targeted primarily toward families of children and young adults with developmental disabilities (Kaufman et al., 1989; Seltzer, Krauss, & Heller, 1991). Knowledge of how best to develop and provide services to aging families is in its own infancy. How case managers currently work with these families can be instructive regarding the state of consensual knowledge.

Another reason for exploring how service providers from the MR/DD network perceive their work with aging clients and their parents is that it is extremely rare for these clinicians to possess formal training in gerontology. Consequently their attitudes and knowledge of aging parents are likely to be distorted by inaccurate societal stereotypes toward the elderly. To the extent that such ageist beliefs exist, they are likely to adversely affect practice with aging adults with this target population (see the discussion by Kaufman et al., 1989).

The views of service providers toward older parents also must be explored because conflicts frequently exist between these two groups,

Table 10.1 Case Management Model for Social Work Practice With Mentally Retarded Aged Living in a Family Unit

Practice Role	Practice Behavior
Outreach worker	Identify families caring for mentally retarded aged who require supportive services
	Identify situation of actual or potential neglect or abuse
Advocate	Assist family unit to overcome obstacles in securing needed services
Teacher	Help family members learn about aging and mental retardation
	Increase family's knowledge of available services and resources
Therapist	Focus on functioning of all members of family unit
	Assist elderly caregivers of mentally retarded clients to cope with their own aging issues
Enabler/facilitator	Help client maximize independent functioning within family unit
	Support efforts of family to keep older mentally retarded person at home
Broker/coordinator	Develop and implement individualized program plan
	Link client to needed community services and monitor service provision
	Involve family in developing and monitoring program plan

SOURCE: Adapted from Kaufman, DeWeaver, and Glicken (1989)

conflicts that may be due, in part, to the existence of ageist stereotypes. During our interviews, parents and practitioners alike have reported that these conflicts often relate to parents' fears that the role of practitioners is to remove adult offspring with developmental disabilities from parents. This erroneous perception by parents distorts communication between the two groups, which, according to practitioners, is compounded because frail older parents are likely to be intimidated by the youthfulness and expertise of many professionals.

It is especially important to know how service providers perceive their assistance to older parents of adults with developmental disabilities in making long-range plans for when these parents can no longer continue caregiving. The problems that confront older parents in long-range planning are both logistically complex and emotionally draining.

Known as "permanency planning," this effort requires resolution of the guilt and anxiety over relinquishing the care of one's dependent offspring, as well as the making of difficult decisions regarding financial security, guardianship, and residential placement (Seltzer & Seltzer, 1985; Smith & Tobin, 1989). Practitioners must assist parents with permanency planning not only to ease parents' uncertainties and ensure smooth transitions for their offspring with mental retardation, but also to ensure that the public sector will not be overwhelmed by a wave of new clientele who unexpectedly need publicly supported residences upon the death of older parents (Janicki & Seltzer, 1991). Unfortunately today's practitioners have no established guidelines to direct their efforts in providing permanency planning assistance.

It is noteworthy that greater use of formal services, particularly respite, case management, and future planning information, increases the probability that caregivers would prefer a residential program placement (Heller & Factor, 1991). This finding, together with the fact that older parents typically prefer continued family care, suggests that use of formal MR/DD services decreases their apprehensiveness toward community residential services and facilitates their ability to engage in long-range planning (Seltzer, Krauss, & Heller, 1991; Smith & Tobin, 1989; Wood & Skiles, 1992). Much less clear, however, is the role of individual service providers in diminishing parents' apprehensiveness toward future placements outside the family. Do practitioners perceive themselves as having deliberate strategies and goals regarding permanency planning assistance? An initial step toward clarifying how service providers can best assist older parents with long-range planning is to query clinicians themselves about such matters.

In summary, it is necessary to obtain a better understanding of how service providers perceive their practice with older parents of adult children with developmental disabilities because working with aging families is a recent, but expanding, phenomenon in which the current cohort of practitioners possesses inadequate experience and training. It is also important to examine how service providers from the MR/DD network perceive practice with older parents of adult children with developmental disabilities because parents are most likely to turn to these professionals with the most pressing task of permanency planning. Assessing the perceptions of practice with older parents is an important first step toward developing pre-professional and continuing education curriculum concerning this new target population.

The service providers that are most likely to have a direct impact on the lives of aging persons with developmental disabilities and their older parents are case managers who work in the MR/DD service system. Although their job description typically states that their primary function is to monitor and arrange supportive services for families with offspring with developmental disabilities, these workers also spend considerable time assisting older parents with permanency planning and serving as confidants to them. Moreover, older parents of offspring with developmental disabilities more frequently turn to this group of practitioners for assistance in meeting their needs than to professionals from the aging services network. This occurs because older parents typically have utilized the MR/DD service system during the life span of their offspring and, thus, generally have developed a reliance on these workers.

Research Questions

The purpose of our exploratory study was to determine how case managers from the MR/DD service system perceive their practice with older parents who provide care at home to offspring with developmental disabilities. In-depth interviews with the case managers addressed several kinds of questions: What, for example, is the impact of case managers' attitudes, feelings, and beliefs on practice with older parents? What differences do they perceive between older and younger parents in service utilization? What, in their opinion, are the most salient issues confronting older parents? What do they consider to be the major obstacles to permanency planning faced by older parents? How do case managers evaluate their effectiveness in assisting older parents with permanency planning? What other professionals do they believe are needed to aid parents with permanency planning? Finally, what innovative programs and services should be developed for older parents?

We anticipated that conducting intensive interviews with a relatively small sample of respondents would yield findings and hypotheses that could be further tested in subsequent studies involving larger and more representative samples.

Method

The Sample

The respondents were 11 case managers from satellite offices of the Oswald D. Heck Developmental Disability Service Office (DDSO) in the capital district area of upstate New York. This agency is one of the 20 DDSOs operated under the auspices of New York State that provide and coordinate an array of formal services to clients with MR/DD and their families. Two criteria were established for selecting the case managers who participated in this study. First, at the time of the interview they were employed at least 1 year as a DDSO case manager and, second, they possessed clinical experience with several families in which parents age 65 and older care for their offspring that have developmental disabilities at home. These criteria ensured that only case managers with a sufficient amount of relevant experience were interviewed.

To recruit this sample, the clinical supervisors from each satellite office of the DDSO were asked to supply the names and phone numbers of interested case managers who met the selection criteria. The first author then phoned each worker to explain the purpose of the study, obtain informed consent, and arrange an interview date.

Of the 11 respondents, 9 were women and 2 were men. The average length of professional service as an MR/DD case manager was 10.5 years (range = 2.5 to 19 years). Nine of the respondents were from satellite offices that served clients in urban and suburban areas, whereas the other 2 served clients in rural environments. All of the respondents had caseloads that contained a mix of clients who resided either in residential programs (e.g., ICF/MRs, group homes) or in the community (e.g., with family or independently). The majority of the caseload for each respondent consisted of clients from residential programs, and none of the respondents reported themselves as having either extensive experience with aging families or formal training in gerontology. Thus, like the majority of MR/DD case managers across the United States, the present sample had virtually no experience or training in working with older parents who provide care at home for offspring with developmental disabilities. Nonetheless, all of the respondents said they anticipated increasing numbers of such families in their future caseloads. They also expressed a strong desire to learn the outcome of the exploratory interviews with their colleagues to guide them in future practice with aging families.

The Interview

The interviews, which averaged about 1.5 hours in duration, were conducted individually by the first author in private office settings that assured respondents' anonymity. As shown in Table 10.2, the focused interview consisted of 12 open-ended queries.

Content Analysis

Responses to each of the 12 queries were transcribed and analyzed for major themes. Initially, the first author read all 11 interview transcripts to identify the themes associated with each question. Next, for each question, a count was made of each theme that occurred among the 11 respondents. (Because themes were not always regarded as mutually exclusive, duplicative counts were possible for some questions.) Then the second author independently read all of the transcripts and themes to assess their coherence. Finally, general themes were derived jointly by the two authors as they reviewed the themes that arose in responses to individual questions.

Results and Discussion

In presenting the results, the major themes associated with each of the interview queries are first described, where the numbers in parentheses indicate the frequency of occurrence for each theme. Then a description of general themes that transcended individual queries is presented. The findings are discussed in terms of their relevance to the model of case management practice with aging families of adults with mental retardation that was delineated by Kaufman and colleagues (1989).

Major Themes in Answers to Queries

When asked, "In what ways are the discussions that you have with parents different as they become older?" 9 of the 11 case managers

Table 10.2 The Interview Queries

Questions
1. In what ways are the discussions that you have with parents different as they become older?
2. In what ways do you see the involvement of parents in case-related activities as being different when they are older?
3. How is the ability of parents to function as caregivers affected by their own aging?
4. How are your own feelings or attitudes about working with parents influenced by their getting older?
5. What services are needed to keep developmentally disabled sons and daughters at home as both parents and offspring get older?
6. Are any of the services used by older families different from those used by younger families?
7. In your opinion, what is the single most important issue faced by parents of developmentally disabled offspring as they get older?
8. Please describe what your discussions with older parents about permanency planning have been like.
9. Do you feel that your discussions with older parents about permanency planning have been helpful?
10. In your opinion, what are the major obstacles that older parents face regarding permanency planning?
11. What types of professionals do you think should provide assistance to parents regarding permanency planning problems and decisions?
12. What unique services or programs do you think your own agency should offer to parents as they grow older?

mentioned that permanency planning is a central issue for these parents (e.g., "From middle age to old age, parents become concerned about who will take care of their offspring when they're gone."). Other themes that emerged from this question include awareness of parents' increasing frailty and disability ($n = 5$), concerns regarding widowhood ($n = 3$), and mistaken expectations that other children will take over caregiving ($n = 3$).

In response to the question, "In what ways do you see the involvement of parents in case-related activities as being different when they are older?" eight of the respondents indicated that parental involvement drops off in old age. The explanations given for this decreased involvement, however, were split between (a) parents' fears and lack of understanding of the service system ($n = 7$) and (b) their physical disabilities ($n = 4$). It is noteworthy that five respondents expressed the belief that decreased involvement on the part of older parents was due to intimidation by professionals.

The question, "How is the ability of parents to function as caregivers affected by their own aging?" revealed unanimous agreement among respondents that aging has adverse effects on caregiving ability (e.g., "Their increasing physical disabilities and health problems cause a breakdown in the family system that they previously maintained."). Some respondents mentioned that older parents who are increasingly disabled become dependent on their offspring with developmental disabilities ($n = 3$; e.g., "Higher functioning clients will often take on some of the parental role, and be frightened by parents' decreased ability."). It also was noted that older parents often continue to resist making permanency planning arrangements despite their increasing frailty ($n = 3$; e.g., "Many can't drive or get around anymore, and caretaking becomes a heavy burden. Yet, they have difficulty with the idea of separating eventually and having their child go off into the world.").

When the case managers were asked, "How are your own feelings or attitudes about working with parents influenced by their getting older?" about half ($n = 5$) of their responses revealed negative affect (e.g., "I'm frustrated when I can't get them to place the offspring before death, or even to talk about a visit to a community residence."). On the other hand, some responses ($n = 4$) involved feelings such as empathy, sympathy, or compassion combined with respect for older parents who have been caregivers for so many years (e.g., "I'm getting older, too, so I understand. You have to be empathic and give credit for keeping the home together and of accepting responsibility.").

The service most frequently cited in response to the question, "What services are needed to keep offspring with developmental disabilities at home as both parents and offspring get older?" was respite ($n = 10$). As one respondent noted, "Respite gives parents rest and can be used to introduce the idea of residential placement." Other services mentioned by respondents were quite varied: home health aides (6), transportation (6), day programs (3), medical/nursing (3), recreation (2), fostering informal supports (2), Meals on Wheels (2), case management (2), and financial support (2). Three respondents stated the need for services to meet the emotional needs of parents.

As a follow-up to the above question, we asked, "Are any of these services different from those used by younger parents?" Nine of the respondents indicated that similar services are needed by older and younger families, but older families need them with greater frequency.

Respondents also pointed out that services are needed for both parent and offspring in older families, unlike for younger families, where services are primarily directed at the offspring (e.g., "Services are the same, but you might prioritize them differently. Specifically, more home health care is needed by older parents. This could help prevent institutionalization. You almost need one home health aide assigned to each older family!").

As expected, the majority of case managers ($n = 9$) raised permanency planning issues in response to the question, "In your opinion, what is the single most important issue faced by parents of children with developmental disabilities as they get older?" The two remaining respondents said that "continuing to provide the same level of care" was the major concern of older parents.

Next we asked the case managers, "Please describe what your discussions about permanency planning have been like." The most common theme ($n = 8$) related to parents' resistance toward planning (e.g., "Initially, there's a hesitancy to talk about it. Their focus is on immediate issues and they procrastinate, especially if everything is okay at the moment."). Four respondents noted that many older parents do not finalize plans until a crisis or precipitating event occurs (e.g., "For a long time, one client refused to talk about the future. She became aware of her own mortality when diagnosed as diabetic, and then began to talk about the future."). Another common theme ($n = 4$) was that permanency planning assistance takes time and occurs in stages (e.g., "I need to assist them to focus on details because these things don't spring to mind. Then, I try to explain our point of view that finding alternate care outside the home is a very difficult and time-consuming process.").

As a follow-up to the above question, we asked, "Do you feel that your discussions with parents about permanency planning have been helpful to them?" Not surprisingly, 10 respondents said that they had been helpful to older parents regarding permanency planning. Typically, the case managers felt that they had been helpful because they gave parents both concrete information and alternative residential placements, in addition to reassurance about their offspring's future well-being as exemplified by the following responses:

> "I can tell that I've helped them by the way they cry and thank me. I give them a lot of information because fear of the unknown is scary. They begin to like and trust me, and they realize that I'll use good judgment. I make the idea of the 'State' seem more personal."

"After their discussions with me, they become more crystallized about permanency planning and they become used to the idea and are more approachable about it."

"It gives parents something concrete, like filling out applications, that they can do about their fears. It also gives them a connection to somebody, so they know that someone is there to call on."

"I help clarify what a community residence is or what a family care home is. This gives parents peace of mind to know not only that their child will be cared for but also where they will be cared for."

These responses imply that case managers view their assistance to parents with permanency planning issues as primarily involving two of the practice roles described by Kaufman and colleagues (1989). On the one hand, case managers must engage in the therapist role to help parents confront the emotion-laden issues surrounding both the anticipation of their own death and worry about what the future holds for their offspring with mental retardation. Simultaneously, the case manager must engage in the teacher role by clarifying for older parents what residential programs are available and how these programs are suited to the needs of their offspring. Indeed, these two roles are interrelated to the extent that older parents will be better able to resolve their uncomfortable feelings regarding the future as they become increasingly aware that residential programs may not be as bad as they have assumed.

With the question, "What are the major obstacles that parents face regarding permanency planning?" two distinct themes emerged with equal frequency. One prominent theme was that the scarcity of community residential placement options hinders planning ($n = 8$; e.g., "If there were more choices then separation wouldn't be so difficult. Some of the community residences don't look very good, and I wouldn't want to put my child in them."). The other frequently expressed theme was that parents' emotions regarding separation from their offspring was a debilitating factor in planning ($n = 8$; e.g., "Their own feelings. It's emotionally tormenting for them, and sometimes they put their own feelings ahead of their child's. Some feel that as long as they live, they won't have to worry about it because someone else will deal with it after they die."). Three respondents mentioned that the offspring's lack of readiness or fear of separation is a barrier to planning (e.g., "About 50% of clients do not want to leave home."). Also mentioned as a barrier to permanency planning were aspects of the system other than too few realistic placement options ($n = 3$; e.g., "It's difficult for parents to deal with agencies because of the energy required to deal with red tape.").

Recognizing the possibility that case managers might feel as though other professionals besides themselves are required to assist parents with permanency planning issues, we asked, "What types of professionals do you think should provide assistance to parents regarding permanency planning problems and decisions?" Not surprisingly, all but 1 of the respondents stated that case managers or social workers are needed to assist parents with permanency planning. These same 10 respondents also expressed the belief that a team approach is needed, with the involvement of diverse professionals including psychologists to deal with offspring's adaptation and parents' feelings toward the transition ($n = 6$), physicians or nurses to judge medical needs ($n = 6$), rehabilitation specialists ($n = 4$), attorneys for legal and financial issues ($n = 4$), and special educators and day-program staff to prepare the offspring for more independent functioning ($n = 3$). There also were several surprising responses to this question. For example, one respondent said gerontology specialists are needed to assist parents with permanency planning. Two respondents felt that professionalism is less important than personal trust and emotional closeness (e.g., "Other family members are more important than professionals."). Another respondent acknowledged the potential value of a team approach but went on to say, "Of course, I think that I can do it all, and I don't call on other professionals too often."

The question, "What unique services or programs do you think your own agency should offer to parents as they get older?" yielded diverse responses, several of which indicated a desire to broaden the involvement of other professionals in assisting older parents. A common theme ($n = 6$) expressed by respondents was the need for individual or group counseling to help parents confront their feelings regarding eventual separation from their offspring (e.g., "Counselors or groups that could help them work through their feelings about aging and their children."). Three respondents mentioned that their agency should provide more community residences so that parents would have more realistic placement options available to them. Four respondents indicated the need for additional case managers to meet the extensive needs of older parents, and one of these respondents mentioned the need for geriatric specialists (e.g., "We need a reassignment of caseloads such that one worker has just or predominantly older parents. When caseloads are so diverse, it's too difficult to provide services adequately. This person should have a background in gerontology."). Three respondents suggested the need for better linkage to other agencies that serve the needs of these families (e.g., "Because we interface with so many other agencies and act as a clearing-house, we should have family education programs and family groups.").

General Themes

When the categories for all 12 questions were reviewed, four ubiqui-tous, general themes were identified: the presence of ageism, aspects of the MR/DD service system that affect older parents unfavorably, distress over situations within aging families that jeopardize clients with developmental disabilities, and attention to the unique needs of aging parents.

Ageism Among Case Managers

One case manager provided the following perspective regarding this general theme: "Ageism exists in the system. In this job, you're judged successful if you give services that result in outcome. So, the feeling is why work with older parents who will die. Your job tenure is threatened if you work too much with older parents."

Although none of the other respondents was as direct in commenting on this issue, their remarks, nevertheless, revealed covert ageism in the MR/DD system. The emphasis on the necessity for quick, positive outcomes, combined with the difficulties in working with aging families that are reflected in the next three global themes, suggests insidious ageism. If the rewards in the system are for efficiency, aging families are surely to be compromised. Assisting older parents in maintaining caregiv-ing, or in making future permanency plans, does not provide immediate and easily measurable outcomes that merit praise by administrators.

Moreover, several of the case managers expressed negative effects regarding interactions with older parents, particularly their frustrations. Also, awareness of heterogeneity among older parents was rarely men-tioned and, indeed, only one respondent verbalized the belief that personality was more important than age in predicting the behaviors of older parents.

Unfavorable Aspects of the MR/DD Service System

The crux of this theme is that several aspects of the MR/DD service system are unintentionally damaging to the best interests of aging families.

A clear example is the observation by case managers of the paucity of residential placements available to offspring of older parents. The fact that there are not enough realistic residential placement options exacerbates parents' psychological resistance toward permanency planning. The following responses were indicative of the scarcity of residential alternatives:

> "If there were more choices, then separation wouldn't be so difficult. Some of the community residences don't look very good and I wouldn't want to put my child in them."
>
> "There are too few openings for community residences. If one of my older parents died today, I don't know where my client would spend the night."
>
> "There are not enough placements of any type available."
>
> "There's a scarcity of community residences for placement. Many spaces are being reserved for those being deinstitutionalized. So, the first that need to be placed are actually the last."
>
> "There aren't enough choices. We only have one or two slots open right now, and they want the perfect person with no behavioral problems. So, older parents with offspring that are difficult to handle are less likely to place that child than parents with a less difficult offspring."

Also noted by the case managers throughout the interview was that practice with aging families is hampered because older mothers frequently are intimidated by the young, female professionals who comprise the majority of MR/DD staff. Elderly mothers are threatened over their belief that they will be regarded as inadequate by younger, better educated, and physically stronger women in such professional roles as case manager, special education teacher, rehabilitation therapist, and so on. In turn, these feelings are likely to restrict the openness and trust that older parents should experience with MR/DD professionals. The following responses reveal this concern:

> "They feel stigma because there are a lot of young female staff who are stronger and more educated than they are."
>
> "They feel that they might be asking questions that professionals will view as foolish."
>
> "There is conflict with young staff. Older parents say 'I've done this my whole life, who are you to tell me what to do?' "
>
> "Often the client may need a day program, but the older parent doesn't want some young professional telling her so. . . . They often cheapen the value of day programs because they don't want to be usurped by the staff."

> "I feel a need to tell them that it's okay to ask for help and that they haven't failed because they can no longer provide care."

> "Older parents are less trusting."

Another concern expressed by the case managers was that it was difficult for parents to deal with some aspects of the MR/DD bureaucracy, which is illustrated by the following responses:

> "Interviews for residential placements are very stressful. It's like going for a job interview. It's competitive and parents know it."

> "Older parents need more case managers to help them get through the red tape and bureaucracy."

> "The system is more overwhelming to older parents."

> "I see a lot of confusion regarding correspondence that they get from agencies."

Clearly these kinds of responses suggest the importance of advocacy by case managers. The respondents strongly vocalized their belief that several aspects of the MR/DD service system need to be changed in order to optimize service to these families. Yet it is puzzling that not one of the respondents expressed the conviction that it was his or her professional obligation to facilitate such changes. Possible reasons for this omission include insufficient time due to prohibitively large caseloads; a sense of futility or pessimism toward changing a large, entrenched bureaucracy; and lack of encouragement from administrators and supervisors. It is important to recall that the sample of case managers in this study had large caseloads that were predominantly comprised of institutionalized clients. Thus a possible dilemma exists regarding the extent to which case managers can be realistically expected to perform the advocacy role delineated by Kaufman and colleagues (1989). To place all of the responsibility for meeting the needs of aging families onto case managers would be detrimental to both groups.

Clients at Jeopardy in Aging Families

Another broad theme throughout the interviews is the tremendous sense of frustration and distress the case managers feel about situations in which parental care jeopardizes the well-being of the clients with developmental disabilities. For example, the following responses reveal that older parents often are so resistant toward permanency planning that uncertainty about the future exists until a precipitating crisis occurs.

> "I haven't had much experience myself, but I've heard from colleagues that older families slide along until crisis occurs. . . . Parents just assume that things will work out without any organized advance discussion."

> "One woman refused to plan and hoped to live as long as her child. Then she became institutionalized. So, now her 60-year-old son is angry, resentful, and living in the hospital with unknown future placement."

> "For a long time, one client refused to talk about the future. She became aware of her own mortality after being diagnosed as diabetic, and only then did she begin to discuss the future."

> "Usually, their mind is made up by some precipitating factor like the death of a spouse."

> "They initially come to a realization when a crisis occurs. There are stages in the crisis. First, they see declines and realize they won't be around forever; then, I may have to stop discussion about placement because of the parent's affect."

The next set of responses reflect case managers' disturbance over the tendency of older parents to place their own needs before those of their offspring with a disability in terms of the avoidance of permanency planning.

> "They can't even get out of bed, but they have the child on the bus by 6:00 a.m. Older parents can't meet the child's needs anymore, yet they don't want to face the realization that after so many years of caring they can't do it anymore. To see someone stronger than them take care of their child leads to a sense of failure."

> "Many can't drive and get around anymore and they become a heavy burden. Yet, they have difficulty with the idea of separating eventually and their child going out into the world."

> "In some cases, I've seen the child helping the parent, who instructs the child regarding what to do. The child often brings financial benefits, too, and the parent would not seek outside placement because of such assistance."

> "I had one mother in her 80s who was unknown to our service system, and was referred by the Department of Social Services. She was very ill for several years, and the daughter would receive respite care during her hospitalizations. But the mother would not accept the reality of need for placement. In fact, the mother wouldn't even let her daughter get medical or dental care!"

"Some parents realize their increasing disabilities and want relief, yet they feel that they must continue to do everything and feel angry and resentful. Then they deny the offspring of some of their needs."

"I hope that if I was their age, and could no longer provide adequate care, I would accept this and let other resources assume responsibility."

"I've always entered the situation with parents already old, and I'm shocked with the living conditions. In one case, the septic tank was broken for weeks and the mentally retarded offspring was caring for the parent. I'm frustrated when I can't get them to place the child before death or even talk about visiting a community residence."

"Some parents put their own feelings ahead of their child's. They feel as long as they're alive they don't have to worry about the future. When they die, someone else will have to deal with it."

"One 80-year-old woman said that she would kill her 47-year-old daughter before placing her. This is not uncommon."

The above responses suggest the salience of the outreach role in case management for older families. As noted by Kaufman and colleagues (1989), "Outreach services may focus upon the identification of and intervention with family units where the older mentally retarded person's health and well-being are at risk because of actual or potential neglectful or abusive behavior on the part of family caregivers or because of problematic situations in the family's environment" (p. 102). Not discussed by Kaufman and colleagues, however, was the mandate for case managers to further identify those aging families who either are underutilizing services or are totally "hidden" from the MR/DD service system (Fullmer, Smith, & Tobin, 1991; Smith & Tobin, 1989). For example, it is not uncommon for case managers to be called upon to suddenly arrange placement for a previously unserved adult with mental retardation, after the parent's death is reported by professionals outside of the MR/DD system such as clergy, police, or hospital staff.

Similar to the observation by Seltzer and Seltzer (1985), our respondents noted that older parents jeopardize the developmental progress of their offspring with a developmental disability by focusing primarily on maintenance or current abilities rather than promoting optimal functioning. This theme is revealed by the following responses:

"They are more accepting of disability than younger parents."

"Older parents do not want to know particulars; instead they only want to know that everything is okay in a general sense."

"In general, older parents are more doubtful when progress or independence is spoken of, which is due to their overprotectiveness."

"The focus of older parents during reviews is on basic needs of the offspring, whereas younger parents are as equally concerned or even more so about helping the child to maximize potential."

"Older parents are also more likely to see the offspring as still a child without potential because, in the past, the service system focused on total care of clients."

"Older parents regard day programs as maintenance, and they don't see any further progress as being possible."

From the perspective of the case management model proposed by Kaufman and colleagues (1989), the above responses suggest that the enabler/facilitator role may be thwarted to some extent in practice with aging families. These authors noted that the focus of this role is "upon helping the client maximize his or her independent functioning within that unit, while helping the unit as a whole maintain its ability to function independently to its maximum potential" (pp. 105-106). Yet as reported by our respondents, older parents frequently are unconcerned about maximizing their offspring's performance. It was further noted by our respondents, however, that this may reflect a cohort effect due to the prior emphasis of the MR/DD service system itself on maintenance rather than on optimization. Thus the case managers were optimistic that future cohorts of older parents will be more open to attempts to promote optimal functioning by the offspring with a developmental disability.

Attention to the Unique Needs of Aging Parents

The final general theme that emerged was the recognition of the special needs faced by families containing older parents. It was common for respondents to note that greater nurturance and emotional support are required when serving older parents, that attention must be given to coordinating services to meet their age-related special needs so they may continue as caregivers, and that modifications in the MR/DD system are warranted to allow case managers to best serve aging families.

It also was apparent from the case managers' response that a variety of practice roles are required to simultaneously meet the diverse needs of older parents and their offspring with mental retardation. The following responses, for example, exemplify the validity of the therapist role:

"I'm more nurturing with older parents than with younger parents. Older parents become more isolated and need more interaction. They need to know that someone is there. In some ways, you become part of the extended family."

"I need to tell them that it's not bad to ask for help and let them know that they haven't failed because they can no longer provide care."

"I try to sympathize with older parents because of their many problems."

"Individual services don't work unless the older parent has someone to nurture them. . . . The worker who sits down and drinks coffee with the parent is saying 'You're still valuable.' You just can't go in once a month to see that everything is okay. Case managers must talk about more than just the child, even though this is not perceived by supervisors as your job. . . . Working with older parents is a true social work task and we'd rather be doing this than a lot of bureaucratic paperwork."

Other responses, such as the following, stressed the importance of the broker/coordinator role in serving aging families:

"The focus in case management becomes a lot more on the needs of older parents, mostly medical needs, so that they can continue to care for the child."

"Older parents often mention the impact of their own disabilities."

"Older parents need more assistance with just about everything."

"If they have to physically care for a multiple handicapped person at home, even simple things like getting meals become difficult. But, they continue to care by arranging services like help from other family members, Meals on Wheels, home health aides, etc."

"A lot of older parents are on medications, they sleep during the day, and they can't do chores. They are totally dependent on offspring, visiting nurses, medicab, DSS, and adult services."

"I have great frustration over matching older parents with service providers. Often, the client and parent have similar needs, but legally we're supposed to only serve the client. In reality, though, we must serve both."

"In my opinion, the best advocate for the child is the parent. So I support and advocate for them. I try to maintain older parents in the caregiver role for as long as possible."

"The single most important issue faced by older parents is support and respite to keep parental care going."

"We need a change in emphasis to family work within the MR/DD system and not just a client-centered approach."

"We need a reassignment of caseloads such that one worker has just or predominantly older parents. When our caseload is so diverse, it's too difficult to provide services adequately. This person should have a background in gerontology."

Implications for Practice and Future Research

Practice Implications

Five broad implications for practice emerge from the findings of our in-depth interviews. First, although the six practice roles of Kaufman and colleagues (1989) are clearly relevant to practice with aging families of adults with developmental disabilities, it is apparent that these roles should not be given equal weight by case managers, nor were they found to be given equal weight. For example, whereas our respondents identified several issues that warranted the advocacy role, none of the case managers indicated her or his own involvement in this particular role. Similarly, although respondents commonly perceived the need for the therapist role in helping parents and offspring deal with their feelings regarding eventual separation, several case managers recommended that other staff, such as psychologists or group workers, be used for this purpose. Thus case managers did not perceive themselves as able to assume the Herculean task of meeting all the needs of aging families through their own resourcefulness. Given the size and diversity of their caseloads, it is apparent that case managers cannot be all things to all families. Most sensible, therefore, may be to expect case managers to be familiar with the purposes of the six practice roles identified by Kaufman and colleagues (1989), but ensure the meeting of family needs through collaboration with other professionals.

A second practice implication from these findings is that case managers employed within the MR/DD service system need preservice, inservice, and continuing education programs in gerontology. This need was revealed by the feelings of frustration and possible ageism that the case managers expressed when describing their interactions with older parents of adults with developmental disabilities. Moreover, in many cases, both the parents and offspring have reached old age either chronologically or in terms of their functional abilities. Thus case managers need to know more about aging issues to understand what age-related changes and transitions face these families. Also, MR/DD case managers must know how to make appropriate referrals to professionals and programs within the aging services network. Fortunately there has been increased recognition of the need for service collaboration and mutual training between the MR/DD and aging networks (Janicki & Seltzer, 1991; Sutton et al., 1992). Congruent with collaborative training is the cultivation of geriatric specialists within the MR/DD service system.

A third practice implication is that case managers must emphasize to parents the need to actuate permanency planning before a crisis occurs within the aging family. Our data, combined with Heller and Factor's (1991) finding that case management increased the probability that caregivers would prefer a residential program placement, suggest that case managers are essential to assisting parents with permanency planning. This assistance is focused primarily on helping parents to confront their own feelings regarding the future, as well on as providing concrete information about available residential, legal, and financial options. It is sensible to include other family members if they are recognized by older parents (Seltzer & Seltzer, 1985). This is particularly true regarding the siblings of the offspring with a developmental disability.

A fourth practice implication is that aging families differ from younger families in that both the clients and the parents may have similar needs. With advancing age, parents are likely to experience increasing difficulty in carrying out activities in daily living. To assume caregiving responsibilities leaves the parents increasingly unable to participate in their own care, while their offspring may be experiencing accelerated aging that ocurs with Down syndrome. In-home services may be essential if the family is to stay intact for as long as possible. An innovative and very successful program was Seltzer's (1992) training of families to be case managers for elders with developmental disabilities. Large caseloads, as well as high turnover among case managers, necessitate programs such as her Family Centered Community Care for the Elderly (FCCCE) model. Unfortunately, as evidenced in our NIA-funded study of 235 mothers, too often an interdependence develops in which the generations care for each other, sometimes with no outside help and with a kind of insularity that makes them less open to seeking assistance in permanency planning. Furthermore, because many of these families do not use MR/DD programs (usually referred to as the "hidden"), reaching out to them, although very difficult, must be considered (Smith & Tobin, 1989).

The fifth and final practice implication is that the MR/DD system must become more meaningful to these families. This meaningfulness must come through policy changes more than through the modification of practice by case managers. A family policy focused on aging families would encompass making the family the client rather than only the adult offspring with a disability, ensuring home care until residential placement is necessary, and having sufficient community residences. Only through a shift in policy will many family caregivers even elect to meet with case managers. Wood and Skiles (1992) found that among 44 family caregivers who were 55 years of age and over, only 17 (38%) met with provider agencies.

Research Implications

Obviously, the generalizability of the present findings is limited given the very restricted and nonrandom sample of respondents interviewed. Thus we recommend an extension of the present study that would include a sample of case managers from both state- and nonstate-operated (e.g., ARC's) MR/DD agencies within several states. A larger study such as this would permit examination of the relationship among important demographic factors and case managers' perceptions of practice. In this vein, the following research questions should be addressed:

1. Do case managers have similar views regarding aging families of adults with developmental disabilites despite variations in agency and state affiliations?
2. Do the perceptions of case managers from rural service locations differ from those located in other geographical areas?
3. Do the perceptions of more experienced case managers reflect an attitude that it is unnecessary to involve other service providers in their work with older parents?
4. Does the age of case managers, after controlling for amount of professional experience, significantly affect their perceptions of practice with older parents?

Possibly, older case managers are more reluctant to work with elderly parents because of anxieties regarding their own aging. On the other hand, older case managers may have greater sensitivity to issues of parental separation because of separations in their own lives.

Future studies also should address the question of what personal skills and traits case managers perceive to be most facilitative in practice with older parents. Some case managers in the present study said the abilities needed in working with older parents are the same as those needed in working with younger parents, whereas others believed that greater patience and knowledge of aging processes is required to work effectively with elderly parents. Indeed, some respondents expressed a need for case managers who specialize in geriatric caseloads. In turn, will those case managers who have had preservice or inservice gerontological education demonstrate more positive attitudes toward practice with elderly parents than those without gerontological training?

Future studies also should focus on the special programs and advocacy efforts that case managers think should be developed by their agency to support aging families. Some respondents in the present study suggested the development of support groups and professional counseling to assist with parents' feelings of separation, others suggested improved interagency coordination with aging network service providers, still others suggested special financial assistance to older parents, and some suggested formal gerontological education for case managers. Whether similar recommendations are made by larger and more representative samples of case managers will be very informative to policy makers and administrators assessing issues related to the care of aging individuals with developmental disabilities.

It is important to survey the practice wisdom that a representative sample of case managers articulate regarding procedures they have found to be effective in assisting older parents with the difficult task of permanency planning. There are no established guidelines in the professional literature regarding this crucial case management activity. Nonetheless respondents in our pilot study demonstrated that they had formulated their own diverse "best practices" such as enhancing parents' feelings of control and predictability, establishing a trusting and warm relationship to eliminate parents' perception of them as the "the State," and recognizing permanency planning as a gradual process that occurs in stages. These approaches obviously are not mutually exclusive and need to be synthesized into an intelligible format.

Finally, evaluation studies are needed regarding the efficacy of practice with aging families. As aptly stated by Seltzer, Krauss, and Heller (1991):

Studies of the impacts of long-term care planning initiatives are particularly needed in order to develop appropriate models that can confront effectively the pronounced propensity of older caregivers to delay the formation of concrete residential, legal, and financial plans. Further, research in this area needs to elucidate the impact of long-term care planning on parental well-being and family functioning. (p. 20)

Case managers represent the group of service providers who can potentially have the greatest impact on the lives of adults with developmental disabilities and their aged parents. In turn, a research agenda that describes the concerns of case managers, identifies their best practice techniques, and evaluates the efficacy of their interventions is needed to ensure their optimal performance.

PART IV

Practice, Research, and Policy Directives

11

Empowering Elderly Caregivers

Practice, Research, and Policy Directives

EDWARD F. ANSELLO
KAREN A. ROBERTO

The process of empowering elderly caregivers must be engaged simultaneously along several fronts. Research must inform policy, which, in
turn, must influence and be influenced by good practice. The practice
of caregiving itself, whether by family members or by regulated outside
personnel, must benefit from ongoing research. Only from such a
continuous interactive loop (research to policy to practice to research)
will effective empowerment truly occur. Advocacy might well speed the
process, but these interactions will provide a solid base.

Consider the following examples. Advocating for public policy to
support research into possible common etiology (Janicki & Dalton, 1992)
of Alzheimer's disease, a late onset disability, and Down syndrome, a
lifelong disability, could result in recognition of commonalities between
currently separate groups such as the Alzheimer's Association and the
American Association for Mental Retardation (AAMR), as well as collaborations in advocacy, training, and innovations related to elderly caregivers of aging adults with these diagnoses. Interviewing elderly
caregivers of different ethnic or racial heritages regarding their perceptions and use of outside day care and in-home care services could result
in specialized training programs for practitioners, more refined targeted
research on ethnic and racial differences among aging caregivers, and

advocacy coalitions among disparate but like-minded subgroups of caregivers.

We hope this book helps to advance the engagement of the continuous loop of research-policy-practice-advocacy that will empower elderly caregivers and their family members. Each of the preceding data-based chapters in this book has included specific suggestions for practice and for future research. In this chapter, we summarize and expand upon the recommendations of our colleagues and provide suggestions for future policy considerations.

Practice Implications

The underlying goal for practitioners, as suggested by the contributors to this volume and others (Ansello & Eustis, 1992; Heller & Factor, 1991; Janicki, 1991; Seltzer, Krauss, & Heller, 1991), is the empowerment of elderly caregivers and care receivers in their quest for a quality life. Based on the results of their research, the authors suggest a variety of approaches for achieving this goal (Table 11.1).

Education, at a variety of levels, is an essential part of the empowerment process. Both family members and practitioners must recognize the physical, psychological, and social changes that individuals experience because of the natural aging process. Providing caregivers with accurate information can help them better comprehend and adapt to the changes both they and their care receivers may experience (e.g., lower energy level, change in work/activity status, loss of a loved one). Education of the public, such as through awareness campaigns, can enlighten the community not only to the needs of elderly caregivers and their families but also to the invaluable and extraordinary work these caregivers perform.

Practitioners working with these families require cross-training in gerontology and rehabilitation. They need to understand the normal aging process, the specific disabilities of their clients, and the multiple service systems. Professionals and paraprofessionals specializing in developmental disabilities and aging should possess knowledge and skills in advocacy, habilitation planning and implementation, and communication (Sutton et al., 1992). Finally, they must be sensitive to the autonomy needs of elderly caregivers and their care recipients. The focus of any strategy, after all, must remain empowerment of the individual—in this context, empowerment of the elder whose caring is

Table 11.1 Summary of Authors' Implications for Direct Practice

Authors	Practice Implications
Heller	Family perspectives at different points in the life cycle; cohort differences when working with families; family support programs; planning for future residential service needs
Roberto	Enhanced gerontological knowledge base; linkages between families and the service community
Brubaker & Brubaker	Family life education; caregiver support groups; activity groups for adults with mental retardation; assessment; case management
Hawkins, Eklund, & Martz	Moderate exercise; low-fat diet; practice cognitive skills; meaningful work, love and companionship, and social/leisure activity
Noelker & Somple	Educational programs and materials for family members and professional caregivers; support for families via appropriate community resources; inclusion of caregivers in all phases of care planning
Wood	Identification of "hidden group"; intersystem cooperation; familiarity with support services
Lehmann & Roberto	Involve families in self-help and educational programs; facilitation of family service use; formal transition planning; involvement of medical practitioners
Rinck & Calkins	Permanency planning; community integrated work experiences; recreation services; financial planning; family-oriented case management
Smith & Tobin	Practitioners' roles; continuing education in gerontology; permanency planning; addressing needs of both parents and offspring; development of family policy

intended to assist the aging care recipient to remain as independent as possible.

Most practitioners in the field of developmental disabilities and aging are either case managers or direct service providers. In either role, they assist families through the use of supportive services. The aging of persons with lifelong disabilities and their caregivers necessitates the development or modification of existing programs to meet the physical and social needs of this growing population. For example, both caregivers and care receivers may require assistance with activities of daily living, nutrition, and transportation to function at their optimal level of independence. For individuals with developmental disabilities, successful "retirement" from paid employment or the sheltered workshop experience requires the availability of alternative programming such as adult day care, recreational opportunities, and structured social activities.

Engaging caregivers in early permanency planning is a challenge facing most practitioners. For example, families often wait until a time of crisis (e.g., death of the primary caregiver) to seek alternative living situations for their dependent members. Practitioners can facilitate the planning process by helping caregivers in identifying and determining housing options, supportive services, and family responsibilities. Through advanced planning, the stress of caregiver and residential transitions for the *entire* family can be minimized.

It is not enough, however, to provide or coordinate services for families caring for relatives with developmental disabilities. Practitioners and families must play an active role in evaluating these services. As agencies strive to build an appropriate service system, both practitioners and families continually need to address questions of effectiveness with respect to program delivery, participant outcomes, and cost.

Direction for Future Research

Despite the growing number of published reports on the issues and concerns of elderly caregivers of family members with developmental disabilities, many gaps remain in the literature. Table 11.2 highlights the recommendations for further research suggested by the contributing authors of this volume. Topics proposed include the refinement of assessment techniques; the importance of lifestyle enhancement (i.e., diet, exercise, social activities); perceptions of family caregivers, persons with lifelong disabilities, and formal service providers; placement preferences compared to actual placement outcomes; skills and abilities of service providers; and the evaluation of intervention strategies.

In addition to their substantive recommendations, several authors agreed on methodological directives. To date, descriptive studies predominate the literature. Although this is a necessary first step, it is now time to move forward and incorporate conceptual frameworks into future work. Theoretically based research paradigms, such as those suggested by several of the contributors to this volume (e.g., Brubaker & Brubaker; Heller; Wood), provide the basis for hypothesis testing and will allow for the study of relationships among variables.

Table 11.2 Summary of Authors' Directives for Future Research

Authors	Research Directives
Heller	Life-span approach; longitudinal studies to examine placement preferences and actual placement decisions; larger and more diverse samples
Roberto	Representative samples; comparison of different family caregivers; social activities and support; longitudinal designs
Brubaker & Brubaker	Caregivers' reactions to crises; comparison of the perceptions of service availability versus actual availability of resources
Hawkins, Eklund, & Martz	Refine measures; gender differences; longitudinal assessment
Noelker & Somple	Genetic research; development of more appropriate and accurate assessment instruments; life-span perspective
Wood	Theory-driven research paradigms; probability samples; longitudinal studies; evaluation research
Lehmann & Roberto	Qualitative methodologies; multivariate analyses; inclusion of persons with disabilities in sample
Rinck & Calkins	Ecological perspective of the study of case management; comparison of perceptions of individual, family, and case manager; evaluation of different case management models
Smith & Tobin	Relationship between demographic factors and case manager's perceptions of practice; personal skills and traits of successful case managers; representative samples; evaluation studies

The authors also suggest the need for advanced sampling procedures. The study of special populations (e.g., elderly caregivers of adults with developmental disabilities) often employs small, homogeneous, convenience samples. The use of larger, random samples that include persons from different socioeconomic, ethnic, and minority groups will strengthen our ability to generalize the findings of future studies. In addition, the majority of individuals studied with lifelong disabilities are persons with mental retardation. In the future researchers must intensify their efforts to include proportionate numbers of individuals with other types of developmental disabilities in their samples. The use of a broader sample population will provide the opportunity for comparing caregiving issues and needs across disabilities.

The representativeness of the caregivers who participate in the study of families caring for aging relatives with developmental disabilities also came into question. Most studies thus far focus only on the primary caregiver's perception of the family situation. In most cases this is the mother. Other primary caregivers, such as fathers and siblings, must be included in future studies to identify similarities and differences in their perceptions of and reactions to their caregiver roles. The use of a family systems approach that includes more than one family member in the data-gathering process would provide greater insight about how these families manage their situations. We also must develop better strategies to identify and include in future studies the "hidden families" who provide in-home care without the support of the formal service system.

The cross-sectional studies presented in this volume and elsewhere (Hogg et al., 1988; Seltzer & Krauss, 1987; Seltzer, Krauss, & Heller, 1991) produced important initial information about the lives of elderly caregivers of adults with developmental disabilities. To advance our knowledge and understanding of the correlates and consequences of family caregiving in later life requires the implementation of longitudinal designs. Mini-longitudinal studies may be beneficial in the study of transitions, such as change in primary caregiver, relocation of aging adults with lifelong disabilities, and entry into the formal service system of both caregivers and their care receivers. The *process* of caregiving, however, requires more long-term examinations to assess the physical, psychological, and social impact of caregiving, and changes in the needs of caregivers and family members with developmental disabilities as they move through the life cycle.

Policy Considerations

Before contemplating the most formidable backdrop against which policy formulation must develop, we should consider salient character-istics of the present elderly caregiving scenario having to do with numbers and qualitative aspects that may shape the direction we pursue. First, the size of the existing population that might benefit from sup-portive services and assistance to elderly caregivers is enormous and may well bring with it needs that exceed projections and policy. Rose and Ansello (1987), Stone (1992), and others have estimated on the basis of their research that some 60% of older adults with lifelong disabilities are aging in family contexts in the community without the use of any aging- or disabilities-related services. Wood, Ansello, Coogle, and Cotter (1992) found that most human service agencies in Virginia have no methodology for outreach to or identification of older clients with developmental disabilities, but rather rely upon the passive process of calls from families and referrals from other agencies.

Second, large numbers of adults with lifelong disabilities are advancing on midlife and later. The latter, the near elderly, are not computed in the staggering projections of late-life disability in the next 30 years recently calculated by Kunkel and Applebaum (1992). These researchers, using the National Long Term Care Survey of 1982, which interviewed persons age 65 and over, and the 1985 National Nursing Home Survey, estimate that the number of elders with functional disabilities will increase from the current 5.1 million to 9.4 million in the year 2020, under the most conservative of four projection models. Unfortunately the databases these researchers relied upon do not include developmental disabilities among the near old. The unprecedented survival of these individuals, however, must be factored into the projections of need for services and personnel.

Third, we have to remember that, as central to aging with lifelong disabilities as it is, the focus upon elderly caregivers may well be a time-limited concern, most essentially associated with caregivers of children with developmental disabilities who were born prior to the mid-1950s. These children, now in their 40s or older, generally did not benefit from legislation introduced at that time that activated a system of improved diagnoses, mainstreaming education, and other funded interventions. So they tended to stay at home, receiving care from the family. This pattern was not necessarily followed by subsequent generations. Not only are there likely to be life-span differences in caregiver burden (Heller, this volume), but also there are meaningful historical and cohort differences among the recipients of this care. Those individuals with developmental disabilities who are approaching midlife from their 20s and 30s today quite often are different from their older counterparts now receiving care from elderly caregivers. Mental retardation, the typical diagnosis among the older population, is a less prevalent diagnosis among younger groups. Arguably, those who are older are more appropriate to receive care, and history has the care being provided in the family home. The younger individuals, in contrast, beneficiaries of mainstreaming interventions and schooled in advocacy, have vocal spokespersons, often have seized responsibility for their own lives and care, and may well transmute the whole issue of elderly family members caring for their aging children with developmental disabilities.

Impact of the Federal Deficit

In considering the policy implications of the research both reported and referenced in the preceding chapters, one must first acknowledge the inescapable matter of the federal deficit, and its associate, recession. The latter may well end, with or without the actions of the nation's leaders. The deficit is another thing altogether. Its size and budgetary impact mean that for the little corner of the world occupied by concern about aging and developmental disabilities, the overriding issue will be the deficit. Any improvement in the relative priority of aging and disabilities as an area of focus for services, research, and personnel will, of necessity, mean decrements in other people's priority areas, in a deficit-driven or deficit-reducing climate. Within the parameters of the aging and disabilities arena itself, obtaining funds for supportive services for elderly caregivers of aging adults with developmental disabilities will require trade-offs from other deserving activities. The key to success would seem to be a multipart strategy that (a) effectively places elderly caregivers and the whole subject of aging and developmental disabilities within a larger arena of public concern, (b) emphasizes nonfederal sources when funds are the issue, and (c) recognizes mechanisms other than new funding when it comes to supporting an activity.

The federal debt exceeded the $4 trillion mark in September 1992. When it reached $1 trillion during the Reagan presidency, the debt was greater than the sum of all of the federal deficits of the preceding 200 years. It has kept growing. At 17 cents of every federal tax dollar, debt service (payment of interest owed) now is greater than any other category of federal spending except Social Security. The numbers are so huge as to be incomprehensible. An analogy would be for the typical U.S. family with a median income of $35,000 to have over $44,000 a year in expenses. The family could reduce its deficit by borrowing money to pay off its debt, but its borrowing and the associated interest would have to continue; or the family could cut future expenses to align them with income. Without a large raise in pay, the family's standard of living would continue to erode. Returning to the federal deficit, it would seem unlikely under the current scenario that real increase in appropriations for broad areas such as aging and developmental disabilities, let alone for narrowly focused interests such as elderly caregivers, would occur without trade-offs and concurrent factionism pitting one group against another.

Both parties in Congress have begun to propose changes in Medicaid and Medicare, from slow growth in spending to major restructuring of the entire health-care system, as a way of saving $50 billion to $100 billion over the next 5 years. Ironically, the time may be right to propose a bold initiative in federal health and long-term care that would include supportive services to elderly caregivers and choices for consumers in personal assistance services throughout the life course. If the overall health and long-term care program were financed by all taxpayers, not just by the elderly as with the ill-fated Medicare Catastrophic Coverage Act of 1988, and if proponents could convince Congress and the administration that a comprehensive program of prevention, early intervention, and participant choice among competing providers would be more cost-effective, such a program might well be palatable. Fitting within this larger agenda, supportive services for elderly caregivers make practical sense. As Gettings (1992) has argued convincingly, tinkering with the current system of federally supported community-based services, even sweeping new legislation that enhanced Medicaid home- and community-based programs, basically would serve to engineer trade-offs among existing services rather than initiation of new services. Between 1988 and 1991, Gettings points out, the number of waivers for home- and community-based services doubled. Although 48 states now have MR/DD waiver programs, waiting lists for these services continue to grow.

Rising health-care costs and the growing public anxiety about them may provide the conditions for a comprehensive, prevention-oriented federal health-care package whose components would accomplish the goals of many proponents of long-term care reform to benefit individuals with lifelong disabilities and their caregivers. These include consumer choice among competing services, access to services and environments that enable one to continue an active life, and priority given to long-term functioning rather than to acute, medically driven, quick-fix interventions (Binstock, 1992). To be sure, the American public is genuinely confused about the health-care issue, but it wants an end to the status quo, and it wants the federal government to take the lead in health-care reform (Kelly & Gemeinhardt, 1992). It would seem prudent to emphasize that, in the bigger picture, support for a broad array of home- and community-based services and, more specifically, assistance to elderly caregivers of aging adults with developmental disabilities are consistent with the financial and philosophical goals of health-care and long-term care reform.

At the same time that the deficit and the inchoate nature of health-care reform characterize the federal role in any future supportive services to elderly caregivers, the role of the states in aging and developmental disabilities has evolved. States are much less the providers of direct services than they were 10 or 15 years ago. Gettings (1992) notes that the numbers of individuals in state mental retardation institutions nationally has dropped from 152,000 in 1977 to 85,000 in 1990 to 72,000 in 1992. States closed 34 MR centers between 1986 and 1990 and 34 more are expected to be closed by June 1995.

States are positioned to play a leadership role in the management of services that may benefit elderly caregivers now and adults with lifelong disabilities over time. Gettings (1992) declares that states need to play leadership roles in conceptualizing services, planning systems, developing resources, and ensuring quality, all of which may mean encouraging alternative services and even competition among providers where feasible. He continues that states need to create a level playing field among the various providers, paying more or less equal levels, for example, for group homes and for supported living arrangements in one's own home; otherwise provider agencies will go where the payments are, and an emphasis upon such "outcomes" as relative independence and community participation will be overshadowed by reimbursement formulas for services. Again, as in the federal scenario, the evolution of the states' roles in aging and developmental disabilities services may mean opportunities to press for, among other things, supportive services for elderly caregivers.

Policy to Create Mechanisms of Support

We cannot stand idle while the above-mentioned federal and state possibilities unfold that may help the big picture of aging and developmental disabilities. Positive results may not occur or may take years in doing so. During this time we must advance in producing mechanisms to reinforce the mainstay of chronic care to our current older adults with developmental disabilities—family caregivers—while at the same time preparing for the subsequent, different cohorts of aging adults with lifelong disabilities. To accomplish both of these ends will require policy that:

1. Strengthens the infrastructure of support for family caregivers
2. Improves the current and builds the future systems of formal caregivers
3. Encourages the autonomy of care recipients

Strengthening the Infrastructure of Support for Caregivers

Bradley and Knoll (n.d.) maintain that the field of developmental disabilities has undergone another paradigm shift, entering its fourth phase. First was emphasis upon segregation and institutionalization, which was followed by deinstitutionalization and the developmental model. The third phase, characterized by community membership and a functional supports model, has given way to a new paradigm with the four major elements of commitment to the community and families, emphasis upon human relationships, person-centered programming, and real choice and control for consumers. If fully insinuated into aging and developmental disabilities services, this emerging paradigm would offer an ethic that is simultaneously sympathetic to the vital role of elderly caregivers and to the different characteristics and needs of younger adults with lifelong disabilities.

Operationally, the paradigm Bradley and Knoll discuss would mean policy that brings together consumers, informal (family) caregivers, and formal (paraprofessional and professional) caregivers in developing, managing, and evaluating a menu of services. The result would be a strengthened infrastructure of support. Besides the examples given in the preceding chapters (e.g., Heller; Lehmann & Roberto; Smith & Tobin), there are a number of initiatives that are or would be consistent with this new paradigm. These include:

1. Experiments with service credit banking: In this undertaking, participants in a community or region provide services to each other that are credited with a service broker who arranges and monitors the type and level of services being contributed. Participants "bank" their volunteered contributions of services to others against future drawdown in time of need. Since 1988, when The Robert Wood Johnson Foundation first awarded grants to six sites to implement this approach to informal care provision, service credit banking has grown to a network of 70 operational and 18 planned service credit programs in 23 states and the District of Columbia (Meiners, McKay, & Helfand, 1992).

2. Shared policy making at the community level, involving the direct service system, families, and consumers: The State of Vermont's Department of Aging and Disabilities began in 1992 a series of regional consortia in five parts of the state to build coalitions and

consensus regarding the direction of long-term care in the state (Charron, 1992). Through grassroots planning, citizens and policy makers are redesigning the entire long-term care system into one more oriented to community-assisted independent living. Questions being asked include experimentation with alternative roles for clients and volunteers, as well as for community institutions such as nursing homes, in assisting clients to maintain community living.

3. Pilot projects that assist family caregivers to continue their care: To aid meaningful policy formulation, state and local service units should be further encouraged to provide and test direct stipends to see whether the quality of caregiving can be prolonged at home and whether demonstrable cost savings over more formalized caregiving (e.g., group homes and institutions) can be observed. Some agencies, such as Maryland's State Office on Aging, already have provided direct stipends to caregivers in pilot projects in the 1980s, but without a policy-driven research design attached to the project, initiators could not validate the benefits of the stipends to an inquisitive state legislature. The Virginia Coalition in Support of Family Caregivers of Older Adults is a recent product of collaborations among the Virginia Department for the Aging; representatives of civic, professional, service, and religious groups; and individual caregivers. This coalition has held regional forums across Virginia to mobilize a grassroots coalition to advocate for needed programs and services, develop educational campaigns and programs for specific target audiences, and establish partnerships to develop and coordinate support programs.

4. Research-influenced policy development: Some states and jurisdictions have shied from research suggested by Wood (this volume) and others into the size of the population of hidden families, thereby allowing policy to be made amidst incomplete information. Progress, however, is being made by others in obtaining realistic estimates of need and resources. Recognizing the "true" size of this population further propels policy arguments for innovations such as service credit banking, coalition building for independent living, and regular interaction of formal and informal caregivers (Noelker & Somple; Smith & Tobin, this volume) regarding consumer health and functional status, and available resources to meet needs.

Building the Present and Future Systems of Formal Caregivers

Large professional organizations are beginning to recognize the issues of aging with developmental disabilities and to state that these will be integrated into the formulation of their policy henceforth. However, the development of personnel for related policy, research, and services will be slow. In 1992 the American Association for Mental Retardation (AAMR) for the first time formally recognized the needs of older persons by setting legislative goals to increase financial assistance and improve services for these elders. Basing their agenda on a quality-of-life and community participation emphasis, AAMR has set goals that include support for senior day programs, senior centers, and other age-integrated activities; comprehensive research on aging with life-long disabilities; advocacy for consumers' retirement from active treatment plans; and aging-related training for staff.

AAMR's commitment is consistent with what Janicki (1991) calls a "top-down" policy approach, wherein officials designate certain constituencies as the focus of organizational activity. Other top-down strategies can be suggested to increase the cadre of professionals who are knowledgeable about aging and developmental disabilities and who constitute a potential resource to elderly caregivers. One of the most straightforward policies, with a fairly quick impact upon elderly caregivers of aging adults with developmental disabilities, would be to advocate for these caregivers to be legislatively mandated targets in the appropriations of existing federal programs. Of course, this strategy may lead to subsequent trade-offs, but it can be argued that designating these caregivers as targets simply broadens the qualifications of those in the program. Examples of a broadened focus to build systems include:

1. In the just-completed 3-year reauthorization of the Health Professions Training Program (H.R. 3508), under which Geriatric Education Centers are funded, Congress directed the parent organization, the Health Resources and Services Administration, to give special consideration to training and education programs for health-care professionals to provide services to those with Alzheimer's disease. Aging and developmental disabilities is certainly a legitimate designee for subsequent reauthorizations.

2. The Health Care Financing Administration (HCFA), under its Rural Health Transitions Grants programs, awarded more than $22 million in 1992 to 517 small rural hospitals in order to, among other things, train their staffs to provide better care to Medicare beneficiaries. Elderly caregivers of adults with developmental disabilities are most likely to be Medicare beneficiaries and deserving of a special focus within this existing initiative. The case also can be made for HCFA to begin another program targeted on elderly caregivers, one that might demonstrate the health-care benefits of linking these caregivers with formal providers or training them to carry out pilot projects for hospitals and health-care professionals, or one that might test other innovations that would multiply the capacity of the formal system to respond to the needs of aging persons with lifelong impairments.

3. The Domestic Volunteer Services Act (P.L. 93-113) enables volunteers to help their homebound counterparts in the community at the modest cost of about $3,000 for a year of volunteered services. ACTION's Senior Companion Program is an example. Low-income (125% of poverty level) older adults contribute 20 hours a week and are paid $2.35 an hour by participating agencies. With amendments to the law, elderly caregivers of aging adults with developmental disabilities can become authorized recipients of volunteered assistance, at the same time empowering caregivers and building the infrastructure of community-based assistance.

Encouraging Autonomy of Care Recipients

Moody (1992) raises fundamental questions about the meaning of autonomy in current social conditions. He observes that "autonomy" of clients in service systems more often is given lip service than it is honored. Although Moody's focus is upon frail elders in nursing homes, his points are equally relevant in any context where individuals have diminished or comprised abilities, as in the crossfire of "autonomy" and "assistance" that characterizes some of the discussion about caregivers and developmental disabilities. Is autonomy or self-control synonymous with being left alone? Conversely, what does it mean when one has diminished power to choose or to exercise choice, whether one is the care recipient or the caregiver? Is autonomy a meaningless goal for older adults with lifelong impairments or for their elderly caregivers?

The fact that Smith and Tobin (this volume) maintain that practitioners have no established guidelines to direct their efforts in assisting families with permanency planning may be emblematic of the tension some concerned providers feel between assistance, thought to be intervention, and nonassistance, thought to be autonomy. Although we can regret this unfortunate misunderstanding of terms and roles, others enmesh the concept of autonomy with the source of services, meaning consumer-selected versus agency-selected, rather than with the consequences of the services. Autonomy in the current discussion of caregiving ought to be conceived of as a negotiated or assisted process leading to an enhanced sense of worth or dignity, whether for the elderly caregiver or the adult child. As policy, agency-provided, even agency-originated, services ought to be seen for what they accomplish.

Several initiatives might serve simultaneously to encourage the autonomy of the care recipient (the aging child with developmental disabilities) and that of the caregiver, especially with the increasing prevalence of both child and parent constituting a "two-generation geriatric family" (Ansello, 1988). Briefly, these include the advocacy of policy that would:

1. Give priority to dissemination of a range of assistive technology devices and home accessibility features shown to help users maintain functioning in the community. These include "low-tech" devices such as wheelchairs, walkers, alphabet boards, raised toilets, and handrails as well as "high-tech" items such as augmentative communication devices, myoelectrically powered prostheses, and computers for memory testing and medical monitoring (Stinson, 1989). LaPlante, Hendershot, and Moss (1992) report that 2.5 million Americans say they need these items but cannot afford them.

2. Promulgate family-oriented case management throughout the life span of the person with a disability. As Rinck and Calkins (this volume) point out, family-oriented case management is mandated for early intervention services by P.L. 99-457, and a life-span approach would assist with the evolution of issues that occur as someone ages in the natural home, including "future planning" that involves the whole family in decision making and permanency planning, found by several contributors to this volume to be frequently lacking. Case management is not the antithesis of autonomy, and can assist all parties to assume the exercise of choice. If conducted properly, case management is time- and goal-limited, with clients as participants in a process of initiating, monitoring, reassessing, and terminating services.

3. Expand the network of shared or matched housing, as a mechanism of opportunity for both elderly caregivers and their aging children (Ansello, 1988). More often associated with aging services, shared or matched housing programs and housing co-ops typically involve an agency to broker the "fit" of two or more unrelated individuals to share housing responsibilities. Sometimes promoted as a means of intergenerational support, these programs can offer the chance for counterbalanced strengths and mutual help for pairs of elderly caregivers.

4. Encourage the development of curricula *for* elderly caregivers and *about* elderly caregivers for professionals and paraprofessionals. Such curriculum development might be a "bottom-up" approach to policy formulation, as participants receive cognitive content and skills training related to such topics as the life-span evolution of caregiving responsibilities (Heller; Wood, this volume); parental needs, roles, and stresses (Brubaker & Brubaker; Roberto, this volume); the behavioral and biological correlates of the disabilities (Hawkins, Eklund, & Martz; Noelker & Somple, this volume); and community opportunities and resources (Lehmann & Roberto; Rinck & Calkins; Smith & Tobin, this volume). Multidisciplinary curricula would benefit preservice and inservice education in human services, gerontology, medicine, nursing, pharmacy, social work, special education, and elsewhere, as well as help caregivers through community or adult education.

5. Support initiatives to enable older adults with developmental disabilities to contribute their time and services to other adults in need of assistance, a theme championed by the 1987 Wingspread Conference on Aging and Lifelong Disabilities (Ansello & Rose, 1989). That aging children with developmental disabilities seldom transcend the categorization of "care recipient" is a misfortune that denies them the opportunity to experience the sense of worth in helping others and denies others the gifts they may need. One of the most crystalline images that continues from the Maryland Partners Project on Aging and Developmental Disabilities (Ansello & Zink, 1990) is that of a near elderly adult with Down syndrome helping a formerly mainstream, now confused elder with Alzheimer's disease to eat and enjoy a meal at an adult day-care center. The communication between them was simple and beautiful. Public policy should encourage, foster, stimulate, and enable such contributions by those who usually are constrained into the role of recipient.

Conclusion

Elderly caregivers of aging adults with developmental disabilities are the mainstay of chronic care in the community. For most of the 20th century, family caregivers have enabled their offspring with developmental disabilities to realize their wishes (Stroud & Sutton, 1988) for everyday things that enrich lives—friendships, employment, and a supportive environment in which to live. Yet, as a group, they have been unrecognized, unrewarded, and unassisted. The public policy of empowerment, mindful of the fiscal and governmental realities around us, considers the characteristics and temporal qualities of caregivers and care recipients in setting directions, and developing a diversity of pathways to attain its goals. The contributors to this volume, through their research and practice initiatives, have advanced our understanding of each of these components.

References

Agosta, J. (1989). Using cash assistance to support family efforts. In G. H. Singer & L. K. Irvin (Eds.), *Support for caregiving families* (pp. 189-205). Baltimore, MD: Paul H. Brookes.

Agosta, J., Bass, A., & Spence, D. (1986, August). *The needs of families: Results of a statewide survey in Massachusetts.* Cambridge, MA: Human Services Research Institute. (ERIC Document Reproduction Service No. ED 305 767)

Albright, L., & Cobb, R. B. (1988). *Assessment of students with handicaps in vocational education: A curriculum based approach.* Alexandria, VA: American Vocational Association.

Alzheimer's Association. (1990). *Alzheimer's disease: An overview.* (Available from the Alzheimer's Association, Cleveland Chapter, 12200 Fairhill Road, Cleveland, OH 44120)

Anderson, D. J. (1989). Trends in health care and other service needs among older persons with mental retardation. In *Proceedings of the 1989 public health conference on records and statistics.* Hyattsville, MD: National Center for Health Statistics.

Anderson, D. J., Lakin, K. C., Hill, B. K., & Chen, T. H. (1992). Social integration of older persons with mental retardation in residential facilities. *American Journal on Mental Retardation, 96,* 488-501.

Ansello, E. (1988). The intersecting of aging and disabilities. *Educational Gerontology, 14,* 351-363.

Ansello, E. (1992). Seeking common ground between aging and developmental disabilities. *Generations, 16*(1), 9-15.

Ansello, E., & Eustis, N. (Eds.). (1992). Aging and disabilities: Seeking common ground [Special issue]. *Generations, 16*(1).

Ansello, E., & Rose, T. (1989). *Aging and lifelong disabilities: Partnership for the twenty-first century.* Palm Springs, CA: Elvirita Lewis Foundation.

Ansello, E., & Zink, M. (1990). The partners project: Targeting community-based research and education on aging and developmental disabilities. In W. R. Rivera & N. W. Clarke (Eds.), *Proceedings of the 1990 Lifelong Learning Research Conference* (pp. 118-124). Fairfax, VA: George Mason University.

Arenberg, D., & Robertson-Tchabo, E. A. (1977). Learning and aging. In J. E. Birren & K. W. Schaie (Eds.), *Handbook of the psychology of aging* (pp. 421-449). New York: Van Nostrand Reinhold.

Asmussen, E., Fruensgaard, K., & Norgaard, S. (1975). A follow-up longitudinal study of selected physiologic functions in former physical education students—forty years. *Journal of the American Geriatric Society, 23,* 442-450.

Backman, S. J., & Mannell, R. C. (1986). Removing attitudinal barriers to leisure behavior and satisfaction: A field experiment among the institutionalized elderly. *Therapeutic Recreation Journal, 20*(3), 46-53.

Barer, B., & Johnson, C. (1990). A critique of the caregiving literature. *The Gerontologist, 30,* 26-29.

Barusch, A., & Spaid, W. (1989). Gender differences in caregiving: Why do wives report greater burden? *The Gerontologist, 29,* 667-676.

Baumeister, A. A., & Kellas, G. (1968). Reaction time and mental retardation. In N. R. Ellis (Ed.), *International review of research in mental retardation,* Vol. 3 (pp. 290-331). New York: Academic Press.

Beckman, P. J. (1983). Influence of selected child characteristics on stress in families of handicapped infants. *American Journal of Mental Deficiency, 88,* 150-156.

Begun, A. (1989). Sibling relationships involving developmentally disabled people. *American Journal of Mental Retardation, 93,* 566-574.

Berger, M., & Foster, M. (1976). Family-level interventions for retarded children: A multivariate approach to issues and strategies. *Multivariate Experimental Clinical Research, 2,* 1-21.

Bertsche, A., & Horejsi, C. (1980). Coordination of client services. *Social Work, 25,* 94-98.

Best-Sigford, B., Bruininks, R., Lakin, L., Hill, B., & Heal, L. (1982). Resident release patterns in a national sample of public residential facilities. *American Journal of Mental Deficiency, 87,* 130-140.

Binstock, R. (1992). Aging, disability and long-term care: The politics of common ground. *Generations, 16*(1), 83-88.

Birenbaum, A. (1971). The mentally retarded child in the home and the family life cycle. *Journal of Health and Social Behavior, 12,* 55-65.

Blacher, J. (1986). *Placement of severely handicapped children: Correlates and consequences* (Grant No. HD21324). Washington, DC: National Institute of Child Health and Human Development.

Blacher, J., Hanneman, R. A., & Rousey, A. B. (1992). Out-of-home placement of children with severe handicaps: A comparison of approaches. *American Journal on Mental Retardation, 96,* 607-616.

Black, M., Cohn, J., Smull, M., & Crites, L. (1985). Individual and family factors associated with risk of institutionalization of mentally retarded adults. *American Journal of Mental Deficiency, 90,* 271-276.

Blieszner, R., & Shifflett, P. (1990). The effects of Alzheimer's disease on close relationships between patients and caregivers. *Family Relations, 39,* 57-62.

Borkan, G. (1980). Assessment of biological aging using a profile of physical parameters. *Journal of Gerontology, 55,* 177-184.

Borthwick-Duffy, S., Eyman, R. K., & White, J. F. (1987). Client characteristics and residential placement patterns. *American Journal of Mental Deficiency, 92,* 24-30.

Boss, P. (1987). Family stress. In M. B. Sussman & S. K. Steinmetz (Eds.), *Handbook of marriage and the family* (pp. 695-723). New York: Plenum.

Botwinick, J. (1977). Intellectual abilities. In J. E. Birren & K. W. Schaie (Eds.), *Handbook of the psychology of aging* (pp. 384-420). New York: Van Nostrand Reinhold.

Bouvier, L., & De Vita, C. (1991). The baby boom: Entering midlife. *Population Bulletin, 46,* 30.

Bowers, B. (1987). Intergenerational caregiving: Adult caregivers and their aging parents. *Advanced Nursing Science, 9,* 20-31.

Bradburn, N. M. (1969). *The structure of psychological well-being.* Chicago: Aldine.

Bradley, V., & Knoll, J. (n.d.). *Shifting paradigms in services to people with developmental disabilities.* Cambridge, MA: Human Services Research Institute.

Bristol, M. M., & Schopler, E. (1984). A developmental perspective on stress and coping in families of autistic children. In J. Blacher (Ed.), *Severely handicapped children and their families: Research in review* (pp. 91-141). New York: Academic Press.

Brody, E. (1985). Parent care as a normative family stress. *The Gerontologist, 25,* 19-29.

Brody, E. (1990). *Women in the middle.* Newbury Park, CA: Sage.

Brody, G., & Stoneman, Z. (1986). Contextual issues in the study of sibling socialization. In J. J. Gallagher & P. M. Vietze (Eds.), *Families of handicapped persons: Research, programs, and policy issues* (pp. 197-218). Baltimore, MD: Paul H. Brookes.

Brody, R. (1974). *A comparative study of four public social service systems.* Ann Arbor: University of Michigan, Microfilms Limited.

Brolin, D. E. (1982). *Vocational preparation of persons with handicaps.* Columbus, OH: Charles E. Merrill.

Bromley, B. E., & Blacher, J. (1991). Parental reasons for out-of-home placement of children with severe handicaps. *Mental Retardation, 29,* 275-280.

Brubaker, T. H. (1990a). Continuity and change in later life families: Grandparenthood, couple relationships and family caregiving. *Gerontology Review, 3,* 24-40.

Brubaker, T. H. (1990b). A contextual approach to the development of stress associated with family caregiving in later life. In M. A. Stephens, J. L. Crowther, S. E. Holofill, & D. L. Tennenbaum (Eds.), *Stress and coping in later life* (pp. 29-47). Washington, DC: Hemisphere.

Brubaker, E., & Brubaker, T. H. (1992). The context of retired women as caregivers. In M. Szinovacz, B. J. Ekerdt, & B. H. Vinick (Eds.), *Families and retirement* (pp. 222-235). Newbury Park, CA: Sage.

Brubaker, T. H., Engelhardt, J. L., Brubaker, E., & Lutzer, V. (1989). Gender differences of older caregivers of adults with mental retardation. *The Journal of Applied Gerontology, 8,* 183-191.

Bruininks, R. H., Hill, B. K., Weatherman, R. F., & Woodcock, R. W. (1986). *Inventory for client and agency planning.* Allen, TX: DLM Teaching Resources.

Brunn, L. C. (1985). Elderly parent and dependent adult child. *Social Casework, 66,* 131-138.

Bullock, C. C., Bedini, L. A., & Driscoll, L. B. (1991). *The WAKE leisure education program: An integral part of special education.* Chapel Hill, NC: Center for Recreation and Disability Studies, Curriculum in Leisure Studies and Recreation Administration.

Cantor, M. (1983). Strain among caregivers: A study of experience in the United States. *The Gerontologist, 23,* 597-604.

Caragonne, P. (1984). Georgia Department of Human Resources Developmental Disabilities case management system evaluation. Austin, TX: Case Management Research.

Carswell, A. T., & Hartig, S. A. (1979). *Older developmentally disabled persons: An investigation of needs and social services.* Athens, GA: Georgia Retardation Center.

Carter, M. J., & Foret, C. (1991). Therapeutic programming for older adults with developmental disabilities. In M. J. Keller (Ed.), *Activities with developmentally disabled elderly and older adults* (pp. 35-52). New York: Haworth.

Caserta, M. S., Connelly, J. R., Lund, D. A., & Poulton, J. L. (1987). Older adult caregivers of developmentally disabled household members: Service needs and fulfillment. *Journal of Gerontological Social Work, 10,* 35-50.

Caserta, M. S., Lund, D. A., Wright, S., & Redburn, D. (1987). Caregivers to dementia patients: The utilization of community services. *The Gerontologist, 27,* 209-214.

Cattell, R. B. (1963). Theory for fluid and crystallized intelligence: A critical experiment. *Journal of Educational Psychology, 54,* 1-22.

Charron, F. (1992). Changing complex long-term care systems. *Generations, 16*(1), 97-99.

Cicirelli, V. (1985). The role of siblings as family caregivers. In W. Sauer & R. Coward (Eds.), *Social support networks and the care of the elderly: Theory, research, and practice* (pp. 93-107). New York: Springer.

Clegg, J. A., & Standen, P. J. (1991). Friendship among adults who have developmental disabilities. *American Journal on Mental Retardation, 95,* 663-671.

Cleveland, D., & Miller, N. (1977). Attitudes and life commitments of older siblings of mentally retarded adults: An exploratory study. *Mental Retardation, 15,* 38-41.

Cohen, D., & Eisdorfer, C. (1986). *The loss of self: A families resource for the care of Alzheimer's disease and related disorders.* New York: Norton.

Cole, D. A. (1986). Out-of-home child placement and family adaptation: A theoretical framework. *American Journal of Mental Deficiency, 91,* 226-236.

Cole, D. A., & Meyer, L. H. (1989). Impact of needs and resources on family plans to seek out-of-home placement. *American Journal on Mental Retardation, 93,* 380-387.

Corso, J. F. (1971). Sensory processes and age effects in normal adults. *Journal of Gerontology, 26,* 90-105.

Cox, W. M., & Wilson, W. L. (1985, March). *Developmentally disabled persons in family settings: Report no. 2.* Olympia: Washington State Department of Social and Health Services, Office of Research and Data Analysis. (ERIC Document Reproduction Services No. ED 266 615)

Coyne, A., Meade, H., Petrone, M., Meinert, L., & Joslin, L. (1990). The diagnosis of dementia: Demographic characteristics. *The Gerontologist, 30,* 339-344.

Craik, F. (1977). Age differences in human memory. In J. E. Birren & K. W. Schaie (Eds.), *Handbook of the psychology of aging* (pp. 384-420). New York: Van Nostrand Reinhold.

Crnic, K., Friedrich, W. N., & Greenberg, M. T. (1983). Adaptations of families with mentally retarded children: A model of stress, coping, and family ecology. *American Journal of Mental Deficiency, 88,* 345-351.

Crossman, L., Landon, C., & Barry, C. (1981). Older women caring for disabled spouses: A model for supportive services. *The Gerontologist, 21,* 464-470.

Dalton, A. J., & Crapper, D. R. (1977). Down's syndrome and aging of the brain. In P. Mittler (Ed.), *Research to practice in mental retardation: Vol. 3. Biomedical aspects* (pp. 391-400). Baltimore, MD: University Park Press.

Dalton, A. J., & Crapper, D. R. (1984). Incidence of memory deterioration in aging persons with Down's syndrome. In J. M. Berg (Ed.), *Perspectives and progress in mental retardation: Vol. 2. Biomedical aspects* (pp. 55-62). Baltimore, MD: University Park Press.

Dalton, A. J., Crapper, D. R., & Schlotterer, G. R. (1974). Alzheimer's disease in Down's syndrome: Visual retention deficits. *Cortex, 10,* 366-377.

Dalton, A. J., & Wisniewski, H. M. (1990). Down's syndrome and the dementia of Alzheimer's disease. *International Review of Psychiatry, 2,* 43-52.

Dattilo, J., & Schleien, S. J. (1991). *Consensus conference on the benefits of therapeutic recreation: A perspective on developmental disabilities.* Working paper. Philadelphia: Temple University.

Davis, S. (1987). *A national status report on waiting lists of people with mental retardation for community services.* Arlington, TX: Association for Retarded Citizens.

Day, A. (1985). *Who cares? Demographic trends challenge family care for the elderly.* Washington, DC: Population Reference Bureau.

Dean, W. (1988). *Biological aging measurement: Clinical application.* Thousand Oaks, CA: Center for Bio-Gerontology.

Dobrof, R. (1985). Some observations from the field of aging. In M. P. Janicki & H. M. Wisniewski (Eds.), *Aging and developmental disabilities: Issues and approaches* (pp. 411-415). Baltimore, MD: Paul H. Brookes.

Dunst, C. J., Trivette, C. M., & Cross, A. H. (1986). Mediating influences of social support: Personal, family, and child outcomes. *American Journal of Mental Deficiency, 90,* 403-417.

Dunst, C. J., Trivette, C. M., & Deal, A. (1988). *Enabling and empowering families: Principles and guidelines for practice.* Cambridge, MA: Brookline Publishing.

Edgerton, R. B. (1967). *The cloak of competence: Stigma in the lives of the mentally retarded.* Berkeley: University of California Press.

Edgerton, R. B., & Gaston, M. A. (1991). *"I've seen it all!": Lives of older persons with mental retardation in the community.* Baltimore, MD: Paul H. Brookes.

Eisner, D. A. (1983). Down's syndrome and aging: Is senile dementia inevitable? *Psychological Reports, 52,* 119-124.

Engelhardt, J., Brubaker, T., & Lutzer, V. (1987, November). *Older caregivers of adults with mental retardation: Service utilization.* Paper presented at the meeting of the American Gerontological Society, Washington, DC.

Engelhardt, J., Brubaker, T., & Lutzer, V. (1988). Older caregivers of adults with mental retardation: Service utilization. *Mental Retardation, 26,* 191-195.

Engelhardt, J., Lutzer, V., & Brubaker, T. (1987). Parents of adults with developmental disabilities: Age and reasons for reluctance to use another caregiver. *Lifestyles: A Journal of Changing Patterns, 8,* 47-54.

Epstein, C. (1983). Down syndrome and Alzheimer's disease: Implications and approaches. *Banbury Report, 15,* 169-182.

Evenhuis, H. (1990). The natural history of dementia in Down syndrome. *Archives of Neurology, 47,* 263-267.

Eyman, R. K., & Call, T. L. (1977). Maladaptive behavior and community placement of mentally retarded persons. *American Journal of Mental Deficiency, 82,* 137-144.

Eyman, R. K., Call, T. L., & White, J. F. (1991). Life expectancy of persons with Down syndrome. *American Journal on Mental Retardation, 95*(6), 603-612.

Factor, A., & Heller, T. (1992, March). *Elderly parents of children with mental retardation: Issues related to burden and placement urgency.* Paper presented at the 38th Annual Meeting of the American Society on Aging, San Diego, CA.

Falvey, M. A. (1989). *Community-based curriculum: Instructional strategies for students with severe handicaps* (2nd ed). Baltimore, MD: Paul H. Brookes.

Farber, B. (1959). Effects of a severely mentally retarded child on family integration. *Monographs of the Society for Research in Child Development, 24*(2, Serial No. 71).

Farber, B. (1986). Historical contexts of research on families with mentally retarded members. In J. J. Gallagher & P. M. Vietze (Eds.), *Families of handicapped persons: Research, programs, and policy issues* (pp. 3-23). Baltimore, MD: Paul H. Brookes.

Fenner, M. E., Hewitt, K. E., & Torpy, D. M. (1987). Down's syndrome: Intellectual and behavioral functioning during adulthood. *Journal of Mental Deficiency Research, 31,* 241-249.

Fisher, M. A., & Zeaman, D. (1970). Growth and decline of retardate intelligence. *International Review of Research in Mental Retardation, 4,* 151-191.

Fitting, M., Rabins, P., Lucas, M., & Eastham, J. (1986). Caregivers for dementia patients: A comparison of husbands and wives. *The Gerontologist, 26,* 248-252.

Flynt, S. W., & Wood, T. A. (1989). Stress and coping of mothers of children with moderate mental retardation. *American Journal on Mental Retardation, 94,* 278-283.

Folkman, S., Lazarus, R. J., Pimley, S., & Novacek, J. (1987). Age differences in stress and coping processes. *Psychology and Aging, 12,* 171-184.

Folstein, M., Folstein, S., & McHugh, R. (1975). Mini mental state: A practical method for grading the cognitive state of patients for the clinician. *Journal of Psychiatric Research, 12,* 189-198.

Friedrich, W. N., Cohen, D. S., & Wilturner, L. S. (1987). Family relations and marital quality when a handicapped child is present. *Psychological Reports, 61,* 911-919.

Fujiura, G. T., Garza, J., & Braddock, D. (1990). *National survey of family support services in developmental disabilities* (Mimeo). Chicago: University of Illinois.

Fullmer, E. M., Smith, G. C., & Tobin, S. S. (1991, November). *Elderly parent caregivers of mentally retarded adults: The "hidden."* Paper presented at the 44th Annual Scientific Meeting of the Gerontological Society of America, San Francisco, CA.

Gallagher, D., Wrabetz, A., Lovett, S., Maestro, S., & Rose, J. (1988). Depression and other negative affects in family caregivers. In E. Light & B. Lebowitz (Eds.), *Alzheimer's disease treatment and family stress: Directions for research* (pp. 218-244). Washington, DC: Government Printing Office.

General Accounting Office. (1977). *Returning the mentally disabled to the community: Government needs to do more* (HRD-76-152). Washington, DC: Government Printing Office.

George, L. K., & Bearon, L. C. (1980). *Quality of life in older persons: Meaning and measurement.* New York: Human Sciences Press.

George, L. K., & Gwyther, L. (1986). Caregiver well-being: A multidimensional examination of family caregivers of demented adults. *The Gerontologist, 26,* 253-259.

German, M. L., & Maisto, A. A. (1982). The relationship of perceived family support system to the institutional placement of mentally retarded children. *Education and Training of the Mentally Retarded, 17,* 17-23.

Gettings, R. M. (1992, September). *Creating a climate for systems change.* Paper presented at the Disability Conference and Technology Fair, Nashville, TN.

Gold, M., Dobrof, R., & Torian, L. (1987). *Parents of the adult developmentally disabled* (Final report presented to the United Hospital Trust Fund). New York: Brookdale Center on Aging.

Goodale, T. L. (1990). Perceived freedom as leisure's antithesis. *Journal of Leisure Research, 22*(4), 296-302.

Goodman, D. M. (1978). Parenting an adult mentally retarded offspring. *Smith College Studies in Social Work, 48,* 209-234.

Grant, G. (1986). Older carers, interdependence and care of mentally handicapped adults. *Aging and Society, 6,* 333-351.

Grant, G. (1990). Elderly parents with handicapped children: Anticipating the future. *Journal of Aging Studies, 4,* 359-374.

Gur, R. C., Mozley, P. D., Resnick, S. M., Gottlieb, G. L., Kohn, M., Zimmerman, R., Herman, G., Atlas, S., Grossman, R., Berretta, D., Erwin, R., & Gur, R. E. (1991). Gender differences in age effect on brain atrophy measured by magnetic resonance imaging. *Proceedings of the National Academy of Sciences, 88,* 2845-2849.

Guralnik, J., Branch, L. G., Cummings, S. R., & Curb, J. D. (1989). Physical performance measures in aging research. *Journal of Gerontology, 44,* M141-146.

Hanson, M. J., & Lynch, E. W. (1989). *Early intervention.* Austin, TX: Pro-Ed.

Hawkins, B. A. (1988). Leisure and recreational programming. In M. P. Janicki, M. W. Krauss, & M. M. Seltzer (Eds.), *Community residences for persons with developmental disabilities* (pp. 217-227). Baltimore, MD: Paul H. Brookes.

Hawkins, B. A., Eklund, S. J., & Martz, B. L. (1991). *Detection of decline in aging adults with developmental disabilities: Research report 1991.* Cincinnati, OH: Research and Training Center Consortium on Aging and Developmental Disabilities.

Heal, L. W., & Chadsey-Rusch, J. (1985). The Lifestyle Satisfaction Scale (LSS): Assessing individuals' satisfaction with residence, community setting and associated services. *Applied Research in Mental Retardation, 6,* 475-490.

Heller, T., & Factor, A. (1987, November). *Elderly parents caring for disabled adult offspring: Issues in permanency planning.* Paper presented at the 40th Annual Scientific Meeting of the Gerontological Society of America, Washington, DC.

Heller, T., & Factor, A. (1988a). Permanency planning among black and white family caregivers of older adults with mental retardation. *Mental Retardation, 96,* 203-208.

Heller, T., & Factor, A. (1988b). *Transition plan for older developmentally disabled persons residing in the natural home with family caregivers.* Public Policy Monograph Series. Chicago: University of Illinois Press.

Heller, T., & Factor, A. (1990, May). *Quality of life of older adults with developmental disabilities living with their parents.* Paper presented at the 114th Annual Meeting of the American Association on Mental Retardation, Atlanta, GA.

Heller, T., & Factor, A. (1991). Permanency planning for adults with mental retardation living with family caregivers. *American Journal on Mental Retardation, 96,* 163-176.

Heller, T., & Factor, A. (in press). Aging family caregivers: Changes in burden and placement desire. *American Journal on Mental Retardation.*

Heller, T., Rowitz, L., & Farber, B. (1992). *The domestic cycle of families of persons with mental retardation.* Chicago: University of Illinois Affiliated Program in Developmental Disabilities and School of Public Health.

Hess, B., & Soldo, B. (1985). Husband and wife networks. In W. Sauer & R. Coward (Eds.), *Social support networks and the care of the elderly* (pp. 67-92). New York: Springer.

Hewitt, K. E., & Jancar, J. (1986). Psychological and clinical aspects of aging in Down's syndrome. In J. M. Berg (Ed.), *Science and service in mental retardation* (pp. 370-379). London: Methuen.

Hill, J. W., Seyfarth, J., Banks, P. D., Wehman, P., & Orelove, F. (1987). Parental attitudes about working conditions of their adult mentally retarded sons and daughters. *Exceptional Children, 54,* 9-23.

Hill, R. (1949). *Families under stress.* New York: Harper & Row.

Hill, R. (1958). Generic features of families under stress. *Social Casework, 39,* 139-150.

Hirst, M. (1985). Dependency and family care of young adults with disabilities. *Child: Care, Health and Development, 2,* 241-257.

Hogg, J., Moss, S., & Cooke, D. (1988). *Aging and mental handicap.* London: Croom Helm.

Hollingsworth, J. W., Hashizume, A., & Jablon, S. (1966). Correlations between tests of aging in Hiroshima subjects: An attempt to define "physiologic age." *Yale Journal of Biology and Medicine, 38,* 11-26.

Holroyd, J., Brown, N., Wikler, L., & Simmons, J. Q. (1975). Stress in families in institutionalized autistic children. *Journal of Community Psychology, 3,* 26-31.

Horn, J. L. (1970). Organization of data on life-span development of human abilities. In L. R. Goulet & P. B. Baltes (Eds.), *Life-span developmental psychology: Research and theory* (pp. 423-466). New York: Academic Press.

Horn, J. L. (1972). State, trait and change dimensions of intelligence. *British Journal of Educational Psychology, 42,* 159-185.

Horn, J. L. (1976). Human abilities: A review of research and theory in the early 1970s. *Annual Review of Psychology, 27,* 437-485.

Horn, J. L. (1985). Remodeling old models of intelligence. In B. B. Wolman (Ed.), *Handbook of intelligence* (pp. 267-300). New York: John Wiley.

Horn, J. L. (1986). Some thoughts about intelligence. In R. J. Sternberg & D. K. Detterman (Eds.), *What is intelligence? Contemporary viewpoints on its nature and definition* (pp. 91-96). Norwood, NJ: Ablex.

Horn, J. L. (1988). Cognitive diversity: A framework for learning. In P. L. Ackerman, R. J. Sternberg, & R. Glazer (Eds.), *Learning and individual differences.* New York: Freeman.

Horn, J. L., & Cattell, R. B. (1966). Refinement and test of the theory of fluid and crystallized intelligence. *Journal of Educational Psychology, 57,* 253-270.

Horowitz, A. (1985). Family caregiving to the frail elderly. *Annual Review of Gerontology and Geriatrics, 5,* 194-246.

Houghton, J., Bronicki, G., & Guess, D. (1987). Opportunities to express preferences and make choices among students with severe disabilities in classroom settings. *Journal of the Association for Persons with Severe Handicaps, 12*(1), 18-27.

Hoyert, D., & Seltzer, M. (1992). Factors related to the well-being and life activities of family caregivers. *Family Relations, 41,* 74-81.

Intagliata, J. (1992). Improving the quality of community care for the chronically mentally disabled: The role of case management. In S. M. Rose (Ed.), *Case management and social work practice* (pp. 25-55). New York: Longman.

Intagliata, J. (1981). Operationalizing a case management system: A multilevel approach. In *National Conference on Social Welfare: Final report. Case management: State of the art* (Grant No. 54-p-71542/3-01). Submitted to U.S. Department of Health and Human Services, Administration on Developmental Disabilities.

Iso-Ahola, S. (1980). *The social psychology of leisure and recreation.* Dubuque, IA: William C. Brown.

Jacobson, J., Sutton, M., & Janicki, M. P. (1985). Demography and characteristics of aging and aged mentally retarded persons. In M. P. Janicki & H. M. Wisniewski (Eds.), *Aging and developmental disabilities: Issues and approaches* (pp. 115-142). Baltimore, MD: Paul H. Brookes.

Janicki, M. P. (1991). *Building the future: Planning and community development in aging and developmental disabilities.* Albany: New York State Office of Mental Retardation and Developmental Disabilities.

Janicki, M. P., & Dalton, A. J. (1992, November). *Alzheimer's disease among a population of adults with mental retardation.* Paper presented at the annual meeting of the Gerontological Society of America, Washington, DC.

Janicki, M. P., & Jacobson, J. W. (1986). Generational trends in sensory, physical, and behavioral abilities among older mentally retarded persons. *American Journal of Mental Deficiency, 90,* 490-500.

Janicki, M. P., & MacEachron, A. (1984). Residential, health, and social service needs of elderly developmentally disabled persons. *The Gerontologist, 24,* 128-137.

Janicki, M. P., Otis, J. P., Puccio, P. S., Rettig, J. S., & Jacobson, J. W. (1985). Service needs among older developmentally disabled persons. In M. P. Janicki & H. M. Wisniewski (Eds.), *Aging and developmental disabilities: Issues and approaches* (pp. 289-304). Baltimore, MD: Paul H. Brookes.

Janicki, M. P., & Seltzer, M. M. (Eds.). (1991). *Aging and developmental disabilities: Challenges for the 1990s* (The proceeding of the Boston Round Table on Research Issues and Applications in Aging and Developmental Disabilities). Washington, DC: American Association on Mental Retardation, Special Interest Group on Aging.

Janicki, M. P., & Wisniewski, H. M. (Eds.). (1985). *Aging and developmental disabilities: Issues and approaches.* Baltimore, MD: Paul H. Brookes.

Jennings, J. (1987). Elderly parents as caregivers for their adult dependent children. *Social Work, 32,* 430-433.

Johnson, C. (1983). Dyadic family relations and social support. *The Gerontologist, 23,* 377-383.

Johnson, C., & Catalano, D. (1983). A longitudinal study of family supports to impaired elderly. *The Gerontologist, 23,* 612-618.

Johnson, D. R., Bruininks, R. H., & Thurlow, M. L. (1987). Meeting the challenge of transition service planning through improved interagency cooperation. *Exceptional Children, 53,* 522-530.

Kaplan, E., Goodglass, H., & Weintraub, S. (1983). *Boston Naming Test.* Philadelphia: Lea & Febiger.

Katz, S., Ford, A., Moskowitz, R., Jackson, B., & Jaffe, M. (1963). Studies of illness in the aged. The index of Alzheimer's disease: A standardized measure of biological and psychological function. *Journal of the American Medical Association, 185,* 94ff.

Kaufman, A. V., Adams, J. P., & Campbell, V. A. (1991). Permanency planning by older parents who care for adult children with mental retardation. *Mental Retardation, 29,* 293-300.

Kaufman, A. V., DeWeaver, K., & Glicken, M. (1989). The mentally retarded aged: Implications for social work practice. *Journal of Gerontological Social Work, 14,* 93-110.

Kaufman, J. M., & Payne, J. S. (1975). *Mental retardation: Introduction and personal perspectives.* Columbus, OH: Charles E. Merrill.

Kaye, L., & Applegate, J. (1990). *Men as caregivers to the elderly: Understanding and aiding unrecognized family support.* Lexington, MA: Lexington Books.

Kelly, C., & Gemeinhardt, E. (1992). Public attitudes on health care reform. *Statistical Bulletin, 23*(4), 2-10.

Kleban, M., Brody, E., Shoonover, C., & Hoffman, C. (1989). Family help to the elderly: Perceptions of sons-in-law regarding parent care. *Journal of Marriage and the Family, 51,* 303-312.

Krauss, M. W. (1990, May). *Later life placements: Precipitating factors and family profiles.* Paper presented at the 114th Annual Meeting of the American Association on Mental Retardation, Atlanta, GA.

Krauss, M. W., Seltzer, M. M., & Goodman, S. J. (1992). Social support network of adults with mental retardation who live at home. *American Journal on Mental Retardation, 96,* 432-441.

Krout, J. (1985). Relationships between informal and formal organizational networks. In W. Sauer & R. Coward (Eds.), *Social support networks and the care of the elderly* (pp. 178-195). New York: Springer.

Krout, J. (1986). *The aged in rural America.* Westport, CT: Greenwood.

Kultgen, P., Rinck, C., Calkins, C., & Intagliata, J. (1986). *Expanding the life chances and social support networks of elderly developmentally disabled adults.* Kansas City: University of Missouri, Institute for Human Development.

Kunkel, S., & Applebaum, R. (1992). Estimating the prevalence of long-term disability for an aging society. *Journal of Gerontology: Social Sciences, 47,* S252-S260.

Labouvie-Vief, G. (1985). Intelligence and cognition. In J. E. Birren & K. W. Schaie (Eds.), *Handbook of the psychology of aging* (2nd ed.) (pp. 500-530). New York: Van Nostrand Reinhold.

Lakin, K. C., Hill, B. K., Chen, T. H., & Stephens, S. A. (1989). *Persons with mental retardation and related conditions in mental retardation facilities: Selected findings from the 1987 National Medicaid Expenditures Survey.* Minneapolis: University of Minnesota, Center for Residential and Community Services.

Lang, A., & Brody, E. (1983). Characteristics of middle-aged daughters and help to their elderly mothers. *Journal of Marriage and the Family, 45,* 193-202.

LaPlante, M., Hendershot, G., & Moss, A. (1992). Assistive technology devices and home accessibility features: Prevalence, payment, need, and trends. *Advanced Data from Vital and Health Statistics,* #217. Hyattsville, MD: National Center for Health Statistics.

Lawton, M. P. (1975). The Philadelphia Geriatric Center Morale Scale: A revision. *Journal of Gerontology, 30,* 85-59.

Lawton, M. P., Moss, M., Kleban, M. H., Glicksman, A., & Rovine, M. (1991). A two-factor model of caregiving appraisal and psychological well-being. *Journal of Gerontology, 46,* P181-P189.

Lawton, M. P., Moss, M., & Fulcomer, M. (1986-1987). Objective and subjective uses of time by older people. *International Journal of Aging and Human Development, 24*(3), 171-187.

Lazarus, R., & Delongis, A. (1983). Psychological stress and coping in aging. *American Psychologist, 38,* 245-254.

Lazarus, R., & Folkman, S. (1984). *Stress, appraisal, and coping.* New York: Springer.

LePore, K., & Janicki, M. P. (1990). *The wit to win.* Albany: New York State Office for the Aging.

Litwak, E. (1985). *Helping the elderly: The complimentary roles of informal networks and formal systems.* New York: Guilford.

Lobato, D. (1983). Siblings of handicapped children: A review. *Journal of Autism and Developmental Disorders, 13,* 347-364.

Lott, I. T. (1982). Down's syndrome, aging, and Alzheimer's disease: A clinical review. *Annals of the New York Academy of Sciences, 396,* 15-27.

Lott, I. T., & Lai, F. (1982). Dementia in Down's syndrome: Observations from a neurology clinic. *Applied Research in Mental Retardation, 3,* 233-239.

Ludwig, F. C., & Masoro, E. J. (1983). The measurement of biological age. *Experimental Aging Research, 9*(4), 219-220.

Lutzer, V. D., & Brubaker, T. H. (1988). Differential respite needs of aging parents of individuals with mental retardation. *Mental Retardation, 26,* 13-15.

Mace, N., & Rabins, P. (1991). *The thirty-six hour day.* Baltimore, MD: Johns Hopkins University Press.

Mahon, M. J., & Bullock, C. C. (1992). Teaching adolescents with mild mental retardation to make decisions in leisure through use of self-control techniques. *Therapeutic Recreation Journal, 26*(1), 9-26.

Mann, D. (1988). Alzheimer's disease and Down syndrome. *Histopathology, 13,* 125-137.

Maverick Corporation. (1976). *The community life association.* Cited in McAnally & Linz (1988).

McCubbin, H. I., & Thompson, A. I. (Eds.). (1987). *Family assessment inventories for research and practice.* Madison: University of Wisconsin, Family Stress Coping and Health Project.

McDade, H. L., & Adler, S. (1980). Down's syndrome and short-term memory impairment: A storage or retrieval deficit? *American Journal of Mental Deficiency, 84,* 561-567.

McGuire, F. A. (1979). *An exploratory study of leisure constraints in advanced adulthood.* Unpublished doctoral dissertation, University of Illinois-Champaign.

McGuire, F. A. (1984). A factor analytic study of leisure constraints in advanced adulthood. *Leisure Sciences, 6,* 313-326.

McHale, S., & Gamble, W. (1987). Sibling relationships and adjustment of children with disabled brothers and sisters. In F. Schacter & R. Stone (Eds.), *Practical concerns about siblings: Bridging the research-practice gap* (pp. 131-158). New York: Haworth.

McKechnie, G. E. (1975). *Manual for the leisure activities blank.* Palo Alto, CA: Consulting Psychology Press.

Meiners, M., McKay, H., & Helfand, L. (1992). *National directory of service credit banking programs.* College Park, MD: University of Maryland Center on Aging.

Meyers, C. E., Borthwick, S. A., & Eyman, R. (1985). Place of residence by age, ethnicity, and level of retardation of the mentally retarded/developmentally disabled population of California. *American Journal of Mental Deficiency, 90,* 266-270.

Miniszek, N. (1983). Development of Alzheimer's disease in Down syndrome individuals. *Journal of Mental Deficiency, 87,* 377-385.

Mints, A. Y., Dubina, T. L., Lysenyk, V. P., & Zhuk, E. V. (1984). Defining the biological age of an individual and an appraisal of the degree of aging. *Physiologichiski Zhurnal, 30*(1), 39-45.

Montgomery, R., Gonyea, J., & Hooyman, N. (1985). Caregiving and the experience of subjective and objective burden. *Family Relations, 34,* 19-26.

Moody, H. R. (1992). *Ethics in an aging society.* Baltimore, MD: Johns Hopkins University Press.

Motenko, A. (1988). Respite care and pride in caregiving: The experience of six older men caring for their disabled wives. In S. Reinharz & G. Rowles (Eds.), *Qualitative gerontology* (pp. 104-127). New York: Springer.

Motenko, A. (1989). The frustrations, gratifications, and well-being of dementia caregivers. *The Gerontologist, 29,* 166-172.

Neulinger, J. (1974). *The psychology of leisure.* New York: Charles C Thomas.

New York State Office of Mental Retardation and Developmental Disabilities. (1987). *Program alternatives for frail elderly and medically fragile.* Albany, NY: Author.

Nisbet, J., & Callahan, M. (1987). Achieving success in integrated workplaces. In S. J. Taylor, D. Biklen, & J. Knoll (Eds.), *Community integration for people with severe disabilities* (pp. 184-201). New York: Teachers College Press.

Noelker, L., & Bass, D. (1989). Home care for elderly persons: Linkages between formal and informal caregivers. *Journal of Gerontology: Social Sciences, 44,* S63-S70.

O'Brien, G. E. (1981). Leisure attributes and retirement satisfaction. *Journal of Applied Psychology, 66*(3), 371-384.

O'Bryant, S. (1988). Sibling support and older widows' well-being. *Journal of Marriage and the Family, 50,* 173-183.

Olson, D. H., & McCubbin, H. I. (1983). *Families: What makes them work.* Beverly Hills, CA: Sage.

Orr, R. R., Cameron, S. J., & Day, D. M. (1991). Coping with stress in families with children who have mental retardation: An evaluation of the double ABCX model. *American Journal of Mental Retardation, 95,* 444-450.

Perlin, L., Lieberman, M., Menaghan, M., & Mullan, J. (1981). The stress process. *Journal of Health and Social Behavior, 22,* 337-356.

Perlman, R. (1975). *Consumers and social services.* New York: John Wiley.

Perlmutter, M. (1986). A life-span view of memory. In P. B. Baltes, D. L. Featherman, & R. M. Lerner (Eds.), *Life span development and behavior,* Vol. 7 (pp. 272-308). Hillsdale, NJ: Lawrence Erlbaum.

Perlmutter, M. (1988). Cognitive potential throughout life. In J. E. Birren & V. Bengston (Eds.), *Emergent theories of aging* (pp. 247-268). New York: Springer.

Perlmutter, M., & Nyquist, L. (1989). Relationships between self-reported physical and mental health and intelligence performances across adulthood. *Journal of Gerontology, 44,* P145-P155.

Poulshock, S. W., & Deimling, G. T. (1984). Families caring for elders in residence: Issues in the measurement of burden. *Journal of Gerontology, 39,* 230-239.

President's Panel on Mental Retardation. (1962). *National action to combat mental retardation.* Washington, DC: Government Printing Office.

Price, D., Whitehouse, P., Struble, R., Coyle, J., Clark, A., Delong, M., Cork, L., & Hedreen, J. (1982). Alzheimer's disease and Down syndrome. *Annals of the New York Academy of Sciences,* 145-162.

Quayhagen, M., & Quayhagen, M. (1988). Alzheimer's stress: Coping with the caregiving role. *The Gerontologist, 28,* 391-396.

Radliff, L. S. (1977). The CES-D Scale: A self-report depression scale for research in the general population. *Applied Psychological Measurement, 1,* 385-401.

Rando, T. A. (1986). *Loss and anticipatory grief.* Lexington, MA: D. C. Heath.

Ray, R. O., & Heppe, G. (1986). Older adult happiness: The contributions of activity breadth and intensity. *Physical and Occupational Therapy in Geriatrics, 4*(4), 31-43.

Reece, D., Walz, T., & Hageboeck, H. (1983). Intergenerational care providers of non-institutionalized frail elderly: Characteristics and consequences. *Journal of Gerontological Social Work, 5,* 21-34.

Riddick, C. A., & Daniel, S. N. (1984). The relative contribution of leisure activities and other factors to the mental health of older women. *Journal of Leisure Research, 16*(2), 136-148.

Rinck, C. (1989). *Level of satisfaction with the Missouri Division of MR/DD case management system: Section I. Family perceptions.* Kansas City, MO: Institute for Human Development.

Rinck, C. (1990). *Needs assessment of St. Louis: Association for Retarded Citizens.* St. Louis, MO: St. Louis Association for Retarded Citizens.

Rinck, C., Eddy, B., Lund, I., & Griggs, P. (1990). *First steps evaluation.* Kansas City: University of Missouri, Institute for Human Development.

Rinck, C., Eddy, B., & Torner, R. (1991). *Independent assessment of the Medicaid Waiver system.* Kansas City: University of Missouri, Institute for Human Development.

Rinck, C., Tintinger, J., & Denman, N. (1990). *Level of satisfaction with the Missouri Division of MR/DD case management system: Section II. Consumer perceptions.* Kansas City, MO: Institute for Human Development.

Roccoforte, J. A. (1991). *Stress, financial burden and coping resources in families providing home care for adults with developmental disabilities.* Unpublished master's thesis, University of Illinois, Chicago.

Rose, T., & Ansello, E. (1987). *Aging and developmental disabilities: Research and planning* (Final report to the Maryland State Planning Council on Developmental Disabilities). College Park: University of Maryland Center on Aging.

Rose, T., & Janicki, M. P. (1986, September/October). Older developmentally disabled adults: A forgotten population (parts 1 & 2). *Aging Network News, 3,* 5-6.

Rosenberg, M., & Brody, R. (1974). *Systems serving people.* Cleveland, OH: Case Western Reserve.

Salthouse, T. (1982). Psychomotor indices of physiological age. In M. E. Reff & E. L. Schneider (Eds.), *Biological markers of aging.* Bethesda, MD: U.S. Department of Health and Human Services, National Institutes of Health, and Public Health Service. Document #82-2221.

Sample, P., Spencer, K., & Bean, G. (1990). *Transition planning: Creating a positive future for students with disabilities.* Fort Collins: Colorado State University, Department of Occupational Therapy, Office of Transition Services.

Schweber, M. (1989). Alzheimer's disease and Down syndrome. *Alzheimer's Disease and Related Disorders, 4,* 247-267.

Scott, J. (1990). Sibling interaction in later life. In T. Brubaker (Ed.), *Family relationships in later life* (2nd ed.) (pp. 86-99). Newbury Park, CA: Sage.

Scott, J., Roberto, K., Hutton, J. T., & Slack, D. (1985). Family conflicts in caring for the Alzheimer's patient. In J. T. Hutton & A. D. Kenny (Eds.), *Senile dementia of the Alzheimer type* (pp. 77-86). New York: Alan R. Liss.

Seltzer, G. B., Begun, A. L., Magan, R., & Luchterhand, C. (1993). Social supports and expectations of family involvement after out of home placements. In E. Sutton, T. Heller, A. R. Factor, B. A. Hawkins, T. Heller, & G. B. Seltzer (Eds.), *Older persons with developmental disabilities: Contemporary perspectives* (pp. 123-140). Baltimore, MD: Paul H. Brookes.

Seltzer, G. B., Begun, A. L., Seltzer, M. M., & Krauss, M. W. (1991). Adults with mental retardation and their aging mothers: Impacts on siblings. *Family Relations, 40,* 310-317.

Seltzer, M. M. (1985). Informal supports for aging mentally retarded persons. *American Journal of Mental Deficiency, 90,* 259-265.

Seltzer, M. M. (1991a, November). *Age-related differences in the impact of lifelong caregiving on middle-aged and older mothers.* Paper presented at the meeting of the Gerontological Society of America, San Francisco, CA.

Seltzer, M. M. (1991b, May). *Families as caregivers: Age-related differences in family characteristics and material well-being.* Paper presented at the annual meeting of the American Association on Mental Retardation, Crystal City, VA.

Seltzer, M. M. (1992). Training families to be case managers for elders with developmental disabilities. *Generations, 16* (1), 65-70.

Seltzer, M. M., & Krauss, M. W. (1984). Placement alternatives for mentally retarded children and their families. In J. Blacher (Ed.), *Severely handicapped children and their families: Research in review* (pp. 143-175). New York: Academic Press.

Seltzer, M. M., & Krauss, M. W. (1987). *Aging and mental retardation: Extending the continuum.* Washington, DC: American Association on Mental Retardation.

Seltzer, M. M., & Krauss, M. W. (1989). Aging parents with mentally retarded children: Family risk factors and sources of support. *American Journal on Mental Retardation, 94,* 303-312.

Seltzer, M. M., Krauss, M. W., & Heller, T. (1991). Family caregiving over the life course. In M. P. Janicki & M. M. Seltzer (Eds.), *Aging and developmental disabilities: Challenges for the 1990s* (pp. 3-24). Washington, DC: American Association on Mental Retardation, Special Interest Group on Aging.

Seltzer, M. M., & Seltzer, G. B. (1985). The elderly mentally retarded: A group in need of service. *Journal of Gerontological Social Work, 8,* 99-118.

Seyfarth, J., Hill, J. W., Orelove, F., McMillan, J., & Wehman, P. (1985). Factors influencing parents' vocational aspirations for their retarded children. In P. Wehman & J. W. Hill (Eds.), *Parent involvement* (pp. 316-331). Richmond: Virginia Commonwealth University, Rehabilitation Research and Training Center. (ERIC Document Reproduction Services No. ED 259 526)

Sherman, B. R. (1988). Predictors of the decision to place developmentally disabled family members in residential care. *American Journal on Mental Retardation, 92,* 344-351.

Sherman, B. R., & Cocozza, J. J. (1984). Stress in families of the developmentally disabled: A literature review of factors affecting the decision to seek out-of-home placements. *Family Relations, 33,* 95-103.

Shevin, M., & Klein, N. (1984). The importance of choice-making skills for students with severe disabilities. *Journal of the Association for Persons with Severe Handicaps, 9,* 159-166.

Shock, N. W. (1981). Indices of functional age. In D. Danon, N. W. Shock, & M. Marois (Eds.), *Aging: A challenge to science and society: Vol. 1. Biology* (pp. 270-286). New York: Oxford University Press.

Shock, N. W., Greulich, R. C., Costa, P. T., Andres, R., Lakatta, E. G., Arenberg, D., & Tobin, J. D. (1984). *Normal human aging: The Baltimore longitudinal study of aging* (NIH Publication No. 84-2450). Washington, DC: Government Printing Office.

Sigelman, C. K., Schoenrock, C. J., Budd, E. C., Winer, J. L., Spanhel, C. L., Martin, P. W., Hronmas, S., & Bensberg, G. J. (1983). *Communicating with mentally retarded persons: Asking questions and getting answers.* Lubbock: Texas Tech University, Research and Training Center in Mental Retardation.

Silliman, R., & Sternberg, J. (1988). Family caregiving: Impact of patient functioning and underlying causes of dependency. *The Gerontologist, 28,* 377-382.

Simeonsson, R., & Bailey, D. (1986). Siblings of handicapped children. In J. J. Gallagher & P. M. Vietze (Eds.), *Families of handicapped persons: Research, programs, and policy issues* (pp. 67-80). Baltimore, MD: Paul H. Brookes.

Singer, G. H., & Irvin, L. K. (1989). Family caregiving, stress, and support. In G. H. Singer & L. K. Irvin (Eds.), *Support for caregiving families* (pp. 3-25). Baltimore, MD: Paul H. Brookes.

Singer, G. H., & Irvin, L. K. (1991). Supporting families of persons with severe disabilities. In L. H. Meyer, C. A. Peck, & L. Brown (Eds.), *Critical issues in the lives of people with severe disabilities* (pp. 271-312). Baltimore, MD: Paul H. Brookes.

Sison, G., & Cotten, P. D. (1989). The elderly mentally retarded person: Current perspectives and future directions. *The Journal of Applied Gerontology, 8,* 151-167.

Smith, G. C., & Tobin, S. S. (1989). Permanency planning among older parents of adults with lifelong disabilities. *Journal of Gerontological Social Work, 14,* 35-59.

Smith, N. R., Kielhofner, G., & Watts, J. H. (1986). The relationship between volition, activity pattern, and life satisfaction in the elderly. *The American Journal of Occupational Therapy, 40*(4), 278-283.

Sneegas, J. J. (1986). Components of life satisfaction in middle and later life adults: Perceived social competence, leisure participation, and leisure satisfaction. *Journal of Leisure Research, 18*(4), 248-258.

Sowers, J. (1989). Critical parent roles in supported employment. In G. H. Singer & L. K. Irvin (Eds.), *Support for caregiving families* (pp. 269-282). Baltimore, MD: Paul H. Brookes.

Springer, D., & Brubaker, T. (1984). *Family caregivers and dependent elderly: Minimizing stress and maximizing independence.* Beverly Hills, CA: Sage.

Stainback, W., & Stainback, S. (1990). *Support networks for inclusive schooling.* Baltimore, MD: Paul H. Brookes.

Stephens, M., Kinney, J., & Ogrocki, P. (1991). Stress and well-being among caregivers to older adults with dementia: The in-home versus nursing home experience. *The Gerontologist, 31,* 217-223.

Stinson, C. (1989). Roles for computers in geriatric health care. *International Journal of Technology and Aging, 2*(1), 77-93.

Stoller, E. (1990). Males as helpers: The role of sons, relatives, and friends. *The Gerontologist, 30,* 228-235.

Stone, J. (1992, September). *Interagency planning for older persons with developmental disabilities: A vision of equal partnership.* Paper presented at the 2nd Lexington Conference on Aging and Developmental Disabilities, Lexington, KY.

Stone, R., Cafferata, G., & Sangl, J. (1987). Caregivers of the frail elderly: A national profile. *The Gerontologist, 27,* 616-626.

Stroud, M., & Sutton, E. (1988). *Expanding options for older adults with developmental disabilities: A practical guide to achieving community access.* Baltimore, MD: Paul H. Brookes.

Sudman, S., & Bradburn, N. M. (1974). *Response effects in surveys: A review and synthesis.* Chicago: Aldine.

Suelzle, M., & Keenan, V. (1981). Changes in family support networks over the life cycle of mentally retarded persons. *American Journal of Mental Deficiency, 3,* 267-274.

Suggs, P. (1985). Discriminators of mutual helping behaviors among older adults and their siblings. *Journal of Applied Gerontology, 4,* 63-70.

Summers, J. A., Behr, S. K., & Turnbull, A. P. (1989). Positive adaptation and coping strengths of families who have children with disabilities. In G. H. Singer & L. K. Irvin (Eds.), *Support for caregiving families* (pp. 27-40). Baltimore, MD: Paul H. Brookes.

Sutton, E., Sterns, H., Schwartz, L., & Roberts, R. (1992). The training of a specialist in developmental disabilities and aging. *Generations, 16*(1), 71-74.

Tausig, M. (1985). Factors in family decision making about placement for developmentally disabled individuals. *American Journal of Mental Deficiency, 89,* 352-361.

Taylor, S. J. (1987). Continuum traps. In S. J. Taylor, D. Biklen, & J. Knoll (Eds.), *Community integration for people with severe disabilities* (pp. 25-36). New York: Teachers College Press.

Taylor, S. J., Knoll, J. A., Lehr, S., & Walker, P. M. (1989). Families for all children: Value-based services for children with disabilities and their families. In G. H. Singer & L. K. Irvin (Eds.), *Support for caregiving families* (pp. 41-54). Baltimore, MD: Paul H. Brookes.

Taylor, S. J., Racino, J., Knoll, J. A., & Lutfiyya, Z. (1987). Down home: Community integration for people with the most severe disabilities. In S. J. Taylor, D. Biklen, & J. Knoll (Eds.), *Community integration for people with severe disabilities* (pp. 36-63). New York: Teachers College Press.

Telleen, S. (1985). *Parenting social support reliability and validity.* Chicago: University of Illinois, School of Public Health.

Test, M. (1979). Continuity of care in community treatment. In L. Stein (Ed.), *Community support systems for the long-term patient* (pp. 15-23). San Francisco: Jossey-Bass.

Tingey, C. (1989). *Implementing early intervention.* Baltimore, MD: Paul H. Brookes.

Tinsley, H., Teaff, J. D., Colbs, S. L., & Kaufman, N. (1985). A system of classifying leisure activities in terms of the psychological benefits of participation reported by older adults. *Journal of Gerontology, 40,* 172-178.

Townsend, A., Noelker, L., Deimling, G., & Bass, D. (1989). Longitudinal impact of interhousehold caregiving on adult children's mental health. *Psychology and Aging, 4,* 393-401.

Turnbull, H. R., Turnbull, A. P., Bronicki, G. J., Summers, J. A., & Roeder-Gordon, C. (1989). *Disability and the family: A guide to decisions for adulthood.* Baltimore, MD: Paul H. Brookes.

Waisbren, S. (1980). Parent reactions after the birth of a developmentally disabled child. *American Journal of Mental Deficiency, 34,* 345-351.

Walker, A. J. (1985). Reconceptualizing family stress. *Journal of Marriage and the Family, 47,* 827-837.

Wallace, S. (1990). The no-care zone: Availability, accessibility, and acceptability in community-based long-term care. *The Gerontologist, 30,* 254-261.

Waltz, T., Harper, D., & Wilson, J. (1986). The aging developmentally disabled person. *The Gerontologist, 26,* 622-629.

Warren, F., & Warren, S. H. (1989). The role of parents in creating and maintaining quality family support services. In G. H. Singer & L. K. Irvin (Eds.), *Support for caregiving families* (pp. 55-68). Baltimore, MD: Paul H. Brookes.

Wehman, P., Kregel, J., & Barcus, J. M. (1985). From school to work: A vocational transition model for handicapped students. *Exceptional Children, 52,* 25-37.

Wehman, P., Moon, M. S., Everson, J. M., Wood, W., & Barcus, J. M. (1988). *Transition from school to work.* Baltimore, MD: Paul H. Brookes.

Weil, M. (1985a). Historical origins and recent developments. In M. Weil & J. Karls (Eds.), *Case management in human service practice* (pp. 1-28). San Francisco: Jossey-Bass.

Weil, M. (1985b). Key components in providing efficient and effective services. In M. Weil & J. Karls (Eds.), *Case management in human service practice* (pp. 29-71). San Francisco: Jossey-Bass.

Wikler, L. (1986). Family stress theory and research on families of children with mental retardation. In J. J. Gallagher & P. M. Vietze (Eds.), *Families of handicapped persons: Research, programs, and policy issues* (pp. 167-195). Baltimore, MD: Paul H. Brookes.

Will, M. (1984). *Bridges from school to working life: Programs for the handicapped.* Washington, DC: U.S. Department of Education, Office of Information and Resources for the Handicapped.

Willer, B., & Intagliata, J. (1984). *Promises and realities for mentally retarded citizens: Life in the community.* Baltimore, MD: University Park Press.

Wisniewski, K., Dalton, A., McLachlan, C., Wen, G., & Wisniewski, H. M. (1985). Alzheimer's disease in Down syndrome: Clinicopathological studies. *Neurology, 35,* 957-961.

Wisniewski, K., Howe, J., Williams, D. G., & Wisniewski, H. M. (1978). Precocious aging and dementia in patients with Down's syndrome. *Biological Psychiatry, 13*(5), 619-627.

Witt, P. A., & Ellis, G. D. (1987). *The leisure diagnostic battery users manual.* State College, PA: Venture.

Wood, J. B. (1991). *The aged and aging developmentally disabled in Virginia: Project report.* Richmond: Virginia Department for the Aging and Virginia Institute for Developmental Disabilities.

Wood, J. B., Ansello, E., Coogle, C., & Cotter, J. (1992, November). *Service for older adults with developmental disabilities: Policy analysis and development.* Paper presented at the annual meeting of the Gerontological Society of America, Washington, DC.

Wood, J. B., & Skiles, L. L. (1992). Planning for the transfer of care. *Generations, 16*(1), 61-62.

Wood, V., Wylie, M., & Sheafer, B. (1969). An analysis of a short self-report measure of life satisfaction: Correlation with rater judgement. *Journal of Gerontology, 24,* 465-469.

Woodcock, R. W., & Johnson, M. B. (1989). *Woodcock-Johnson Psycho-Educational Battery—Revised.* Allen, TX: DLM Teaching Resources.

Woodcock, R. W., & Mather, N. (1989). WJ-R Tests of Cognitive Ability—Standard and supplemental batteries: Examiner's manual. In R. W. Woodcock & M. B. Johnson, *Woodcock-Johnson Psycho-Educational Battery—Revised.* Allen, TX: DLM Teaching Resources.

Young, E. C., & Kramer, B. M. (1991). Characteristics of age-related language decline in adults with Down syndrome. *Mental Retardation, 29*(2), 75 79.

Young, R., & Kahana, E. (1989). Specifying caregiver outcomes: Gender and relationship aspects of caregiving strain. *The Gerontologist, 29,* 660-666.

Zarit, S., Orr, N., & Zarit, J. M. (1985). *The hidden victims of Alzheimer's disease: Families under stress.* New York: New York University Press.

Zarit, S., Reever, K., & Back-Peterson, J. (1980). Relatives of the impaired elderly: Correlates of feelings of burden. *The Gerontologist, 20,* 649-655.

Zarit, S., Todd, P., & Zarit, J. M. (1986). Subjective burden of husbands and wives as caregivers: A longitudinal study. *The Gerontologist, 26,* 260-266.

Zarit, S., & Zarit, J. M. (1983). *The burden interview.* University Park: Pennsylvania State University Press.

Zeltin, A. (1986). Mentally retarded adults and their siblings. *American Journal of Mental Deficiency, 9,* 217-225.

Zigman, W., Schupf, N., Lubin, R. Q., & Silverman, W. P. (1987). Premature regression of adults with Down syndrome. *American Journal of Mental Deficiency, 92*(2), 161-168.

Zigman, W., Seltzer, G., Adlin, M., & Silverman, W. P. (1991). Physical, behavioral, and mental health changes associated with aging. In M. P. Janicki & M. Seltzer (Eds.), *Aging and developmental disabilities: Challenges for the 1990s* (pp. 52-75). Washington, DC: American Association on Mental Retardation, Special Interest Group on Aging.

Index

About the Contributors

Edward F. Ansello, Ph.D., is Director of the Virginia Center on Aging, Medical College of Virginia, at the Virginia Commonwealth University in Richmond. His gerontological focuses include elder caregiving; pre-retirement education; disabilities and aging; geropharmacy; coalition building; and the humanities, media, and aging. He is the author of 12 books, monographs, special issues, and book chapters, and 36 published articles, and he has made over 400 presentations before professional and civic groups nationally and internationally.

Ellie Brubaker, M.S.W., Ph.D., is Associate Professor in the Department of Sociology and Anthropology at Miami University, Oxford, Ohio. She has written several journal articles and book chapters on the topic of family care in the later years. She is also the author of the book *Working With the Elderly: A Social System's Approach.*

Timothy H. Brubaker, Ph.D., is Professor and Director of the Family and Child Studies Center at Miami University, Oxford, Ohio. He has written two books and edited four other volumes on family life in the later years. In addition, he has published several journal articles and numerous book chapters focusing on caregiving issues facing older families.

Carl Calkins, Ph.D., is Director of the University of Missouri-Kansas City Institute for Human Development, a university affiliated program. He has served as principal investigator on a number of federal grants in the area of aging and developmental disabilities, including both demonstration and training grants. He has presented to national audiences and published on the topic of aging and developmental disabilities.

Susan J. Eklund, Ph.D., is Professor of Counseling and Educational Psychology, Byron Root Professor on Aging, and Director of the Indiana University Center on Aging and Aged. Her areas of professional expertise include adult development and aging, life-span development, school psychology, and the aging/aged developmentally disabled. She has authored more than 40 publications and is active in both aging and educational professional associations.

Barbara A. Hawkins, Re.D., is Associate Professor of Health, Physical Education, and Recreation and Research Coordinator of the Program on Aging and Developmental Disabilities at the Indiana University Institute for the Study of Developmental Disabilities. She is principal investigator of a training grant in the area of aging and developmental disabilities from the U.S. Department of Health and Human Services (U.S. DHHS), has completed a curriculum development grant from the Administration on Aging (U.S. DHHS), and is the lead principal investigator for a study of bio-psycho-social aspects of aging-related decline in persons with mental retardation and Down syndrome. She has authored more than 35 publications and delivered more than 50 presentations on state, national, and international levels.

Tamar Heller, Ph.D., is Associate Professor of Community Health Services and Psychology at the University of Illinois at Chicago and Coordinator of the Family Studies and Service Program at the Illinois University Affiliated Program in Developmental Disabilities. She has been the principal investigator of numerous federal and state grants including the Residential Transition Project and the Later Life Planning Project of the Rehabilitation Research and Training Center Consortium on Aging and Developmental Disabilities. She has conducted research and published widely on residential transition and future planning issues for persons with disabilities, elderly persons, and family caregivers.

Jean P. Lehmann, Ph.D., is Assistant Professor in the School of Occupational and Educational Studies at Colorado State University. Her interest in families of persons with disabilities has evolved from experiences working with these families as a community case manager for persons with disabilities and as a secondary special education teacher. Her most recent research examines factors associated with mothers' expectations for their adolescent children.

B. L. Martz, M.D., is Professor Emeritus of Medicine at the Indiana University School of Medicine and former Director of the Indiana University Center on Aging and Aged. He continues private practice as a geriatrician with the Marion County General Hospital and the Indiana Masonic Home Hospital. He is co-principal investigator with Susan Eklund and Barbara Hawkins on a longitudinal research project with aging adults who have developmental disabilities. He is an active member of more than 15 professional organizations and has authored more than 50 publications in a variety of areas including cardiology and geriatric medicine.

Elizabeth A. Noelker, R.N.C., M.S.N., is a Gerontological Clinical Nurse Specialist at the University Foley ElderHealth Center of University Hospitals of Cleveland. She also works at the University Alzheimer's Center as an educator and is on the clinical faculty at Frances Payne Bolton School of Nursing at Case Western Reserve University. She is certified by the American Nurses Association in gerontological nursing.

Christine Rinck, Ph.D., is Director of Research at the University of Missouri-Kansas City Institute for Human Development. She was Research Associate on an AoA/ADD demonstration grant and was a coauthor of the *Training Guide for Aging Specialists.* She has conducted a number of needs assessments for the State of Missouri and various regions on the prevalence and needs of older persons with developmental disabilities. She is the author of *Aging and Developmental Disabilities in Rural America* and co-editor of the publication *Dialogue on Drugs, Behavior, and Developmental Disabilities.*

Karen A. Roberto, Ph.D., is Professor and Coordinator of the Gerontology Program at the University of Northern Colorado. Her research focuses on family and friend relationships in later life and the influence of chronic illness on the lives of older women. Her work has been published in a variety of scholarly journals including *The Journal of Gerontology: Psychological Sciences, The Journal of Women and Aging, The Journal of Applied Gerontology, The Gerontologist,* and *The Journal of Gerontological Social Work.*

Gregory C. Smith, Ed.D., is Assistant Professor in the Department of Human Development at the University of Maryland, College Park. His research interests are in the field of applied gerontology, including interventions for family caregivers of the frail elderly, psychosocial environments within geriatric residences, and aging among developmentally disabled adults and their parents. He has published numerous articles in such scholarly journals as *The Gerontologist, Psychology and Aging, Clinical Gerontologist, Educational Gerontology,* and *The Journal of Gerontological Social Work.*

Lauren C. Somple, M.S.W., L.I.S.W., A.C.S.W., is employed as a Clinical Social Worker at University Foley ElderHealth Center, University Hospitals of Cleveland. She received her master's degree in Social Work from the University of Pittsburgh in 1982 and Certificate in Gerontology from Case Western Reserve University in 1984. She has served as an instructor and consultant for the Western Reserve Geriatric Education Center and Mandel School of Applied Social Sciences.

Sheldon S. Tobin, Ph.D., is Professor in the School of Social Welfare at the Rockefeller College of Public Affairs and Policy of the University at Albany, State University of New York. He also is a Professor in the School of Public Health, the Department of Psychology, and an Adjunct Professor of Medicine at Albany College. Among his nearly 100 publications, focused on psychological aspects of aging and services for the elderly, are the following books: *Last Home for the Aged* and *The Experience of Aging* (both with M. A. Leibman), *Effective Social Services for the Elderly* (with S. Davidson and A. Sack), *Current Gerontology: Long Term Care* (editor), *Enabling the Elderly: Religious Institutions Within the Community Service System* (with J. W. Ellor and S. Anderson-Ray), and *Health in Aging: Sociological Issues and Policy Directions* (co-edited with R. A. Ward).

Joan B. Wood, Ph.D., is Associate Professor of Gerontology and Psychology and Associate Director of the Virginia Geriatric Education Center at Virginia Commonwealth University (VCU). She also serves as Gerontology Discipline Coordinator for the Virginia Institute for Developmental Disabilities, the university-affiliated program for develpmental disabilities in Virginia, at VCU. She was Director of the first statewide project on aging and developmental disabilities in Virginia, at VCU, and she was Codirector of a project funded by the Administration on Aging (1990-1992) on policy, training, and service related to aging and developmental disabilities. Her primary research interest is family caregiving for older adults with disabilities.